S0-BJW-440

Computer Security

ACM MONOGRAPH SERIES

Published under the auspices of the Association for Computing Machinery Inc.

Editor ROBERT L. ASHENHURST *The University of Chicago*

A. FINERMAN (Ed.)   University Education in Computing Science, 1968
A. GINZBURG   Algebraic Theory of Automata, 1968
E. F. CODD   Cellular Automata, 1968
G. ERNST AND A. NEWELL   GPS: A Case Study in Generality and Problem Solving, 1969
M. A. GAVRILOV AND A. D. ZAKREVSKII (Eds.)   LYaPAS: A Programming Language for Logic and Coding Algorithms, 1969
THEODOR D. STERLING, EDGAR A. BERING, JR., SEYMOUR V. POLLACK, AND HERBERT VAUGHAN, JR. (Eds.)   Visual Prosthesis: The Interdisciplinary Dialogue, 1971
JOHN R. RICE (Ed.)   Mathematical Software, 1971
ELLIOTT I. ORGANICK   Computer System Organization: The B5700/B6700 Series, 1973
NEIL D. JONES   Computability Theory: An Introduction, 1973
ARTO SALOMAA   Formal Languages, 1973
HARVEY ABRAMSON   Theory and Application of a Bottom-Up Syntax-Directed Translator, 1973
GLEN G. LANGDON, JR.   Logic Design: A Review of Theory and Practice, 1974
MONROE NEWBORN   Computer Chess, 1975
ASHOK K. AGRAWALA AND TOMLINSON G. RAUSCHER   Foundations of Microprogramming: Architecture, Software, and Applications, 1975
P. J. COURTOIS   Decomposability: Queueing and Computer System Applications, 1977
JOHN R. METZNER AND BRUCE H. BARNES   Decision Table Languages and Systems, 1977
ANITA K. JONES (Ed.)   Perspectives on Computer Science: From the 10th Anniversary Symposium at the Computer Science Department, Carnegie-Mellon University, 1978
DAVID K. HSIAO, DOUGLAS S. KERR, AND STUART E. MADNICK   Computer Security, 1979

Previously published and available from The Macmillan Company, New York City
V. KRYLOV Approximate Calculation of Integrals (Translated by A. H. Stroud), 1962

Computer Security

DAVID K. HSIAO

Department of Computer and Information Science
Ohio State University
Columbus, Ohio

DOUGLAS S. KERR

Department of Computer and Information Science
Ohio State University
Columbus, Ohio

STUART E. MADNICK

Sloan School of Management
Massachusetts Institute of Technology
Cambridge, Massachusetts

ACADEMIC PRESS   New York   San Francisco   London   1979

A Subsidiary of Harcourt Brace Jovanovich, Publishers

'359063 658.4
$H873c$

COPYRIGHT © 1979, BY ACADEMIC PRESS, INC.
ALL RIGHTS RESERVED.
NO PART OF THIS PUBLICATION MAY BE REPRODUCED OR
TRANSMITTED IN ANY FORM OR BY ANY MEANS, ELECTRONIC
OR MECHANICAL, INCLUDING PHOTOCOPY, RECORDING, OR ANY
INFORMATION STORAGE AND RETRIEVAL SYSTEM, WITHOUT
PERMISSION IN WRITING FROM THE PUBLISHER.

ACADEMIC PRESS, INC.
111 Fifth Avenue, New York, New York 10003

United Kingdom Edition published by
ACADEMIC PRESS, INC. (LONDON) LTD.
24/28 Oval Road, London NW1 7DX

Library of Congress Cataloging in Publication Data

Hsiao, David K   Date
    Computer security·

    Includes bibliographies.
    1. Computers——Access control. 2. Electronic data
processing departments——Security measures.   I. Kerr,
Douglas S., joint author. II. Madnick, Stuart E.,
joint author. III. Title.
QA76.9.A25H74   658.4'7   79-14503
ISBN 0-12-357650-4

PRINTED IN THE UNITED STATES OF AMERICA

79 80 81 82   9 8 7 6 5 4 3 2 1

RIDER COLLEGE LIBRARY

TO DORA, ETHEL, AND WAUNETA

CONTENTS

FOREWORD

The Office of Naval Research program in computer security has had the objective, not simply of ensuring the integrity of stored data, but also of encouraging information sharing by building managerial confidence in our ability to control the sharing process. Along with other DOD and nondefense government funding agencies, ONR has a long history of investing resources in creating approaches or solutions for the multiplicity of problems germane to achieving a secure computational environment. While there have been some successes over the past 10 years, time has taught us the lessons both of the illusive nature of a total solution to the security problem, and of the enormous complexity of the many issues and interactions that impact on the matter of computer security.

It is the purpose of this ONR supported book to examine and report on the history of security research. Our deeper interest, constituting a challenge to the authors, was to distill from the past insights into promising directions for future research. Growing national concern with computer security and privacy, extending beyond the conventional military requirement to cover the entire civilian and business community, has underscored the urgency of reinforcing and redefining research activity. We are convinced that this book establishes research objectives and directions—the long-term realization of which will represent important progress in resolving the national concern with security and privacy issues.

MARVIN DENICOFF
Director of Information Systems Program
Office of Naval Research

PREFACE

Huck, have you ever told anybody about—that?
'Bout what?
You know what.
Oh—course I haven't.
Never a word?
Never a solitary word, so help me. What makes you ask?

Mark Twain—*The Adventures of Tom Sawyer*

The work reported in this monograph was suggested by Marvin Denicoff, Director of the Information Systems Program of the Office of Naval Research in the Summer of 1976. The work is intended to produce a technical review of recent research in the area of computer security. Furthermore, it is intended to provide some assessment and evaluation of the work reviewed. Some projections and speculations of future activities in computer security research are also included.

Because the monograph is written for technical managers, program monitors, and other managerial people who are not directly conducting such research, we have tried to present the review in a tutorial and illustrative manner. We have also attempted to introduce some of the necessary terminology with intuitive and informal definitions. To allow readers to have a comprehensive and coherent coverage of computer security research, we endeavored to give our personal views on various subjects and attempted to include all relevant areas for consideration. We would like the reader to bear with us in our expression of these views.

To allow further pursuit of recent work in computer security, we have also provided a rather complete bibliography with annotations. Although the bibliography covers published work in computer security from 1974 through 1978, much of the work covered up to 1977 was compiled and annotated by Philip F. Sherburne. The authors would like to thank him for the assistance.

The authors would also like to thank Shelley Green, Robyn Lerch-backer, and Nancy Parkinson for typing several drafts of the manuscript. Last, but not least, the authors would like to thank ONR for their support of the work.

ACKNOWLEDGMENTS

Figure 5–2 is adapted from Madnick, Stuart E. and Donovan, John J., *Operating Systems*, © 1974, McGraw-Hill, New York, p. 45.

Adapted from Hsiao, David K., *Systems Programming—Concepts of Operating and Database Systems*, © 1975, Addison-Wesley, pp. 192, 194, 302, 308, 306 are the following, respectively: Figure 5–4, Figure 5–5, Figure 8–8, Figure 8–9, Section 8.3.2, 28 lines of textual material.

Adapted from Hoffman, Lance J., *Modern Methods for Computer Security and Privacy*, © 1977 by Prentice-Hall, Englewood Cliffs, New Jersey, pp. 122, 110, 44, 40 are the following, respectively: Figure 5–3, Figure 5–13, Figures 6–1 and 6–4, and Figure 7–1. Figure 5–1 is from p. 113.

Figure 5–7 is adapted from Organick, Elliott, J., *The Multics System: An Examination of Its Structure*, © 1972, M.I.T. Press, pages 148, 152, 153. By permission of M.I.T. Press.

Figure 5–12 is adapted from Lipner, Steve, "A Minicomputer Security Control System," in *Proceedings of the Ieee COMPCON Conference*, 1974, San Francisco, California. By permission of the Institute of Electrical and Electronics Engineers, Inc.

Figure 6–2 is adapted from Feistel, H., "Cryptography and Computer Privacy," *Scientific American, 228*, No. 5 (May, 1973), pp. 21 and 22.

Figure 7–2 is adapted from Lampson, Butler, "Protection," in *Proceedings of the Fifth Princeton Symposium on Information Sciences and Systems*, Princeton University, March 1971, pp. 437–443, and reprinted in *Operating Systems Review*, *8*, 1, January, 1974, p. 22.

Figure 7–3 is adapted from Scherr, A. L., "Functional Structure of IBM Virtual Storage Operatings Systems, Part II: OS/VS2–2 Concepts and Philosophies," *IBM Systems Journal*, *12*, No. 4, 1973, p. 390. Reprinted by permission from IBM Systems Journal © 1973 by International Business Machines Corporation.

The sample statistical database in Section 8.1.2 is adapted (with simplication) from Denning, Dorothy, "Are Statistical Data Bases Secure?" *AFIPS Conference Proceedings—1978 NCC*, *47*, 1978, pp. 525–530. © 1978 AFIPS Press, Montvale, New Jersey.

Figure 8–5a is adapted from Wong, E. and Chiang, F., "Canonical Structures in Attribute-Based File Organization," *Communications of the ACM*, *14*, No. 9 (Sept. 1971), pp. 593–597. Copyright 1971, Association for Computing Machinery, Inc., reprinted by permission.

Figure 8–14 is copied from a figure in Baum, Richard R. and Hsiao, David K., "Data Base Computers—A Step Toward Data Utilities," *IEEE Transactions on Computers*, c-25, 12 (Dec., 1976), 1254–1259. Reprinted by permission of the Institute of Electrical and Electronics Engineers, Inc.

Computer Security

Chapter 1

INTRODUCTION

(Computer security deals with the managerial procedures and technological safeguards applied to computer hardware, software, and data to assure against accidental or deliberate unauthorized access to and dissemination of computer system data.)Computer privacy, on the other hand, is concerned with the moral and legal requirements to protect data from unauthorized access and dissemination. The issues involved in computer privacy are therefore political decisions regarding who may have access to what and who may disseminate what, whereas the issues involved in computer security are procedures and safeguards for enforcing the privacy decisions.) The motivations for security and privacy can be found in the desire for secrecy in military affairs, for nondisclosure in industrial applications, and for information-sharing in modern society. These motivations have become particularly acute where computers are used since computers play a major and important role in processing and storing of secret and proprietary information and in providing effective sharing of useful information.

The relationships between privacy issues and security measures are depicted in Fig. 1–1. By referring to it, we note that through legislative measures (privacy issues affect all aspects of computer security.)With due consideration of its social implications, legislation for computer privacy determines the type of information collected and by whom, the type of access and dissemination, the subject rights, the penalties, and the licensing matters. In Chapter 2, a discussion on privacy issues, legislative measures, and their implications on security

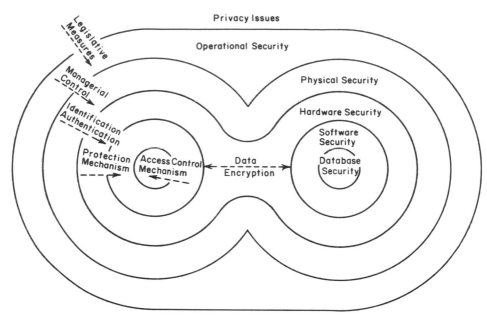

FIGURE 1-1. A computer system environment consisting of two information nodes.

is given. Based on the legislation, it is then possible to establish some form of operational security. The operational security allows the management of a computer installation to exercise control and be responsible for the installation.

Guidelines and procedures may be established for accountability, levels of control, type of control (in terms of data classification and system configuration, information flow, and inventory), rules, and checklists. Preventive measures and recovery due to internal threats and external intrusions are also a part of the operational security. For these threats and intrusions, the causes, effects, and means must be studied. More difficult aspects of operational security research include risk analysis, assessment, and insurance. By knowing the risks involved, the operational security may be expressed in terms of quantitative indicators, cost factors, and options. Finally, the psychological security of the operational staff is necessary to successful operational security. These discussions are included in Chapter 3.

Through managerial control, the operational security allows the user to be physically close to the computer installation as depicted in Fig. 1–1. Unless the computer system is physically secure, any further attempts to protect the computer system and system data will be futile.

There are several areas of concern for physical security: control of physical access, prevention and recovery from loss due to natural disasters, electromagnetic and electronic tampering, and malicious entry and destruction. In Chapter 4, the subject of physical security is treated.

With proper identification and authentication, a user may gain access to a computer system (again see Fig. 1–1). Identification and authentication can be accomplished (a) via something that the user knows (simple passwords, complex passwords, one-time passwords, handshaking through a question–answer session or dynamic program invocation, (b) via something that the user carries (keys, magnetic-stripe cards, or badges), or (c) via physical characteristics of the user (voiceprints, fingerprints, or hand and facial geometry). Furthermore, actions upon intruder identification should also be considered as a part of the physical security. In order to provide a more coherent introduction, the discussion on identification and authentication is also included in Chapter 4.

Once the computer system begins its work for a user, security is facilitated at three levels: the hardware level, the software level, and the data level. In addition, if the computer system consists of terminals or several computers, then intercommunications between terminals and computers and among computers require security considerations.

Computer hardware security can be accomplished by means of (real and virtual) memory protection, multiple execution states, microprocessors, and minicomputers. In memory protection, access to areas of memory may be controlled by bounds registers (e.g., CDC 6000 computers), locks and keys (e.g., IBM 360 series), and access bits in real memory (e.g., tag-oriented architecture), in page table entries (e.g., UNIVAC system 70/46), and in segment table entries (e.g., IBM 370 series). The use of multiple execution states enables programs to be run not only in either supervisor or user state (where the supervisor state is endowed with more access privileges), but also in a hierarchy of states (where programs in a higher state are endowed with more access privileges than those in a lower one; Honeywell's Multics is a system with such hierarchies, known as protection rings). As hardware security aids, microprocessors may be placed between input–output (I/O) channels and main memory for access control. They can be used as specialized processors for postprocessing of data in order to enforce field-level and bit-level access control. As hardware security controllers, minicomputers may be used to perform periods processing—a Department of Defense (DOD) requirement for secure processing. They can also be used for monitoring the activity of a host computer. The monitoring may include the logging of the transactions and the alarming of the operator. In Chapter 5, we deal with the hardware security.

One of the main goals of computer software security has been the design and implementation of secure software systems. First, we need a design methodology for secure software (e.g., the security kernel approach). Second, we must be able to verify and to test that the software produced is indeed the software intended (e.g., proof of correctness and penetration tests). Finally, we must have secure software which can carry out a wide range of security policies (say, separation of policy and mechanism). Once we have learned how to design and produce secure software, we can then implement various software mechanisms to achieve desired security. There are essentially two types of mechanisms available—those which rely on surveillance (such as logging, access control, and treat monitoring) and those which rely on isolation (such as virtual machines). Software security is expounded on in Chapter 7.

The most unique aspect of database security is where the semantics of (at least, some of) the data must be made confidential. Thus, the main concern in database security is safeguarding the confidentiality of the data semantics. To protect the confidentiality of the data, two principal problems must be resolved by the computer systems. The first is to conceal the data in user–computer and computer–computer communications (using encryption); the second is to determine who can perform what operations on which data (providing access control). Encryption is, therefore, a technique for encoding the data to hide its meaning. On the other hand, access control to a data aggregate requires the system to identify the user, to determine the data aggregate, and to enforce the authorized operations. Unless a user is properly identified, the system will not be able to establish the authorized data operations for the user. In order to determine the data aggregate on which the user is allowed to operate, the system must comprehend the content of the data. Without such comprehension, the system will not be able to determine the exact data aggregate involved. Thus the semantics of the data plays an important role in access control. An "intelligent" access control mechanism of a computer system is one which can determine the proper data aggregate for access considerations despite the complicated semantics of the data involved.

Since data are handled as messages in user–computer (and computer–computer) communications, the classical cryptographic techniques have been used for encryption. Here, the data are enciphered at the time and place of the entry. The encipherment involves the data, a key, and an operation. By performing the operation on the data digits and the key digits, the data entry terminal produces enciphered messages which will then be sent to the central computer system. An enciphered message returned by the system is deciphered at the data exit terminal. The decipherment involves the enciphered message, the same or related key, and the same operation. By performing the operation on the enciphered digits and the key digits, the data exit terminal produces the original data. Because both of the operations performed at the data entry and the data exit terminals are the same, it is possible to use a single terminal for both data entry and data exit. Furthermore, the same operation may be built in the hardware, rather than software, for more rapid and reliable performance. However, the key (say, on a card with magnetic stripe) must be guarded by the user and changed frequently. Research has been directed toward the development of data terminals with encryption capability. Cryptographic techniques utilizing classical ciphers such as transpositions and substitutions (either monographic or polyalphabetic) have been in use. However, frequent changes of keys require a way to produce random patterns of keys. Research into using pseudorandom number generators for producing keys has been noted. When databases are large and messages are long, there is a need for longer keys. Research into utilizing multiple short key tapes to produce a long compound key has been conducted. Because certain information such as numerical data is critical in some data operations and because errors in this information cannot be detected by context, there is need for a technique in which the enciphered messages are sensitive to any change of a single digit position. Such techniques not only can provide high message confidentiality, but also can provide an acute alert for the detection of errors. When data are required at the central site, the data aggregate may have to be deciphered either in part or in whole for subsequent data management. To decipher a data aggregate either in part or in whole for processing purposes, the system must have access to keys. A fundamental problem is therefore the capability of the system to protect the keys. The subject of encryption is treated in Chapter 6.

In handling data in a computer system, the user will first want the data to be represented in formatted form in order to refer to it in terms of logical aggregates such as fields, arrays, tables, records, subfiles, and files. These aggregates are logical units of information which may have little resemblance to their physical or virtual storage images. By allowing the user to associate access control requirements and security measures with the logical units, the access control mechanism can facilitate direct control and protection of the data regardless of the location of that data. Furthermore, the mechanism does not require the user to be familiar with the physical or virtual storage structure of the computer system. For these reasons, such mechanisms in computer systems are referred to as logical access control mechanisms. Logical access control mechanisms must therefore have the facility for the user to specify shareable and private data in terms of logical aggregates of the database, to assign access rights and security requirements to these aggregates and the types of access that other users may have, and to incorporate additional authentication and checking measures.

The capability for the user to specify shareable and confidential data is directly related to the level of authorization and enforcement of the computer system. For example, some systems facilitate an authorization hierarchy which enables different users to have different rights for granting other access to the common data. Such a facility is particularly useful in a military environment where multilevel authorization is a necessity. The level of enforcement is primarily reflected in its granularity. In other words, access control to large data aggregates, such as files, as well as small aggregates, such as fields, should be facilitated without severe overhead.

The determination of data aggregates for access control purposes may require resolution on the part of the computer system. Resolution is needed when more than one (possibly conflicting) security requirement is applicable to the same data. To provide automatic resolution, the system must have a known resolution policy (e.g., least disclosures and need-to-know policies). With the known policy, the system can then resolve the subsequent accesses to authorized data by either modifying the user request (known as the query-modification technique) or a posteriori checking (i.e., giving access only to those data which have been resolved for all applicable security requirements).

Because the database resides on secondary storage, considerations of data security also include compartmentalization of the database for the elimination of the "pass-through problem." Ideally, data that have the same security requirement are stored in the same storage area (say, the same disk drive). Access to data satisfying one security requirement does not involve access to data satisfying other security requirements. In this way, both physical security and access control can be jointly provided for in the database.

In addition to the pass-through problem, database security also involves problems of inference even when the data are used only for statistical purposes. Since the database is full of semantics, inference on the basis of these semantics can breach the confidentiality of the data. Again, the knowledge of the computer system in terms of the data semantics plays an important role in statistical and inferential control of data access. The complex problems of database security and some solutions to database security are treated in Chapter 8.

In conclusion, we would like to emphasize that computer security and privacy covers a broad range of problems and issues which make the implementation of the security measures difficult and complex. Without a thorough understanding of the problems and issues involved, attempts to provide solutions in isolated areas may render the computer security inadequate. In this book, we have tried to survey the entire spectrum of computer security and privacy so that its complexity and comprehensiveness are put in some perspective. Furthermore, we include an up-to-date annotated and cross-referenced bibliography of technical material for those who would like to pursue the study of computer security.

POSTSCRIPT[1]

There are a number of books, monographs, and bibliographies on the subject of computer security and privacy which we shall annotate herewith. However, in contrast to existing literature, this monograph is intended as a review of computer security research. In order to cover the entire computer security field, we attempt to provide a comprehensive review. Because of the diversity and newness of the research, we also try to provide a coherent view or perspective. In other words, the characterizations, treatments, and critiques of various security research work are our own. This view or perspective will become more pronounced in the last few chapters of the monograph. We would like the reader to bear with us.

On operational and physical security, we have many books and monographs to refer to. There is the classical and comprehensive one by [Martin 73], the not so comprehensive ones by [Hemphi 73] and [Hoyt 73], and more recent ones by [Leibho 76] and [Walker 77]. There are specialized treatments on operational security. On medical applica-

---

[1] In reading either the Postscript or References at the end of a chapter, one may encounter citations of other references. Some of these cited items are not included in the same chapter. They are, instead, listed in the references of other chapters. There are two reasons in doing so: (1) they are more relevant to the subject matter of that chapter; and (2) they are not repeated in other chapters in order to conserve space.

The best way to locate a cited reference is first to look over the references in the same chapter. If it is not there, then use the Author Index at the end of the monograph. For each author, a list of references on the author and the pages in which the references appeared are provided.

tions of security, we have [Laska 75]. For municipal and other
managers of computer facilities, we have [Dial 75]. On databanks, we
have [Westin 72]. A livelihood has been made compiling computer
related crimes [Parker 76c]. [Whites 78] has also reported on computer crimes. Some procedures to prevent such crimes are proposed in
[Leibho 76].

The book that perhaps influenced us most is the one by [Hoffma
77a] which has good coverages on all aspects of the computer security
except data security.

Bibliographies on computer security are many. However, they all
owe their origin to [Bergar 72] and [Scherf 74]. The former deals with
only technical papers on security published prior to 1972. The latter includes also nontechnical papers up to 1974. Since then, there are
specialized ones on operating system security [Abbott 74], [Carlst 78],
and [Huskam 76], on privacy [Eichma 77], and on databanks [Hunt 74].
A more comprehensive one can be found in [Pfiste 76]. Abstracts from
NTIS and the Engineering Index Data Base appear in [Reimhe 78a],
[Reimhe 78b], and [Reimhe 78c].

REFERENCES—BOOKS AND MONOGRAPHS

Dial 75

Dial, O. E., and Goldberg, E. M., *Privacy, Security, and Computers:
Guidelines for Municipal and Other Public Information Systems.*
Praeger, New York, 1975.

> Written as a guide for city officials, the book is designed to introduce
> unknowledgeable people to the problems of individual privacy and the
> way individual privacy is affected by municipal information systems. The
> chapters cover such topics as the problem of privacy, auditing data pro-
> cessing operations, and the standards which should be used in the design
> and operation of municipal information systems to protect privacy.
>
> The texts of ordinances passed in the cities of Wichita Falls, Texas,
> and Charlotte, North Carolina, to control data access are included in the
> appendices. Their use as guidelines for administrations in other cities
> makes these valuable. Additionally, statements of policy regarding data
> access control in the previously mentioned cities and Dayton, Ohio, are
> contained in the appendices.

Hemphi 73

Hemphill, C. F., Jr., and Hemphill, J. M., *Security Procedures for Computer Systems.* Dow Jones-Irwin, Homewood, Illinois, 1973.

In many cases the individual responsible for the security of a computer facility may not be totally familiar with the computer and its operation. This book is designed to assist this type of person in developing adequate security measures for the installation. Reviewing most areas of operational and physical security this book provides reasonably complete coverage of the material in a nontechnical manner. The book, organized well, includes chapters on physical security, fire, computer access, sabotage, procedural controls, disaster planning, legal protection, and insurance. Each chapter includes a security checklist for the corresponding material.

The major contribution of this book is that the presentations are readable and the explanations of technical details are clear but not oversimplified.

Hoffma 73

Hoffman, L. J., *Security and Privacy in Computer Systems.* Melville Publishing Co., Los Angeles, 1973.

This book is a compendium of 23 papers compiled by Hoffman. These papers represent some of the work done in computer security and privacy before 1973. The book is divided into seven sections entitled: Civil Liberties Threats, A Cram Course in Threats and Countermeasures, Privacy Transformations, Models for Secure Systems, "Statistical" Data Banks, Is There Hope in Hardware?, and Security in Existing Systems.

Hoffma 77a

Hoffman, L. J., *Modern Methods for Computer Security and Privacy.* Prentice-Hall, Inc., Englewood Cliffs, New Jersey, 1977.

This book represents one of the best and most recent surveys of the technical aspects of computer security. Valuable as a reference, the book is also designed to be used as a textbook for a high-level class in computer security techniques. Questions are included at the end of each chapter and sample answers to these may be found at the end of the book.

The book contains chapters covering authentication and identification, authorization policies, logging, traditional and modern methods of cryptography (including a section on the Federal data encryption standard), operating systems, machine architecture, mathematical models, and future research areas. The book also contains a chapter on the nontechnical aspects of computer security (operational and physical concerns) and one discussing the legal aspects of computer privacy. Additionally, the book contains an up-to-date and reasonably complete bibliography.

Hoyt 73

Computer Security Research Group—Hoyt, D. B., Chairman, *Computer Security Handbook.* Macmillan, New York, 1973.

Written to inform managers of computer installations of the need for security and the methods that may be used, this book covers the physical and operational aspects of computer security. The chapters, each written by an expert in a specific area of security, discuss such topics as management's role in computer security, auditing computerized systems, computer risk insurance, and computer facility physical security. With the chapters each being written by a separate individual, a certain amount of overlap occurs. While this overlap is bothersome when reading the book as a whole, it does help make the book valuable as a reference tool since the chapters are not dependent on one another.

Katzan 73

Katzan, H., Jr., *Computer Data Security*. Van Nostrand Reinhold, New York, 1973.

Laska 75

Laska, E. M., and Bank, R., eds., *Safeguarding Psychiatric Privacy—Computer Systems and Their Uses*. John Wiley and Sons, New York, 1975.

A collection of papers, most dealing with the Multi-State Information System (MSIS), are presented in this book. The MSIS was created in 1967 through the Department of Health, Education, and Welfare (HEW) to collect and maintain records about individuals receiving mental health care and about the delivery of that care. Terminals were set up in mental health care facilities around the country to supply these records to the main computer located at the Rockland Research Institute in New York. The system was designed for use in administrative and research efforts to improve the therapeutic rehabilitation of patients.

Included in the book are sections on the design of the system and its applications. A good section on the legal and social issues surrounding a central databank containing personal records of psychiatric patients is included as well. Typical questions to be asked are the following: Should the patient be allowed to see his own records? What if the patient feels the information is incorrect? Who else should be allowed access to the records? The New York General Assembly has passed a bill forbidding the MSIS to release any personally identifiable records although this certainly does not protect the records from disclosure at their source.

The book provides a detailed view of one specific information system, why it exists, how it is used, and what measures exist to protect the confidentiality of the information within it.

Leibho 76

Leibholz, S. W., and Wilson, L. D., *User's Guide to Computer Crime: Its Commission, Detection and Prevention*. Chilton, Radnor, Pennsylvania, 1976.

Written as a businessman's guide to computer security focusing on computer crime, the book introduces the businessman to the risks of computer operations and some of the protective measures available. The book is organized into four sections: the problems including case histories of computer crimes, methods of protection, methods of detection, and a section on programs of action needed in accounting and legislative areas to facilitate development of secure computers. Although providing a reasonable introduction into these areas, the presentations are far less than detailed. [Parker 76c] and [Martin 73] provide far more in depth coverage of the material than contained in this book.

Martin 73

Martin, J., *Security, Accuracy, and Privacy in Computer Systems.* Prentice-Hall, Inc., Englewood Cliffs, New Jersey, 1973.

This book covers practically all issues related to operational and physical computer security. The book is comprised of five sections: Introduction to the Problem, Design of the Computer System, Physical Security, Administrative Controls, and the Legal and Social Environment. The book gives a good introduction to the topics as well as in-depth coverage of most of the material. However, it does not cover actual operating or database system design in detailed fashion.

While the book discusses the computer system itself, the sections entitled "Physical Security" and "Administrative Controls" are particularly important. Included in these sections are chapters on locks, vaults, and protected areas; electronic security devices; fire; sabotage; vital records program and system recovery; control of programmers; physiological security; and auditors.

Although some of the material presented is out of date, the book is one of the best reference tools available on physical and operational security. Especially valuable are the appendices which include 91 pages of security checklists.

Parker 76c

Parker, D. B., *Crime by Computer.* Charles Scribner's Sons, New York, 1976.

The result of Parker's studies since 1970 at Stanford Research Institute (SRI), the book is based mostly on the earlier report "Computer Abuse." Detailed are the four roles Parker feels the computer may play in acts of computer abuse: the computer as the object of the act, creating the unique environment for the act, becoming a tool used in the act, and the use of the computer as a symbol.

Chapters are included which profile the typical computer criminal, describe methods for safeguarding the computer, and predict the incidence of computer abuse and its effect on computer usage. The major portion of the book is spent detailing various computer crimes and their perpetrators. Included are detailed case history reports of two of the more infamous computer crimes: the Equity Funding Fraud and Jerry Schneider's theft of a million dollars in telephone equipment.

The book represents the most detailed and one of the latest accounts of Parker's compilation activities at SRI where he has collected and documented 375 cases of computer abuse. (For a brief summary of the conclusions of this research see [Parker 76b].) Well written, the book provides some interesting views of man's immoral, sometimes illegal, but most certainly ingeneous use (perhaps misuse) of computers.

Walker 77

Walker, B. J., and Blake, I. F., *Computer Security and Protection Structures.* Dowden, Hutchinson and Ross, Inc., Stroudsburg, Pennsylvania, 1977.

The authors state that increasing dependence on computers by the military and business communities along with public concerns over protection of individual privacy has led to increasing interest in computer security. This book attempts to provide the reader with introductory material to all aspects of computer security. Additionally, certain areas are dealt with in more detail.

The book is divided in three major sections: threats, countermeasures, and a survey of implemented systems. Within the first section on threats are chapters on natural disaster, accidental threats, and deliberate threats.

Topics covered in the second section on countermeasures include safeguards for the installation, hardware, operating systems, terminals, and files.

Among the systems reviewed in the third portion of the book are Rush, Adept-50, RSS, Atlas II, and Multics. The comments in this section tend to be quite brief.

Westin 72

Westin, A. F., *DATABANKS in a Free Society: Computers, Record-Keeping and Privacy,* Quadrangle Books, New York, 1972.

The result of a three-year study (1970–1972) of computerized databanks and their implications in the area of civil rights and public policy, the book represents the first comprehensive study regarding these issues. The study is based on questionnaires sent to over 1500 organizations and visits to 55 of the most advanced users of computerized information systems. Conclusions reached in the study are that organizations are not, as a result of using computers, collecting or exchanging more detailed personal information than in the years before widespread use of computers. Individual rights, as they existed in manual systems, are being carried over to automated systems and these systems have been responsive when changes occur in how these rights should be protected. The study did find the public genuinely concerned over databanks of personal information but felt the concerns would have existed with or without computers. Recommendations are given for the protection of individual rights in the context of any type of personal record keeping system.

The book, objectively written, is organized into five sections: an introduction to records, computers, and civil liberties; detailed profiles of 14 information systems in government, business, and nonprofit organizations; findings of the visits to 55 organizations mentioned previously; a chapter on future trends in computer technology; and a final chapter on the implications for public policy determined by the study. This book and the Department of HEW report [Ware 73] are the major contributions in the study of computerized personal information systems.

Whites 78

Whiteside, T., *Computer Capers*. Crowell, New York, 1978.

This book describes many computer crimes. Many of the incidents were taken from [Parker 76].

REFERENCES—BIBLIOGRAPHIES

Abbott 74

Abbott, R. P., Bloone, L. W., Morvay, I. M., and Tokubo, S., "A Bibliography on Computer Operating System Security." Technical Report, Lawrence Livermore Laboratory, University of California at Livermore, April 15, 1976.

Containing 750 references, this bibliography is organized into two parts. The first contains a KWIC index of the references based on title and author name. The second is a list of the references.

Bergar 72

Bergart, J. G., Denicoff, M., and Hsiao, D. K., "An Annotated and Cross-Referenced Bibliography on Computer Security and Access Control in Computer Systems." Technical Report, The Ohio State University, OSU–CISRC–72–12, November 1972, (NTIS AD–755 225).

Based on Bergart's Masters thesis, this bibliography contains annotated references to 85 important papers in computer security published previous to 1972. The bibliography is organized into four major sections (Privacy Protection and Access Control in Computer Systems, Computer Security, Business and Management Overview to Computer Security, and Social and Legal Implications) with the majority of the articles contained in the first two. While this bibliography is excellent in its references to early work in computer security, it is not suitable for the individual interested in the nontechnical side of the topic.

Carlst 78

Carlstedt, J., "Protection Errors in Operating Systems: A Selected Annotated Bibliography and Index to Terminology." Information Sciences Institute, University of Southern California, Los Angeles, March 1978, ISI/SR–78–10 (NTIS AD A053 016).

> This bibliography contains short annotations of 173 selected documents on operating system security.

Eichma 77

Eichman, B., "A Bibliography on Privacy," *The Privacy Report—ACLU*, Vol. V, No. 2, Sept. 1977, pp. 1–15.

> This issue of the *Privacy Report* contains an extensive bibliography covering the broad topic of individual privacy. Although it does include books published since 1964 and articles published since 1970, the bibliography emphasizes material published since 1974. The references are organized into three broad categories: General and Introductory Works, Specialized Works, and Reference Works, with each reference containing a short annotation about the material covered. One of the subsections of the Specialized Works category is particularly directed towards computer security and computer crime.

Hunt 74

Hunt, M. K., and Turn, R., "Privacy and Security in Databank Systems: An Annotated Bibliography, 1970–1973." Rand Corp. Report R–1361–NSF, March 1974.

> This bibliography contains 740 briefly annotated references to papers and reports published for the most part between 1970 and 1973. The bibliography also contains an index by a set of relevant keywords. Although [Scherf 74] contains a larger set of references with more extensive annotations, the well organized index makes this bibliography a valuable contribution.

Huskam 76

Huskamp, J. C., "A Partially Annotated Bibliography for Computer Protection and Related Topics." Lawrence Livermore Laboratory, UCID–17198, July 1976.

> This bibliography contains partial annotations of about 150 documents on operating system, hardware, and database security.

Pfiste 76

Pfister, J. J., "An Annotated and Cross-Referenced Bibliography on Computer Security and Privacy (1973–1975)." Masters thesis, Industrial Engineering Dept. of Texas A & M University, College Station, March 1976.

Pfister presents a well organized bibliography of 102 articles relating to computer security and privacy. The report is organized into sections on computer security and privacy with the former broken down into General System Software Design; Database Management Systems; Cryptography and Privacy Transformations; Test, Evaluation, and Certification; and Miscellaneous. Although the references do contain annotations they are in most cases original or modified versions of the author's abstract.

Reimhe 78a

Reimherr, G. W., "Computer Information Security and Protection. Vol. 1, 1964–June 1977." NTIS, U.S. Department of Commerce, Washington, D.C., NTIS PS–78/0859.

Reports on computer security and privacy available from NTIS published before June 1977 are listed with their abstracts. These reports are the results of federally funded research.

Reimhe 78b

Reimherr, G. W., "Computer Information Security and Protection. Vol. 2, July 1977–May 1978." NTIS, U.S. Department of Commerce, Washington, D.C., August 1978, NTIS PS–78/0860.

A continuation of [Reimhe 78a].

Reimhe 78c

Reimherr, G. W., "Computer Information Security and Protection (Citations from the Engineering Index Data Base)." NTIS, U.S. Department of Commerce, Washington, D.C., August 1978, NTIS PS–78/0861.

This bibliography contains 182 abstracts from a wide variety of sources.

Scherf 74

Scherf, J. A., "Computer and Data Security: A Comprehensive Annotated Bibliography." Massachusetts Institute of Technology Project MAC, MAC TR–122, Cambridge, January 1974.

Scherf's bibliography contains one of the most complete sets of references to work on computer security and privacy published before 1974. There are over 1000 references with over half being extensively annotated. These have also been rated by Scherf as to their usefulness and uniqueness.

This bibliography also contains a subject indexing scheme which, although clever, is awkward to utilize. In addition, for the individual strictly interested in the technical side of computer security, this bibliography is difficult to use since a good portion of the references are to articles relating to business and management issues.

Chapter 2

PRIVACY AND ITS TECHNICAL
IMPLICATIONS ON SECURITY

The increased use of computers by government agencies and private organizations has prompted recent concern with the invasion of privacy. A large amount of information is being collected and disseminated without, always, the necessary concern for its relevance or reliability. Thus, there is an effort to control this situation. A definition of the *right to privacy* has been given in the 1973 HEW's report as follows: "the right of individuals to participate in decisions regarding the collection, use, and disclosure of information personally identifiable to that individual." It is important to note that the individual does not have the sole right to determine the collection, use, and disclosure of the information.

2.1 BACKGROUND

The strong concern over privacy arose during the 1960s. The first official recognition of this concern may have been the hearings of a House of Representatives Subcommittee on The Computer and Invasion of Privacy in 1965 and 1966. These hearings were prompted by a concern over the proposed creation of a "National Data Bank." In addition, several studies were commissioned. The National Academy of Science 1972 study surveyed the then current state of the art in computerized systems. It looked at 55 advanced systems and studied 14 in detail, choosing a wide variety of organizations, including the Social

Security Administration, the FBI, the Kansas City Police Department, the Bank of America, TRW-Credit Data Corporation, the Church of Latter-Day Saints, and the Kaiser-Permanente Medical Care Program. This report was mainly intended to show the current status rather than to propose solutions.

The 1973 report for the Department of Health, Education, and Welfare proposed several actions that should be taken to help protect individual privacy. This report first proposed the following set of five "fundamental principles of fair information practice" to guide the development of regulations and laws concerning privacy:

- There must be no personal-data record-keeping systems whose very existence is secret.
- There must be a way for an individual to find out what information about him is in a record and how it is used.
- There must be a way for an individual to prevent information about him obtained for one purpose from being used or made available for other purposes without his consent.
- There must be a way for an individual to correct or amend a record of identifiable information about him.
- Any organization creating, maintaining, using, or disseminating records of identifiable personal data must assure the reliability of the data for their intended use and must take reasonable precautions to prevent misuse of the data.

This study distinguished two types of data systems: one for *automated personal data* systems and the other for *statistical reporting and research*. It recommended the enactment of legislation establishing a *Code of Fair Information Practice* for all automated personal data systems as follows:

- The Code should define fair information practice as adherence to specified safeguard requirements.
- The Code should prohibit violation of any safeguard requirement as an unfair information practice.
- The Code should provide that an unfair information practice be subject to both civil and criminal penalties.
- The Code should provide for injunctions to prevent violation of any safeguard requirement.
- The Code should give individuals the right to bring suits for unfair information practices to recover actual, liquidated, and punitive damages, in individual or class actions. It should also provide for recovery of reasonable attorneys' fees and other costs of litigation incurred by individuals who bring successful suits.

Many of their specific recommendations have been included in the Privacy Act of 1974. At the same time, there was also considerable concern shown in Canada and Western Europe, particularly in Great Britain, Sweden, and France.

2.2 LEGISLATION

The concern about privacy described in the previous section has prompted several recent laws at both the state and national levels. In addition, several other countries have also enacted privacy legislation.

2.2.1 Fair Credit Reporting Act of 1971

Prior to the Privacy Act of 1974, the *1971 Fair Credit Reporting Act* established regulations for credit-reporting agencies. Individuals have the right to be informed about and to contest information in their files. This information is required to be accurate and timely. It may only be used in response to a court order, to determine credit, insurance, or employment eligibility, or to meet the needs of a business transaction involving the individual.

2.2.2 Privacy Act of 1974

The *Privacy Act of 1974* can be summarized as follows:

1. The Act applies to federal agencies and their contractors which have information (whether computerized or not), which is stored in personally identifiable records about individuals.
2. Agencies are allowed to collect and maintain only relevant and necessary information.
3. A description of each system must be published. This description must specify what routine uses will be made of the information by other agencies.
4. An individual has the right to access and request deletions or corrections to information about him or her. An appeal process is provided.
5. Nonroutine disclosure of information outside the agency requires the individual's consent. An account of each disclosure outside the agency, whether or not routine, must be maintained.
6. An individual may sue to force an amendment to a record. In addition, an agency or individual who willfully discloses personally identifiable information or who maintains a system of

records without meeting the Act's notice requirements can be fined up to $5000.

7. Law enforcement, investigatory, and national security files are exempted from the Act.

8. Individuals may refuse to reveal their social security numbers unless required by statute or unless they were used in the systems prior to 1975.

9. A 2-year Privacy Protection Study Commission to study and recommend legislation and regulation applicable to all governmental, regional, and private organizations was established. (A later section discusses the report of this commission.)

2.2.3 The States

Many states including Arkansas, California, Connecticut, Massachusetts, Minnesota, Ohio, Utah, and Virginia have enacted privacy legislation regulating state (and sometimes local) agencies. The objectives and requirements of this legislation are similar to that of the Privacy Act of 1974. In addition, there are state statutes affecting fair credit reporting and the disclosure of bank information. A few states have statutes governing the collection, use, and disclosure of information about private-sector employees. Finally, some states regulate access to medical records.

2.2.4 Privacy Legislation in Other Countries

National laws have also been enacted in Sweden (1973), Germany (1976), and France (1978) and more are expected. The Swedish Data Act is summarized in the following:

1. The Data Inspection Board must issue a permit for any computerized information system containing information that can be assigned to an individual. (It should be noted that this Act applies to all systems, not just government ones.)

2. The Board has the power to regulate the content, use, and security of the systems.

3. The collection of information about convictions, medical history, and political or religious views is restricted.

4. Individuals have the right to access and challenge their own records.

5. Recipients of incorrect information must be notified of any corrections.

6. The Board has the right to visit computer centers and to examine documentation about covered systems.
7. The crime of data trespass is defined as the unauthorized access to covered information.

Despite their concern about privacy, Canada and Great Britain have not yet enacted any privacy legislation. The major distinction between American and Western European laws is that the latter provide a board, such as the Swedish Data Inspection Board, with extensive administrative powers. In the United States, on the other hand, the individual must pursue his or her own case.

2.3 COST OF PRIVACY

As part of its activities, the Privacy Protection Study Commission of 1974 investigated the cost of implementing the Privacy Act of 1974. The Office of Management and Budget has estimated that start-up costs were about $30 million over a 9-month period, and that the first-year operating expenses were about $36.6 million. These costs are broken down in Table 2–1. It should be noted that the cost of security and control amounted to only 7.4% of the start-up cost and 3.7% of the operating cost.

TABLE 2-1
Cost of Implementing the Privacy Act of 1974

	Summary—all agencies (Outlays in thousands of dollars)			
	Start-up		Operations	
Publication requirements	$13,549	46.0%	$ 4,405	12.0%
Training	6,825	23.2	3,282	9.0
Granting access	914	3.1	10,670	29.2
Correcting records	483	1.6	2,116	5.8
Security and control	2,175	7.4	1,345	3.7
Accounting for disclosures	667	2.3	9,415	25.7
New data collection procedures	1,164	4.0	1,507	4.1
All other costs	3,728	12.7	4,012	11.0
Reductions from records/ systems eliminated	− 45	− .2	− 62	− .2
Collections	− 2		− 91	− .2
Total	$29,459	100.00%	$36,599	100.00%

Source: Federal Personal Data Systems Subject to the Privacy Act of 1974, Second Annual Report of the President, Calendar Year 1976, p. 23.

2.4 FUTURE DEVELOPMENTS

Since the enactment of the Privacy Act of 1974, two Commissions, the Privacy Protection Study Commission and the National Commission on Electronic Fund Transfers have reported with recommendations on privacy.

2.4.1 Privacy Protection Study Commission

As stated earlier, the five principles outlined in the HEW report were the basis for the Privacy Act of 1974, and also for many of the state acts. In its review of the history of the Privacy Act, the Privacy Protection Study Commission refined these principles to be as follows:

The Openness Principle.   There shall be no personal-data record-keeping system whose very existence is secret and there shall be a policy of openness about an organization's personal-data record-keeping policies, practices, and systems.

The Individual Access Principle.   An individual about whom information is maintained by a record-keeping organization in individually identifiable form shall have a right to see and copy that information.

The Individual Participation Principle.   An individual about whom information is maintained by a record-keeping organization shall have a right to correct or amend the substance of that information.

The Collection Limitation Principle.   There shall be limits on the types of information an organization may collect about an individual, as well as certain requirements with respect to the manner in which it collects such information.

The Use Limitation Principle.   There shall be limits on the internal uses of information about an individual within a record-keeping organization.

The Disclosure Limitation Principle.   There shall be limits on the external disclosures of information about an individual a record-keeping organization may make.

The Information Management Principle. A record-keeping organization shall bear an affirmative responsibility for establishing reasonable and proper information management policies and practices which assure that its collection, maintenance, use, and dissemination of information about an individual is necessary and lawful and the information itself is current and accurate.

The Accountability Principle. A record-keeping organization shall be accountable for its personal-data record-keeping policies, practices, and systems.

The Commission felt that the Act has been generally good. It recommended the Act's provisions not be extended to state and local governments or to the private sector. Instead, the states should continue to devise their own privacy protections. For the private sector, mostly voluntary compliance is recommended. However, some modifications to the Fair Credit Reporting Act are proposed. In addition, it is also proposed that individually identifiable information in electronic funds transfer data communication networks be controlled.

However, the Commission did point out several shortcomings. Ambiguities in language should be clarified. *Reasonable tests* should be included to allow flexibility. The definition of *system of records* should be replaced because of two problems. First, the Act now applies only to records that are retrieved by a unique identifier. Thus, information retrievable by algorithm or attribute search is not included. Second, different categories of records should be defined so that different rules can be applied to the different categories. Finally, the Act should be extended to include the identification of routine internal use, not just external use as now required. Most individual's concerns are really with the internal uses.

2.4.2 National Commission on Electronic Fund Transfers

The National Commission on Electronic Fund Transfers (EFT) was established in 1974 and began work in 1976 to study the effect of EFT on financial institutions, the public, and the government's economic and monetary policy. Included in the report are recommendations on both privacy and security.

2.5 TECHNICAL IMPLICATIONS FOR SECURITY

The enactment of privacy legislation has several technical implications. Policies and procedures must be established to assure the *operational security* of the computer system. The *physical security* of the system must be maintained. The computer *hardware* must have features that augment security. Information transmitted to or from remote sites must be protected, possibly using *data encryption*. The *operating system* and the *data management system* must also have features to augment security. The problems of each of these areas are described in the following chapters.

Specifically, the Privacy Protection Study Commission reported that

> a major technical implication of privacy protection is the requirement to restrict system functions so that they operate either on subsets of a file—that is, particular records or records with particular characteristics or attributes—or on subsets of a record—that is, particular data items or data items with particular characteristics or attributes.

Thus, future systems must be able to control access down to the data item level.

In addition to the control of access required by the privacy legislation, there must be a means to determine who has received information, so that later corrections may also be forwarded to those who have received the incorrect information. Thus, automatic *logging* of the transfer of information is necessary.

2.6 POSTSCRIPT

Concern about individual privacy arose in the late 1960s culminating in several studies of the problem. The most important of those in the United States were done for the National Academy of Sciences [Westin 72] and for the Secretary of the Department of Health, Education and Welfare [Ware 73]. Canada and Great Britain also had studies at the same time. The first federal statute affecting individual privacy was the Fair Credit Reporting Act of 1971 [Patric 74]. It was followed by the Privacy Act of 1974 [Privac 74]. Discussion of the implications and motivations for this act can be found in [ACLU 75] and [Flato 74]. Guidelines for implementing the act can be found in [Bushki 76a]. Other technical implications are considered in [Bushki 75], [Bushki 76b], [Higgin 76], [NBS 75c], [Salasi 76], [Turn 76], and [Ware 77c]. In addition to these federal statutes, there are also several state laws [Linowe 77, Appendix 1] and European laws which are discussed in [Hoffma 77b].

Following the enactment of these laws there has continued to be further concern about privacy. See for example [Dougla 76], [Flato 75], [Laska 75], [Ombuds 76], and [Rosenb 76]. In particular the possible creation of a universal identifier has received much attention [Ware

73], [ACLU 77b], [Bushki 76b], and [Flato 76a]. In addition, the National Bureau of Standards alone [Rennin 74a] and [Rennin 74b], and in conjunction with the Association for Computing Machinery [Trigg 75] has sponsored several conferences either completely or partially devoted to computers and privacy.

The cost of implementation of privacy controls has been of continued concern [Berg 75] and [Jansse 77]. Some research has been done to develop models for estimating costs [Goldst 75], [Goldst 76], and [Lobel 75]. Further work is needed.

The Privacy Protection Study Commission was established by the Privacy Act of 1974. Its report [Linowe 77] contains many recommendations for the future. The reports of the National Commission on Electronic Fund Transfers, [Nation 77a] and [Nation 77b], contain recommendations on both privacy and security. Other discussion of electronic fund transfers is included in [Dewey 78], [Kaufma 76], [Kling 78], [Mazzet 76], [Thomps 76], and [Ware 77b]. The possible abuse of privacy by multinational corporations is discussed by [Goldwa 77]. The Privacy Protection Study Commission, in Appendix 5, also discusses technical implications of the Privacy Act with respect to computer security. Other such discussions can be found in [ACLU 77a], [Davis 76], and [Ingema 76b].

REFERENCES

ACLU 75

American Civil Liberties Union, "The Privacy Act of 1974: What Are Your Rights." *The Privacy Report,* Vol. 2, No. 5, March 1975, pp. 1–9.

> This article presents a very readable summary of the Privacy Act of 1974 covering all the important sections. This is one of the best references available outside of reading the Act itself.

ACLU 77a

American Civil Liberties Union. "Privacy and Computer Security." *The Privacy Report,* Vol. 4, No. 11, June 1977, pp. 2–4.

> This article comments on computer security and how it interrelates with privacy noting that lax computer security undermines any attempt to protect personal privacy. The article also notes that methods used to increase computer security may conflict with other civil liberties.

ACLU 77b

American Civil Liberties Union, "Who Are You? Identifiers and Identity Documents." *The Privacy Report,* Vol. 4, No. 10, May 1977, pp. 1–9.

The ACLU examines the concept of a standard universal identifier (SUI) focusing on the social security number (SSN) and its approximation of an SUI. The use of the SSN in the Child Support Enforcement Program's Parent Locator Service to find parents who avoid paying child support is discussed. A section on the implications of a National Identity Document is included.

ACLU 77c

American Civil Liberties Union, "Report of the Privacy Commission," *The Privacy Report,* Vol. 4, No. 11, June 1977, pp. 8–9.

Berg 75

Berg, J. L., "Exploring Privacy and Data Security Costs." *National Bureau of Standards,* August 1975, NBS TN 876.

A summary of a February 1975 workshop on the costs of complying with the Privacy Act of 1974 sponsored by NBS is given. The participants included nine individuals, about half from the Federal government, the rest from private industry or academe. The questions discussed were (a) what benefits to computer users would accrue? (b) what costs would there be? (c) how would these costs be allocated?

Bushki 75

Bushkin, A. A., "The Security Implications of Privacy." System Development Corporation, SP–3823, June 1975 (NTIS PB–253 050).

Bushkin, in this report, attempts to clarify the technical implications of privacy legislation such as the Privacy Act of 1974 (Privac 74). Bushkin feels that with respect to personal information, unauthorized penetrators with strong technical knowledge are not typical threats. Instead, Bushkin thinks that the threats to a personal information system will come from authorized, but dishonest, individuals. Auditing and logging procedures are suggested as solutions to these types of threats.

Bushki 76a

Bushkin, A. A., and Schaen, S. I., *The Privacy Act of 1974: A Reference Manual for Compliance.* System Develoment Corp., Santa Monica, California, 1976.

This report provides a most valuable reference work for any individual interested or affected by the technical implications of the Privacy Act of 1974. The report is divided into five major sections entitled Introduction, Coverage of the Act, Basic Compliance Requirements of the Act, Technical Considerations in the Implementation of the Act, and Establishing "Appropriate Safeguards."

Background and definitions used in the Act are provided in the first two sections. The third section discusses in detail the important portions of the Act. This section is excellent in that it describes the requirements of the Act with respect to the Act itself and Office of Management and Budget Guidelines.

The fourth chapter is written specifically for automated information systems and examines the implementation of the provisions of the Act on such a system.

The final chapter addresses the problem of accidental or malicious use of data stored in an information system and safeguards available to prevent this.

Several appendices are included which contain references, the actual text of the Privacy Act, and an outline of section three.

Bushki 76b

Bushkin, A. A., and Schaen, S. I., "Some Technical Difficulties in the Implementation of The Privacy Act of 1974," 15th Annual Technical Symposium: Directions and Challenges, Washington, D.C., Chapter ACM and Institute for Computer Science and Technology, June 17, 1976.

> Several difficulties encountered in implementing the Privacy Act of 1974 are explained in this paper. The first topic is the coverage of the Act which is any Federal record system in which the information is retrieved by an individual identifier. The implication is that coverage of the Act is based on the method of information retrieval rather than the type of records. This means that when a new program is developed for accessing a record system, it may imply a need to notify Congress under the provision of the Act calling for notification when a new system is developed.

The problems of personal identification and the requirements of the Act that an individual not be required to know a specialized identification number and in many cases not be required to provide his social security number are examined. The development of a *standard universal identifier* is examined [Ware 73].

Also studied is the problem of granularity, that is the need to access and protect the information in a record at the field level. The problems of appending an individual's comments about disputed information are also looked at.

This paper provides an interesting look at technical difficulties that can arise when complying with seemingly nontechnical privacy legislation.

Davis 76a

Davis, R. M., "Implications of Privacy Legislation on the Use of Computer Technology in Business." National Bureau of Standards, Fall 1976 (NTIS PB–259 714).

Dewey 78

Dewey, R., "Systems Auditability and Control in EFTS Environment." *AFIPS Conference Proceedings–1978 NCC,* Vol. 47, 1978, pp. 185–189.

A review of auditing tools and specific system controls applicable to EFT systems are presented. Controls can be applied to data entry, data communications, computer processing, data storage and retrieval, and output processing.

Dougla 76

Douglas, A. S., "The U.K. Privacy White Paper." *AFIPS Conference Proceedings-1976 NCC,* Vol. 45, 1976, pp. 33–38.

In 1975 the British government issued a White Paper on privacy which includes specific proposals for computerized information systems. In this paper, Douglas reviews the history of the White Paper and examines its implications on individual privacy. The paper is interesting in its account of action taken in countries outside the United States to protect individual privacy.

Flato 74

Flato, L., "Behind the Privacy Bill." *Computer Decisions,* Vol. 6, No. 9, September 1974, pp. 24–26.

This paper contains the text of discussions held with Representatives Koch and Goldwater after their introduction of what was to become the Privacy Act of 1974 [Privac 74]. The article is interesting for the historical perspective it provides.

Flato 75

Flato, L., "Privacy: The ACLU Takes a Stand." *Computer Decisions* Vol. 7, No. 4, April 1975, pp. 32–34.

This article is a report on Aryeh Neier, head of the American Civil Liberties Union, and his attitudes and efforts regarding current privacy issues. Neier feels that with passage of the Privacy Act of 1974 much has been accomplished. He still believes more regulations are needed regarding information collected by law enforcement agencies and private organizations. According to Neier, laws today generally affect personal data already collected and more laws are necessary to control the actual collection of this data.

Flato 76a

Flato, L., "A Crisis of Identity." *Computer Decisions,* Vol. 8, No. 5, May 1976, pp. 22–26.

The problem of false identification is providing many government agencies with the incentive to develop ID cards that would be needed in order to receive services. Examined in particular is the desire of the Immigration and Naturalization Service to require resident and border crossing aliens to carry special "tamper-proof" ID cards. Card readers, which would be installed at high-volume entry points, would be tied to a central computer and used in verifying the alien's identity. Flato explains that the Agriculture Department is considering the use of similar cards in its food stamp program. The article relates many of the concerns raised in Congress and elsewhere that these systems would eventually lead to a national ID card system.

Goldst 75

Goldstein, R. C., "The Costs of Privacy." *Datamation,* Vol. 21, No. 10, October 1975, pp. 65–69.

Goldstein asserts that companies using computers may no longer ask "Will we be affected by privacy legislation?" but they must more appropriately ask "How much will it cost?" Although current privacy legislation [Privac 74] affects only government computer facilities, it seems likely that the private sector will soon be included. Goldstein presents a summary of a privacy cost model he developed based on his Ph.D. dissertation. He uses this to analyze the costs to six personal data systems of implementing regulations such as the Privacy Act of 1974.

Using Goldstein's model the major costs appear to result from maintaining the accuracy of the information and the handling of inquiries and complaints from individuals about the contents of their records. The former requires much clerical time and the latter a large amount of executive time. Goldstein notes that the privacy costs in terms of computer resources (data storage, processing time, programming, etc.) will actually be a very small percentage of the total cost.

The results of this work are also reported in [Lobel 75].

Goldst 76

Goldstein, R. C., Seward, H. H., and Nolan, R. L., "A Methodology for Evaluating Alternative Technical and Information Management Approaches to Privacy Requirements." D. P. Management Corp., Lexington, Massachusetts, NBS TN–906, June 1976 (NTIS PB–254 048).

Described in this report is a methodology for evaluating alternatives for complying with the requirements of the Privacy Act of 1974. The methodology provides for "(a) identifying actions which must be taken to comply, and (b) estimating the cost of these actions to see if low cost techniques are being utilized."

The authors stress four major requirements of the Privacy Act: (a) agencies must obtain disclosure consent from data subject, (b) maintain accounting of disclosures and be able to inform individuals of disclosures upon request, (c) allow an individual access to his records and a right to amend them, (d) general requirements to maintain accurate data and security. Based on their experiences in this field, the authors have developed a system which is given information about a specific agency's information system. Based on a set of algorithms described in the report, a set of actions to comply with the four major requirements outlined above are produced. These actions are multiplied by cost factors to obtain an estimate of what it would cost the agency to comply.

Much of the work described in this report is an extension of earlier work by Goldstein discussed in [Goldst 75].

Goldwa 77

Goldwater, B. M., Jr., "Data Haven: International Privacy Threat." *Computer Decisions*, Vol. 9, No. 6, June 1977, pp. 22–24.

Representative Barry Goldwater, Jr., long an advocate of personal privacy, relates the problem that exists today with information systems in one country containing records on citizens of another. With the lack of any international law regarding such systems it is unclear who is responsible for the use and maintenance of these systems. Additionally, there is the problem of insufficient technological safeguards to prevent interception of transmission of such data.

Goldwater states that while some nations are beginning to approach these problems some of the proposed laws would discriminate against the technical or commercial presence of foreign companies thus affecting U.S. interests.

There are efforts under way to study these matters and Goldwater specifically points out the Task Force on Information, Computers, and Communication Policy formed by the U.S. State Department and the Information and Privacy Research Center at Purdue University.

Higgin 76

Higgins, W. H., "Review of the Air Force Privacy Act Tracking System (PATS)." Office of the Executive Secretary, Defense Privacy Board, March 1976.

The Air Force Privacy Act Tracking System (PATS), located at Randolph AFB, is a logical procedure that is interleaved with existing software in the Air Force Advanced Personnel Data System. This memo reviews the parts of the Privacy Act of 1974 that the Air Force has complied with and the operational features of PATS. Most of the features center around the update and disclosure portions of the Act.

Hoffma 77b

Hoffman, L. J., "Privacy Laws Affecting System Design." *Computers and Society*, Fall 1977, pp. 3–6.

In the paper Hoffman provides a good, although brief, review of the various privacy laws in effect in the United States. These include the Privacy Act of 1974, the 1974 Minnesota Privacy Law, and the 1974

Berkeley, California, Social Impact Statement. Also, Hoffman outlines the common features of current legislation.

Ingema 76b

Ingemarsson, I., Fak, V., Forchheimer, R., and Blom, R., "Computer Security 1981." Internal Publication LiTH–ISY–I–0116, Department of Electrical Engineering, Linkoping University, Linkoping, Sweden, No. 4, 1976.

Ingemarsson and fellow researchers conducted a series of interviews with a small number of data processing users to determine their security needs in the near future. This report, containing the results of the survey, is broken into five sections: an introduction, a short section on current trends in computer systems, a description of the survey, results of the interviews, and personal comments by the authors on the subject.

Jansse 77

Janssens, C. J., "Privacy Legislation and Its Implication Toward the Computer Industry." M.S. thesis, Naval Post Graduate School, June 1977 (NTIS AD A042 280).

Effects of the Privacy Act of 1974 on management, requirements for accuracy and flow of data, computer hardware and software, and costs are considered.

Kaufma 76

Kaufman, D., and Auerbach, K., "A Secure, National System for Electronic Funds Transfer." *AFIPS Conference Proceedings–1976 NCC,* Vol. 45, 1976, pp. 129–138.

A system level design of a secure local and national EFT network is described based on the following security principles: (a) The personal identification number (PIN) should be known only by the cardholder. (b) There should be no way to derive the PIN from identification on the card. (c) Exposure of the PIN should be minimized during a transaction. (d) Sensitive or private transaction data should not be subject to unauthorized exposure. (e) Transaction data should not be subject to unauthorized alteration. (f) All transaction requests and transaction authorizations should be authenticated at their destination.

Kling 78

Kling, R., "Value Conflicts and Social Choice in Electronic Funds Transfer System Development." *Communications of the ACM,* Vol. 21, No. 8, August 1978, pp. 642–657.

Among the problems of EFT systems discussed are those of security and privacy.

Linowe 77

Linowes, D. F. (Chairman), *Personal Privacy in an Information Society: The Report of the Privacy Protection Study Commission.* GPO Catalog No. Y3. P93/5:1/.

> One provision of the Privacy Act of 1974 was to establish a Privacy Protection Study Commission to make a "study of the databanks, automatic data processing programs, and information systems of governmental, regional and private organizations, in order to determine the standards and procedures in force for the protection of personal information." This report contains the final findings and recommendations of that commission. Based on these studies, the commission was also to recommend what extensions should be made to the Privacy Act of 1974 that would be applicable to institutions outside the Federal government. The report is organized in 14 chapters entitled: Introduction, The Consumer–Credit Relationship, The Depository Relationship, Mailing Lists, The Insurance Relationship, The Employment Relationship, Record Keeping in the Medical Care Relationship, Investigative Reporting Agencies, Government Access to Personal Records and "Private Papers," Record Keeping in the Education Relationship, The Citizen as Beneficiary of Government Assistance, The State Role in Privacy Protection, The Relationship between Citizen and Government: The Privacy Act of 1974, The Relationship between Citizen and Government: The Citizen as Taxpayer, The Relationship between Citizen and Government: The Citizen as Participant in Research and Statistical Studies, and The Social Security Number. In each of these chapters, the results of the findings are presented and specific recommendations are made. A discussion and criticism of this report may be found in [ACLU 77c].

Lobel 75

Lobel, J., "The Cost of Computer Privacy." *AFIPS Conference Proceedings–1975 NCC,* Vol. 44, 1975, pp. 935–940.

> Presented in this paper is a summary of a study performed by Robert Goldstein to determine the potential costs of privacy legislation. Included are explanations of the model used and the findings reached.
> A similar summary by Goldstein is presented in [Goldst 75].

Mazzet 76

Mazzetti, J. P., "Design Considerations for Electronic Funds Transfer System Development." *AFIPS Conference Proceedings–1976 NCC,* Vol. 45, 1976, pp. 139–146.

> An EFT switch permits sharing of customer terminals among financial institutions by switching each transaction to the appropriate host in-

stitution. Particular problems of security are discussed briefly in addition to the other considerations for switch design.

Nation 77a

National Commission on Electronic Fund Transfers, "EFT and the Public Interest." U.S. Government Printing Office, Washington, D.C., February 1977 (NTIS PB 272 575).

Nation 77b

National Commission on Electronic Fund Transfers, "EFT in the United States: Policy Recommendations and the Public Interest," Final Report, U.S. Government Printing Office, Washington, D.C., October 1977.

Included in this final report are several recommendations related to privacy and computer security of electronic fund transfer (EFT) systems. The Commission concluded that current privacy safeguards are inadequate because (a) new kinds of financial records are being kept, (b) an increasing number of records are available, (c) these records are easier to retrieve, (d) it is now possible to physically locate individuals who use an EFT system, and (e) an increasing number of institutions have access to EFT information. Thus the Commission recommended stricter controls of both government and private access to EFT information.

Particular recommendations include: (a) The government should minimize requirements to maintain and report information and should minimize requests to collect information that is not needed as part of the EFT system. (b) The government should not use the system for surveillance to determine consumer location or pattern of behavior. (c) Government agencies, including law enforcement agencies, should be required to obtain a judicial subpoena or court order, or an administrative summons to obtain information about an individual, and, except in limited cases, the individual should be notified of and be allowed to challenge any such request. (d) Individual information should be released to private third parties only if either it is required for the operation of the system or the individual has given permission for such a release. (e) Individuals should have the right to challenge and correct their own information.

The security vulnerabilities were identified as being located at the terminals, on communication links, and at the central computer. The Commission concluded that the loss from fraud has been low. It did however recommend that state and federal financial regulatory agencies develop joint regulations for security. The Commission also concluded that state and federal laws were needed to cover general misuse of computers, in particular (a) the introduction of fraudulent data, (b) the unauthorized use of computer facilities, (c) the fraudulent or malicious alteration or destruction of data, or (d) the theft of funds, data or programs.

NBS 75a

National Bureau of Standards, "Privacy Mandate: Planning for Action." Symposium/Workshop April 2–4, 1975, National Bureau of Standards/Mitre Corp..

Currently the Privacy Act of 1974 is in effect for the Federal government and proposals are being made to extend these regulations to the private sector. With planning for this extension of regulations in mind, a symposium/workshop cosponsored by the National Bureau of Standards and the Mitre Corporation was held. Individuals from all levels of government and industry gathered to consider nine different perspectives on the issues (managerial, judiciary, economic, technological, etc.) presented by experts in the various areas. The text of these presentations is contained in the proceedings. Four panels then convened resulting in recommendations based on institutional considerations, individual rights, technological implications, and economic factors. The four panel summaries, which present a perspective of the issues and include specific recommendations, are well worth reading.

The overall recommendations reached by the workshop are very general in nature. These are made in two parts: (a) institutional actions and (b) research actions. The first includes establishment of policies for individuals to access and review their records along with methods to determine responsibility for the records use. Recommended for research action are investigations into better computer security techniques and determining the nature of privacy and the costs of providing it.

NBS 75c

National Bureau of Standards, "Index of Automated System Design Requirements as Derived from the OMB Privacy Act Implementation Guidelines." October 1975, NBSIR 75–909.

The Federal Information Processing Standards Task Group 15 (Computer Systems Security) prepared this index to Office of Management and Budget guidelines for implementing the Privacy Act of 1974.

Ombuds 76

Ombudsman Committee on Privacy, Los Angeles Chapter ACM, Gerberick, D. A. (Chairman), *Privacy, Security and the Information Processing Industry.* Association for Computing Machinery, 1976.

With much of their information coming from the Department of HEW's report "Records, Computers, and the Rights of Citizens" [Ware 73], the Ombudsmen Committee on Privacy sets forth guidelines for implementing security and privacy in information systems. The report is broken into two major sections covering privacy and security. Although generally focusing on those activities of interest in the state of California, the material contained in the report is of broader interest. The security section provides reasonable coverage of the physical and operational aspects of computer security while the privacy section covers most of the issues fairly well.

Half of the report is appendices which by themselves would provide a valuable reference tool. These include a good bibliography, glossary, and a checklist for security. Also included is the text of the Privacy Act of 1974 and the Comprehensive Right to Privacy bill.

Patric 74

Patrick, R. L., "Privacy, People and Credit Services." *Datamation*, Vol. 20, No. 1, January 1974, pp. 48–50.

Credit grantors (department stores, banks, etc.) are relying more and more on databanks to determine the credit worthiness of their customers. These credit databanks are managed by single companies who rely on subscribers (the banks and stores) for information about individuals. Patrick explains how a subscriber, when deciding whether to grant credit or not, interrogates the credit bank. Based on the individual's past performance, as recorded in the databank, the credit grantor then makes the decision.

With enactment of the Fair Credit Reporting Act in 1971, individuals now have the right to find out what information is being kept on them in these credit banks. Patrick relates his experiences in obtaining the contents of his records and how appalled he was with the sparseness of the information in them. At TRW Credit Data in Anaheim, California, the largest such service in the country, Patrick found information on property ownership, automobiles, and bank accounts missing. This was apparently because he did not do business with companies who were TRW subscribers thus making him appear as a less than good credit risk in the TRW files.

Patrick details some changes he feels are necessary in legislation affecting these computerized credit services. Views supporting the use of the social security number as a universal identifier are also offered.

Privac 74

Congress, 93rd—2nd Session, "Privacy Act of 1974." PL 93–579.

The Privacy Act of 1974 is by far the most important United States legislation passed to date affecting information systems containing records on individuals. Adopted by Congress in late 1974 and signed into law by President Ford, the Act took effect in late September 1975.

The Privacy Act is based on the recommendations contained in the 1973 Department of Health, Education and Welfare report "Records, Computers, and the Rights of Citizens" [Ware 73]. The review of the Privacy Act by the American Civil Liberties Union (ACLU) [ACLU 75] is recommended reading for anyone interested in finding out the details of the act without actually having to read it.

Rennin 74a

Renninger, C. R., and Branstad, D. K., eds., "Government Looks at Privacy and Security in Computer Systems." NBS Technical Note 809, Washington, D.C., February 1974, GPO SD Catalog Number C 13.10:404.

The first of two conferences held by the National Bureau of Standards on Privacy and Security in Computer Systems was an attempt to identify the needs and problems confronting governmental agencies in safeguarding individual privacy and protecting data. Presentations were made outlining the need for uniform Federal, state, and local legislation; standards in complying with the legislation; and improved access control mechanisms.

Rennin 74b

Renninger, C. R., ed., "Approaches to Privacy and Security in Computer Systems." *National Bureau of Standards,* September 1974, NBS SP 404.

The second of two national conferences on Privacy and Security in Computer Systems was held so that individuals and organizations could offer views and proposals on how the issues realized at the first conference [Rennin 74a] might be resolved. This publication contains a good summary of the conference as well as the text of the presentations made. These included talks on legislative proposals, industry views, computer architecture and access controls, and efforts by professional societies.

Much of the discussion on legislative proposals affecting privacy requirements revolved around what type of legislation should or should not be passed. This discussion is somewhat outdated with the passage of the Privacy Act of 1974.

Rosenb 76

Rosenberg, J. M., "Human and Organizational Implications of Computer Privacy." *AFIPS Conference Proceedings–1976 NCC,* Vol. 45, 1976, pp. 39–43.

With the advances in computer technology in recent years the ability of society as a whole to invade an individual's privacy has become greatly enhanced. This paper explains the implication of this potential loss of privacy and why, for the "greater" good of its people, society is reluctant to prevent this erosion of privacy. Rosenberg outlines 10 rules of conduct which he feels all computerized data centers should follow to prevent misuse of personal data. He also suggests several areas where further research is needed before establishment of large data bases of personal records.

Salasi 76

Salasin, J., "A Control Systems Model of Privacy." *AFIPS Conference Proceedings–1976 NCC*, Vol. 45, 1976, pp. 45–51.

Computerized systems that can store large numbers of personal records and their ability to process these records have raised many concerns about infringements on individual privacy. Many problems with these automated information systems stem from a lack of understanding about the nature of privacy by those responsible for these systems. Salasin suggests using a feedback control systems model to study the relationship of privacy and automated information systems. He explains that a feedback control system is one in which control is partially determined by response from the system being controlled. The ability of individuals or groups to modify the behavior of a social system may be taken to represent feedback in the control of social systems objections to the type of information being gathered on an individual, the accuracy of that information, as well as objections as to whom the material is being distributed. Salasin feels the inability of an individual to provide this feedback may be expressed as a loss of privacy.

The author then describes how this model allows regulations that are intended to protect privacy to be examined with regard to how they assist or hinder feedback from individuals or groups. Recommendations of the Department of HEW Secretary's Advisory Committee on Automated Personal Data Systems [WARE 73] are analyzed in terms of how they affect feedback in government data systems. Salasin suggests several other potential uses for the model.

Sterli 76

Sterling, T. D., and Laudon, K., "Humanizing Information Systems." *Datamation*, Vol. 22, No. 12, December 1976, pp. 53–59.

Criteria to "humanize" computerized information systems and the development of an interface (Computer Ombudsman) between the end user and the system are examined. Suggested criteria for privacy protection, user interface to the system, exception handling, and inclusion of ethics in system design are outlined. These include elimination of routine clerical tasks, inclusion of procedures to override the system, and provisions for allowing examination and correction of information in the system.

In an effort to enforce some of the above criteria the Computer Ombudsman Service (COS) came into service in Canada in 1974. With its headquarters at Simon Fraser University in Vancouver, B.C., the COS was staffed by members of the Canadian Information Processing Society. Some of the typical cases handled by the COS are looked at and a few of the problems encountered are related. The major problem the authors see is the small number of cases that have been handled by the COS. The authors state that public feeling that nothing can be done when the "computer" fouls up along with a lack of publicity are the reasons for little response to the service.

Thomps 76

Thompson, S. F., "The Invasion of Privacy and Electronic Fund Transfer Systems: Spotlight on Invaders." *Computers and People*, Vol. 25, No. 9, September 1976.

Thompson presents his view that concerns about individual privacy in automated information should focus on the invaders of privacy (FBI, CIA, IRS, etc.). Thompson feels legislation should be directed at controlling these organizations rather than the information they have gathered.

Trigg 75

Trigg, C. D. (Chairman), "Impact of Government Regulations." Panel Report from Proceedings DataBase Directions Workshop, NBS and ACM, Fort Lauderdale, Florida, October 1975, pp. 67–78.

The panel was formed to predict which governmental rules or statutes will relate to information systems. In particular they were to identify and assess the impact of proposed regulations on database management systems, procedures, and methods.

One quite obvious result reached by the panel is that existing and proposed regulations will affect organizations whether or not database management systems are used. They do note that such systems may facilitate the implementation of regulations. The one regulation felt to be unreasonable if adopted is that requiring notification be sent to all previous recipients of data when subsequent changes to that data are made. The panel felt this should only be required if requested by the data subject. In addition it was felt there was no need to require notification of all data subjects that a file exists since Federal law [Privac 74] requires that descriptions of all information systems be published in the Federal Register.

The panel concludes its finding with a statement that the lack of a universal identifier [Ware 73] complicates the problem of insuring accuracy and completeness of data in information systems. This increases the cost of these systems which will eventually be borne by the consumer.

Turn 75a

Turn, R., and Ware, W. H., "Privacy and Security in Computer Systems," *American Scientist*, Vol. 63, No. 2, March–April 1975, pp. 196–203 (NTIS AD–A016 493).

Turn 76

Turn, R., "Classification of Personal Information for Privacy Protection Purposes." *AFIPS Conference Proceedings–1976 NCC*, Vol. 45, 1976, pp. 301–307.

This paper suggests that in light of laws such as the Privacy Act of 1974 a need exists for a standard system with which to classify personal records in order to implement these effectively. A review of previously proposed systems is presented whereupon Turn suggests his own generalized sensitivity levels with dissemination rules and security requirements for each level. It is noted that the same security requirements may be used for more than one category.

Methods for assigning sensitivity levels to specific records are discussed, with Turn noting that sensitivity is highly subjective and context-dependant. Automatic classification proposals include those that would assign systems (i.e., name, date of birth, etc.) or those that assign levels to categories of information (identifiers, physical characteristics, etc.).

Ware 73

Ware, W. H. (Chairman), *Records, Computers and the Rights of Citizens.* Report of the Secretary's Advisory Committee on Automated Personal Data Systems, U.S. Government Printing Office, Washington, D.C., 1973.

The Secretary's Advisory Committee on Automated Personal Data Systems was appointed to study the impact of computers used in keeping records on people. This report represents the results of that study and includes recommendations by the committee for safeguards against possible adverse results from using computers in this manner.

The report begins with a brief summary of the report and the set of recommendations by the committee. These recommendations include enactment of a Federal "Code of Fair Information Practice." This code would be based on five principles.

1. No secret personal data record keeping systems.
2. Ways for an individual to find out what information is being kept on him and how it is used.
3. Ways for an individual to keep information obtained for one purpose from being used for another without that person's consent.
4. Ways for individuals to correct or amend information kept on them.
5. Organizations maintaining or using these data banks are responsible for the reliability and use of the data.

The report continues with a short, interesting history of records and record keepers. The report discusses the origins of the three basic types of records (administrative, intelligence, and statistical) and practices surrounding them, noting that the use of computers is affecting these practices drastically.

The actual effects of computers on record keeping and changes in concept of privacy are pointed out. The report pays particular attention to the trend of using the social security number as a de facto universal

identifier and problems associated with this. Specific recommendations
on the issuance and use of the social security number are given.

Reports on specific record keeping systems are included in the appendix.

It should be noted that this report represents the major study of computers and their impact on information systems containing personal
records. Many of the recommendations made in this report were included
in the Privacy Act of 1974 [Privac 74].

Ware 74

Ware, W. H., "Computer Privacy and Computer Security." Rand Corporation, Santa Monica, California, Paper P–5354, October 1974 (NTIS
AD–A010 965).

Ware 75

Ware, W. H., "Privacy: The Private Sector and Society's Needs." Rand
Corporation, Santa Monica, California, Paper P–5414, March 1975
(NTIS AD–A022 233).

Ware 76

Ware, W. H., "Privacy Issues and the Private Sector." Rand Corporation, Santa Monica, California, July 1976, Paper P–5685.

> The paper gives a review of current privacy issues with an overview
> of related legislation. This paper was presented as the keynote address to
> the GUIDE meeting in Washington, D.C., May 26, 1976. This is probably
> the best of Ware's many reviews of the privacy issues.

Ware 77a

Ware, W. H., "Federal and State Regulations Concerning the Privacy of
Health Care Data." Rand Corporation, Santa Monica, California,
January 1977, Paper P–5783.

> In this paper Ware briefly covers the various state regulations re-
> garding access to medical records and comments on the general lack of
> privacy protection they provide. The Privacy Act of 1974 and the
> Freedom of Information Act as they apply to medical records maintained
> by the Federal government are also discussed. Ware feels the Federal
> regulations provide adequate protection while allowing the patient access
> rights to his own records. Ware suggests similar statutes are necessary in a
> consistent manner on the state and private level.

Ware 77b

Ware, W. H., "Testimony Before the National Commission on Electronic Fund Transfers." Computers and Society, Vol. 8, No. 1, Spring
1977, pp. 2–5.

This article contains the text of Ware's testimony before the National Commission on Electronic Fund Transfer given in October 1976. In this testimony Ware explains the terms security, privacy, and confidentiality. Ware discusses each of these in general terms and then examines each related to EFT systems. He appeals to the Commission to consider the seriousness of the privacy and security problems in EFT systems when making their recommendations.

Ware 77c

Ware, W. H., "State of the Privacy Act: An Overview of Technological and Social Science Developments," *Computers and Society,* Vol. 8, No. 1, Spring 1977, pp. 6–9.

This paper was presented as the keynote address to the University of Southern California Conference "Expanding the Right to Privacy" held in Washington, D.C., October 14, 1976. Ware discusses record systems and the goals of privacy safeguards as they relate to them. The Privacy Act of 1974 [Privac 74] and the goals of the Privacy Protection Study Commission [Linowe 77] formed as part of the Act are also discussed.

Chapter 3

OPERATIONAL SECURITY

Although many security issues are controlled by legislative ruling and social standards or are constrained by technological limitations, there are many important matters of operational security that are directly or indirectly under management control. In this chapter these issues are identified and possible actions are proposed.

3.1 INTRODUCTION

In general, much of the literature and research on security-related matters has focused on either privacy and its associated social and legislative implications or technical mechanisms to enforce a specific security objective. In comparison, the managerial and organizational issues, lacking the emotional tone of the privacy issues and the precision of the technical solutions, have received more limited attention. This situation is especially unfortunate because even after generally accepted privacy legislation is enacted and the major technological security mechanisms refined, the operational security issues, by their very nature, will persist.

3.1.1 Internal Policies and Objectives

Operational security is concerned with the policies and procedures adopted by management to ensure the security of their data and computer installation. Although certain of these policies and procedures may be externally defined, such as those relating to privacy laws or government regulations (e.g., IRS rules), most are internally defined within the managerial organization.

A typical (definition of data security found in the literature might be "protection of data against accidental or intentional disclosure to *unauthorized* persons, or *unauthorized* modifications or destruction.") The key to such a definition is the notion of authorization. Major managerial control issues arc the questions of who should be authorized, how this is determined, and how the authorization process is operated.

3.1.2 Misconceptions

One of the major problems plaguing effective managerial security control is the presence of many widely held misconceptions. At one extreme, data security is sometimes viewed as a completely new and unique managerial problem; whereas most of the general issues regarding data security have always existed in manual systems even before the advent of the computer.

On the other hand, there have been many changes in society and technology that have changed the nature of the data security problem. For example, the activities of data gathering, processing, and dissemination in our society, sometimes collectively referred to as the "information industry," have increased to the point where they have been reported to represent 46% of the United States Gross National Product (GNP) and 53% of all United States wages. This growth of the information industry has occurred so rapidly that many individuals and organizations have not fully adjusted to the changes.

The technology supporting the information industry, such as computers, communications, etc., has also introduced new situations and capabilities that have not previously existed. Many of these changes affect accepted social and organizational norms. For example, an employee, out of curiosity, may not see any harm in glancing at the company's product plan report sitting on the top of his manager's desk. Actually opening a desk or file drawer, even if unlocked, to look at the report is quite likely to be viewed as less acceptable behavior, while breaking into a locked area to read such a report might be viewed as wrong, if not illegal, even by a person who felt that glancing at the report on the manager's desk was a harmless act. When we consider remote access to computerized corporate databases, we find that there are often very few security measures actually used or that they are quite different from the manual procedures that the organization has been familiar with. Thus, norms for behavior are ill defined.

The speed and precision of computers also introduce new risks. With manual data systems, the amount of copying or changes possible was physically limited by human capabilities. It would take a small army with copying machines weeks to copy the millions of documents that make up a typical corporation's records. A single individual, using the computer itself, could make such a copy in a relatively small amount of time.

As noted earlier, a key management issue regarding data security is authorization. As the volume of data and operational complexity of most organizations have increased considerably, the process of authorization has become very difficult. Furthermore, computers, lacking the discretionary capabilities of the humans that operated earlier manual systems, require more precise authorization rules.

The authorization process requires managerial decisions or actions that were often not needed, at least not explicitly, in earlier smaller manual systems. For example, let us briefly consider the issue of the importance of specific information. At first thought we might consider all of the organization's records to be important—otherwise, why keep the information? The National Fire Protection Association defines four levels of importance:

1. Vital—irreplaceable information that is crucial to the operation of the organization.

2. Important—information that could be replaced but at great cost and difficulty.

3. Useful—information that is useful and would be difficult to replace but the organization could operate effectively without it.

4. Nonessential—information no longer needed by the organization.

Actually characterizing information in this way can be quite difficult because the information may be used by many different parts of the organization, each with a different assessment of the information's importance. Furthermore, the importance rating for a piece of information is usually time-varying (e.g., the blueprints of a new potential product probably become much less important if that project is cancelled—recall that Boeing had difficulties finding someone to take away the prototype for their SST after that project was cancelled).

The degree of sophistication and consideration given computer security by management varies widely from organization to organization. It has been noted, on several occasions, that many businesses rely on nothing more than the ignorance of outside individuals to be their principal defense against loss of computerized information.

3.1.3 Highly Secured Facilities of the Future

(It has been proposed that computer facilities of the future be essentially automatic in their day-to-day operation. By using on-line files and comprehensive operating systems, the need for computer operators could be eliminated) In fact, many current-day, time-sharing installations operate for several days at a time (e.g., over the weekend) without manual intervention. (By using high reliability components and computer designs, maintenance and repair personnel will be needed only rarely.) Finally, (all data access, for input and output, low-speed and high-speed, can be restricted to controlled communication lines. Thus, there is no need for any on-site personnel and the installation can be placed in a highly secured location) (e.g., under a mountain).

Although such a facility may have greatly improved physical security and be (much less susceptible to certain human actions) (e.g., an operator walking off with the master tape), most of the issues regarding operational security, such as (who should be authorized to do what, etc., will remain.)

In the following sections we will explore various facets of operational security in more detail.

3.1.4 Categorization of Management Policies and Procedures

In recent years various individuals have attempted to address some of the operational security policy and procedure issues. With few exceptions these studies have either been imbedded within elaborate privacy or technical security reports or have been intended to serve as introductions to certain aspects of the problem areas. As a result, the literature on managerial security is largely diffuse and unorganized. This chapter attempts to introduce a comprehensive framework for organizing and studying the diverse aspects of managerial security. This framework, depicted in Fig. 3–1, places issues of operational security policies and procedures into four categories: (1) operational considerations, (2) organizational impact, (3) economics, and (4) objectives and accountability.

Each of these categories will be discussed in a separate section of this chapter.

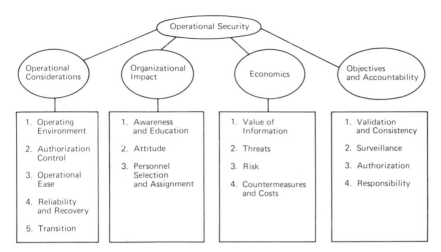

FIGURE 3-1.   Operational security categorization.

3.2 OPERATIONAL CONSIDERATIONS

There are many managerial decisions that must be made regarding the procedures to be used in the operation of an organization's computer facility. Although many of these decisions impact the degree of data security, they must be viewed in the light of the organization's overall objectives.

3.2.1 Operating Environment

The physical and operational procedures can be used to significantly limit the number of people that have any access to the computer facility. Three major categories are the following:

1. Closed—Only a very small number of operators have direct access to the computer facility. All computation to be performed is submitted to one of the operators who will then oversee the actual run.

2. Open—In principle, any member of the organization may have access to the computer facility. The user must physically appear at the computer facility to perform his computations and may be screened at that time.

3. Unlimited—Access to the computer facility is via communication lines, usually the public telephone network. The user need not ever

physically appear at the computer facility nor have any personal contact with the operators of the facility.

There are, of course, many variations on the operating environments listed above. Each environment has implications for the organization's data security as well as the utility of the computer facility. By severely limiting access, such as in a closed environment, controls similar to those used for a bank vault can be enforced. In fact, most high security military installations use this approach and the "computer room" is often actually a vault.

Although a closed environment can provide high physical security, it may not be consistent with the organization's needs. For example, an account verification system to be used by 3000 tellers in a bank's 600 branch offices does not lend itself to closed operation. Thus, many of the important modern applications of computers are dependent upon the concept of online access—leading essentially to an unlimited access environment.

The open and unlimited access environments introduce different types of risks. In an open environment it is still possible to screen out external intruders but the computer facility is very exposed to the actions of internal users who have legitimate physical access to it. An unlimited access environment cannot easily constrain access by external intruders but direct physical contact with the computer can be prevented and the actions that can be performed via communication lines can be restricted in various ways.

3.2.2 Types of Authorization Control

As noted previously, operational security is primarily concerned with the authorization process. This issue has many aspects. The first is the six W's: who, which, what, when, where, and why (see Fig. 3–2).

1. Who—The most obvious control relates to *who* wishes to access or alter information.
2. Which—The second important issue relates to *which* information is to be affected.
3. What—The third important issue relates to *what* operation (e.g., read, modify) is to be performed on the information.
4. When—An additional issue is *when* (i.e., at what time) the action is allowed to take place. This is similar to the use of time-locks on bank vaults.
5. Where—We may also wish to control *where* (i.e., the source) requests may originate. For example, certain terminals may be specifi-

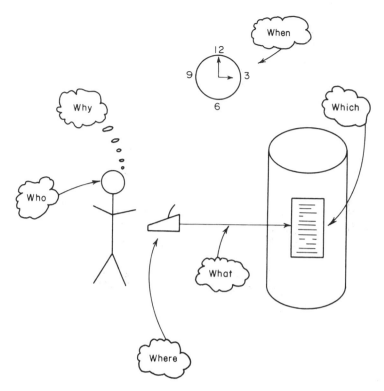

FIGURE 3-2. The six W's of authorization control.

cally identified, such as by unique codes built into the terminals or by the fact that they are connected to specific communication lines.

6. Why—Relating to the "need-to-know" concept, we may wish to know *why* a specific action is requested.

We will look at the critical who, which, and what questions in more detail below.

A. Identification and Verification

In order to enforce a "who" control, it is necessary to be able to identify and verify the identity of the user. The verification process usually involves something that the user (a) knows (e.g., a password), (b) carries (e.g., a badge), or (c) is (e.g., physical characteristic, such as fingerprint). The various verification procedures and technologies are discussed in more detail in Section 4.3.

Once the user has successfully passed the identification and verification procedure, he may be viewed as (a) an individual, (b) a role, or (c) a function. In the first case, the specific individual is identified (e.g., "John Jones") and the authorizations are tied to specific individuals. In many organizations it is the role (e.g., "assistant purchasing agent") rather than the individual that is important. By tying authorizations to roles rather than individuals it is much easier to accommodate personnel turnovers in the organization. Furthermore, it may be conceptually simpler to consider the question "what information should the assistant purchasing agent be able to access" rather than "what information should John Jones be able to access."

Going one step further, we may be interested only in the broad functionality of the user (e.g., a teller or a data entry clerk). Although functional identification is less precise than the earlier two approaches mentioned, in an organization of 100,000 or more employees it may make far more sense to define 100 functional categories and carefully determine the appropriate authorization for each category than attempt to realistically categorize the entire 100,000 employees, either as individuals or as roles.

Another situation that is common in most organizations is the use of "surrogates." That is, it is usually rare to see the president of a company personally seated at a terminal requesting and waiting for the printout of a report. More typically, his secretary, an administrative assistant, or some other staff employee will actually obtain the report. Thus, a single individual may have more than one role, such as "administrative assistant" and "acting for the president."

Both the technical mechanism for assigning roles, such as giving someone the "president's badge," and the procedural mechanisms for ensuring the correct and legitimate behavior of an individual acting as a surrogate for someone with more security warrant considerable attention. In many systems there is no way to distinguish between the multiple individuals that are allowed to take on a specific role (e.g., acting for the president). Without such a differentiation procedure it is difficult to effectively audit such a system or trace responsibility. This point will be pursued further in Section 3.5.

Obviously, combinations of the individual, role, and function identifications and authorizations can be utilized as desired by an organization. These are primarily managerial decisions that affect the type of security operationally desired.

B. Classification of Information

The "which" control, in many ways, parallels the discussion above. In particular, a specific document or piece of information may be identified and authorized either as (a) a specific document, (b) a role, or (c) a functional area. In the first case, we assume that each document is uniquely identified (e.g., document no. 110789) and the authorizations are related to it on that basis. Alternatively, we can tie authorizations to the role of the document (e.g., Current Production Plan Report). Conceptually, it may be administratively simpler to be concerned about a document's role rather than the specific document number.

Many organizations have millions and even hundreds of millions of corporate records. It is quite common to divide such documents into a fairly small number of functional categories (e.g., personnel, accounting, production). Matching the user's function with the information's function can provide the basis for an administratively simple authorization policy.

The classification of information can be complicated by many factors, such as granularity and security level. By *granularity* we mean the level of detail of information to be classified, such as an entire document, a record, or a specific data item. A single document may contain a variety of information that may warrant separate classifications. Furthermore, in certain types of computerized databases the concepts of documents or even records may not explicitly exist. In such a situation it becomes necessary to authorize on the basis of specific data items or data types.

The use of *security levels* is largely motivated by the military concept of security classifications such as confidential, secret, top secret, etc. Most nonmilitary organizations also use this concept to some extent (e.g., company confidential, company registered confidential, etc.).

Various combinations of information classification schemes could be employed in an organization. For example, combining "horizontal" partitioning (i.e., functional) with a "vertical" partitioning (i.e., security level) is a common choice.

Other aspects of the information classification issue can be found in Chapter 8.

C. Operations upon Information

Once we have established the "who" and the "which," we must consider what actions are to be allowed. In the simplest case, we can distinguish between the operations "read" and "write." In the first case, one may be authorized to read certain information, such as a customer's bank balance, but not be allowed to change it. In the latter case, one may be authorized to change the information, such as changing the customer's bank balance.

There are many variations of these two basic operations. For example, "creating" or "destroying" records is often treated differently from "reading" and "writing." An inventory control clerk may be authorized to update the inventory balances, but only the engineering department personnel may be authorized to create new part records.

There are also many versions of "reading." For example, some systems allow access to statistical information (e.g., average salary) without providing access to the individual salary information. Also, especially for proprietary software, there is the notion of "execute-only" access, whereby someone may be authorized to use the program but not be allowed to modify the program or read the program (reading the program would allow it to be copied and thereby stolen).

Further examples of operations upon information can be found in Chapters 7 and 8.

3.2.3 Operational Ease

(Many people fail to recognize the fact that security mechanisms may cause additional hardship or inconvenience for their users.)If such mechanisms are not easy to operate, it is most likely that they will not be used effectively. For example, in a noncomputer environment, if a door requires 30 minutes to lock and 30 minutes to unlock and this door must be used frequently, it is likely that the employee will rapidly learn to leave the door open—thus defeating the purpose of the lock.

Although the one-hour lock situation described above may seem farfetched, situations with similar effects can exist in computerized systems. This is because, for most users, security is not their primary job function. For example, an inventory control clerk's primary responsibility is to maintain up-to-date information on the company's inventory. If the security mechanism requires him to take extra time to update the inventory status, it will be at odds with his primary job function and, implicitly, encourage him to find shortcuts that may compromise the security mechanism.

One common problem area is the login (identification and verification) procedure on many systems. Let us consider one example. At a fairly advanced medical clinic a computerized medical records system had been installed. Due to the sensitive nature of the information in the system, the designers had developed an extensive identification and verification procedure relying upon user-provided passwords. Since most standard reports were prepared by the computer staff, many doctors used the system only rarely. The system had been designed with infrequent users in mind. It was "menu-selection" oriented whereby the user would be asked what was wanted and would be led through the necessary steps. Unfortunately, the login procedure, and especially the assigned passwords, were frequently forgotten. Thus, doctors might spend considerable time trying to remember this information or finding someone to help them. This problem was solved by the medical staff by taping an instruction sheet to each terminal that explained the login procedure along with a complete list of all the doctors and their assigned passwords!

When one is devising an authorization and security mechanism it is important to consider the operational environment and pick an approach that is likely to be easy and convenient to use. This decision may involve compromises between degree of security and ease of use.

3.2.4 Reliability and Recovery

As information systems have increased in their capabilities and cost effectiveness, they have become closely integrated into the operation of many organizations. This has, in turn, increased the concern regarding reliability and recovery. Consider the immediate impact upon an airline if its computer system were to stop operation: it would not be possible to accept new reservations, it would be difficult to assign seats (especially for those airlines that rely upon computer seat assignment and record keeping), and many important related processes, such as meal scheduling, fuel loading and scheduling, etc., would be disrupted. Many businesses are similarly dependent upon computer operations.

On another matter, in many organizations, the key records, such as inventory levels, sales orders, or accounts balances, are kept on computer files. If these files were to be destroyed, it might be very difficult and time-consuming, if not impossible, to reconstruct the information.

For these reasons, it is important that systems be as reliable as possible to minimize the possibility of their malfunction or the destruction of information. Furthermore, it is very desirable to have effective recovery procedures that allow normal operations to be resumed as soon as possible after a failure.

In some cases such reliability and recovery procedures are concordant with security procedures, in other cases they may be discordant. For example, many reliability mechanisms are based upon including additional tests for potential errors in either the hardware or software. Some of these tests may directly, or with minor extension, also be used to test for potential security violations.

On the other hand, many of the mechanisms are based upon redundancy and duplication. For example, one way to safeguard a company's key files and provide for effective recovery is to make one or more duplicate copies. Thus, if the original does get destroyed, a copy can be used. Unfortunately, these copies may increase the exposure to security violations. In fact, since under normal operation the duplicate copies are not used, if such a copy were stolen or replaced it is possible that it may never be missed! In order to address this specific problem, many companies are adopting new procedures whereby both the original and copy are used in normal operation, such as on alternate days. In this way it is more likely that missing information will be detected. In addition, the reliability of the copies can be confirmed. In one organization a spot check of their "backup copies" revealed that 25% were not usable due either to errors during the copying operation or to deterioration during storage.

A somewhat diabolical scheme used on several occasions by disgruntled former computer employees is to leave a "time bomb" behind. That is, prior to leaving the company the employee systematically destroyed the key backup tapes. In one case this was easily done since one of the employee's responsibilities was sending the backup tapes to the protected storage area—the employee merely sent blank tapes instead of the actual backup tapes. After the employee left it was merely a matter of time until a serious computer problem occurred which required recourse to the backup tapes. At that time, possibly months later, the company would be in for a big surprise!

One simple approach, though often not used, is to periodically and systematically test all security, reliability, and recovery procedures. This issue will be discussed further in Section 3.5.

3.2.5 Transition

At periods of transition, the system is extremely vulnerable to security violations, especially if it is a transition from a manual system to a computerized system.

This vulnerability is caused by many factors, such as (a) most users are not used to the new system and are likely to be careless, (b) the system itself may not include all of the "ultimately desired" security facilities and the facilities provided may not be fully tested, and (c) the operational and technical problems that usually accompany a transition may act as significant diversions of attention away from any concurrent security violation activities. Thus, security considerations must be carefully factored into the transition plan to minimize these vulnerabilities.

3.3 ORGANIZATIONAL IMPACT

Computer system security often requires or causes organizational changes. Some of these changes are desirable and are concordant with the security objectives. There are also impacts that may be detrimental to the security objectives and, possibly, to the organization as a whole. Several of these key issues are discussed in this section.

3.3.1 Awareness and Education

As noted earlier, the degree of awareness of data security as an issue and of the possibility of security threats varies widely. Although awareness is increasing, it is likely that the situation has not changed significantly from that reported in a study a few years ago. At that time it was concluded that only a small proportion of computer users use security features. As one senior manager of a time-sharing firm stated, "some customers are concerned about security, some are not; but they are all naive."

It has been found that, in organizational settings, those individuals who work closely with the computer system tend to be more aware of potential security problems than other individuals in the organization. Furthermore, it has been found that the degree of security demanded by a user depends upon the user's awareness of security threats. In this regard, it appears that users perceive the instigators of security violations as mirrors of themselves. If they know thousands of ways to subvert their system's security, they assume that their "enemies" are equally knowledgeable. Conversely, if they are not aware of any defects in their security system, they assume that the system cannot be penetrated.

This situation has been demonstrated in several studies. In one study several system staff and user department managers were interviewed. Three of the questions were as follows:

1. *How would you describe your exposure to and/or use of the company's computer system?*
   Extensive   5   4   3   2   1   Negligible

2. *Generally, how would you describe your personal concern for such things as security leaks, bugging, and the invasion of privacy?*
   Extremely   5   4   3   2   1   Not
   Concerned   Concerned

3.   *How would you rate the company's present system in regard to the security of computerized information?*
     Excellent   5   4   3   2   1   Poor

Systems staff personnel (i.e., those with a high sophistication of use and computer-related knowledge) responded near the extremes of "extensive," "extremely concerned," and "poor;" whereas user department managers, who had little or no exposure to the computer system, fell at the other end of the spectrum with responses of "negligible," "not concerned," and "excellent."

These observations are consistent with the attribution theory of psychology. That is, individuals evaluate the motivations and behavior of others by attributing to them their knowledge, values, and feelings. Consequently, an individual who is knowledgeable about computer systems is aware of their shortcomings and possible ways that they may be compromised; this knowledge can influence his attribution process.

A. Awareness

(Despite increasing concerns regarding computer security, many users are still unaware of the possible threats and the available countermeasures.) For example, in the time-sharing service bureau study mentioned above, it was found that although most systems provided various special security mechanisms, only a handful were actually used and those used were used by the most sophisticated users. The majority of the users assumed that the computer system was secure and that they were adequately protected.

One might be tempted to discount such a finding on the basis that many time-sharing users may be new to the computer field or are not especially sophisticated (neither of these possibilities is necessarily true). A study was conducted a few years ago at the Massachusetts Institute of Technology (M.I.T.), a community of about 5000 fairly sophisticated computer users (note: the majority of the users, although fairly sophisticated, are "users" rather than computer specialists). At that time M.I.T. was considering the installation of IBM's experimental Resource Security System (RSS) to be used in conjunction with IBM's Time-Sharing Option (TSO) that had been in use at M.I.T. for several years. When users were asked how much more valuable the system would be if no one else could read or write their files, a large majority was surprised to find that this was not already the case!

B. Education

From the above observations, it seems that user education is an important prerequisite to improved and effective security procedures and enforcement. Part of this increased education and awareness will come about as a result of external factors, such as (a) press and media coverage, (b) increases in direct personal contact with computer systems as they become more pervasive in organizations, and (c) advances, both in technique and cost-effectiveness, in security which makes it a more natural and easier to use aspect of modern systems.

In addition to these external factors, organizations may find it valuable to accelerate the awareness process by developing or sponsoring specific security education activities.

3.3.2 Attitude

When extensive computer security is introduced into an organization, some personnel may react in a negative manner because of difficulty in getting their work accomplished and/or a feeling of loss of power. The first problem was briefly discussed earlier in Section 3.2.3.

In a secure system people no longer can have unlimited, unrestricted access to the entire system. Management must explicitly determine each individual's access rights. To the extent that possession of information is a form of "power," individuals may resist and resent any decrease in their information access rights—even if the information is not necessary for the normal operation of their job. Furthermore, restrictions on or the elimination of "hands-on" computer access by most applications and systems programmers is often a serious blow to their egos.

In these regards, increased awareness and education can be very helpful. If each employee realizes that there are potential threats and that his information is better protected by increased security procedures, he is more willing to accept his own limitations.

3.3.3 Personnel Selection and Assignment

To a large extent the security-related aspects of personnel selection and assignment are very similar in both the computer and noncomputer environments; thus, much of the existing literature of such subjects (e.g., embezzlement) is applicable.

Two of the basic personnel concepts relating to security are division of responsibilities and provisions for checks and balances. The checks and balances imply that a security violation, to be successful, must pass several steps. At any of these steps the violation may either be prevented, if it is a preliminary step, or be detected, if it is a posterior step. The division of responsibility implies that different individuals be responsible for different steps. Thus, a successful security violation would require the active collusion of several individuals. This makes a security violation much more difficult and risky, thereby significantly decreasing the threat.

Computerized systems have introduced several new problems. First, a computerized system often allows for much more streamlined and efficient operation by eliminating many of the traditional steps. For example, an on-line order entry system may allow a company salesman to directly place a production order to the plant without requiring any processing by his sales manager or an order entry file clerk. In such a situation, although rapid order entry may be desirable and should be allowed, a parallel process whereby the computer produces timely reports to the sales manager and/or sales order clerk would reintroduce certain of these checks and balances. Furthermore, in many cases, such information may be very useful for planning, trend identification, and other auxiliary purposes.

Second, the operation of computerized systems introduces many new roles and procedures for which the concepts of division of responsibility are not well established from experiences with prior manual systems. For example, computer programs, to a large extent, act as surrogates for what were traditionally manual steps. Thus, if a single individual were to write the program for disbursements as well as the program for auditing disbursements, the implied checks and balances do not really exist since "collusion" between these programs could be easily accomplished (e.g., "authorized" disbursements can be issued to the programmer and ignored during the auditing process by appropriate modifications to both programs).

Another such area involves the separation of responsibilities between computer programmers and operators. For example, a programmer may feel uncomfortable about printing a hundred or so checks for himself if there is a chance that the computer operator might, even by accident, notice this peculiarity. Similarly, it is usually desirable to prevent the operator, who has physical access to the computer, from writing programs. One way to accomplish this is to hire only operators that have no programming ability. However, this could cause various organization, personnel, and performance problems. First, a knowledge of programming, although not necessarily essential, can be helpful to operators in performing their job effectively, especially in diagnosing problem situations. Second, in terms of career advancement, many operators aspire to positions as programmers; thus, many companies encourage and provide such training for their operators. The correct balancing of these potentially conflicting objectives must be carefully studied. Various additional procedures and checks and balances can be developed to lessen the potential exposure due to security violations by computer operators.

3.3.4 Responsibility

As can be seen from the preceding discussions, effective security requires considerable managerial concern and planning. Yet, in many companies the responsibilities for such planning and decisions are not well defined.

For example, in a study of several financial institutions, over 60% of the managers surveyed stated that a central decision maker is required in data security matters, but there was wide disagreement as to where in the organization this decision maker should be—both in terms of functional area and level of management! This issue is discussed further in Section 3.5.

3.4 ECONOMICS

As the preceding discussion has indicated, there are many managerial decisions regarding computer security that an organization must make. It is useful to consider ways to frame these decisions as economic-investment-type decisions to which organizations are more accustomed.

Key issues that must be resolved in order to determine security economics include (a) determination of the value of information, (b) assessment of likely threats to the information, and (c) determination of the cost of available security mechanisms and their effectiveness. Aspects of these issues are discussed in the following.

3.4.1 Value of Information

It should seem obvious that determination of the value of information is a crucial step in any security decision as well as in normal information management. Although there have been various efforts to formalize this process, using techniques such as those of information theory and decision analysis, the evaluation process remains very subjective.

The evaluation process not only requires placing a value on information (four levels of importance were identified in Section 3.1.2) but also requires consideration of the fact that the same information may

be perceived to have different values by different groups of individuals.

Let us consider three different groups involved:

1. Keeper—The organization that has and uses the information.

2. Source—The organization, or individual, that provided the information, or to whom the information pertains.

3. Intruder—An individual or organization that may wish the information, but which would normally not have access to it.

Different types of information may have different values to these
different groups. For example:

1. *Critical* operating information, such as this week's sales order
and production schedule, may have a very high value to the keeper
compared with its value to its sources (i.e., the customers) or potential
intruders.

2. *Personal* information, such as an individual's census data or
medical information in his employee personnel file, may have a much
higher value to the source (i.e., the individual) than to either the keeper
or intruder.

3. *Proprietary* information, such as marketing forecast data
gathered by a company, may be much more valuable to an intruder,
such as a competing company, than to either the sources (i.e., sample
customers) or the keeper who may have already finished analyzing the
data.

The categories listed here are aggregations. The value of a specific
type of information may be perceived differently by different keepers
(or different individuals or groups within the "keeper" organization),
sources, and intruders.

3.4.2 Threats

Just as the value of information may be different for different
groups, there are also differences depending on what is done with the
information. In Section 3.2.2 various types of operations upon information were discussed. In evaluating threats, one wants to know what is
the economic impact (usually interpreted as a loss or expense to the
keeper or source) if a certain operation were to be performed on certain information. For example, if the one and only master copy of the
1978 Boston telephone book were stolen before it was published, it
could be very costly to reconstruct it and its unavailability would
disrupt operations, such as Directory Assistance. On the other hand, if

an intruder were to copy a published directory, it is unlikely to be of much concern to the telephone company. In fact, in view of the printing costs, the telephone company may be pleased if the "intruder" made copies for the rest of his relatives and neighbors.

Threat operations can be divided into major categories, such as:

1. Interrupt—to disrupt the normal processing of the information, such as by bombing the computer (there are less drastic actions that could cause interruptions of various durations). Note that an interruption may be an important concern even though the information itself may not be affected in any way.

2. Steal or disclose—to read or copy information, either for use by the intruder or a third party (such as publishing the psychiatric records of a competitor).

3. Alter—to change information, such as the intruder's bank balance. This is probably the most obvious threat to most people.

4. Destroy—to permanently destroy the information, such as by erasing a magnetic tape.

Thus, an information valuation procedure should consider both the information, the threat, and the interested party. For example, specific cases would be "value to keeper to protect information x against disclosure" and "value to intruder to alter information y." All possibilities could be enumerated in the form of a three-dimensional table as illustrated in Fig. 3–3.

There are, of course, alternative categorizations of threats as well as additional factors that may be considered, such as whether the ac-

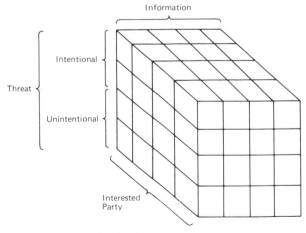

FIGURE 3-3. Information valuation factors.

tion was intentional (e.g., an intruder breaking in) or unintentional (e.g., someone lost the data). Although the intentional threats are often of most concern, the unintentional may be more frequent, and possibly have greater overall economic impact.

3.4.3 Risk

The threat assessment is intended to determine the value of a certain action upon information. In order to develop a rational security plan, it is necessary to assess the probability of each threat occurring. For example, the physical theft of an entire computer center might represent a very large threat in terms of the cash value of the equipment, the information lost, and the disruption of normal operations. On the other hand, although pieces of equipment may have been stolen, we are unaware of any previous occurrence of a wholesale theft of an entire computer center. Thus, one might reasonably associate a low probability with the likelihood of such a threat occurring.

A common objective of most risk assessment strategies proposed is to arrive at a quantitative statement of risk. A fairly obvious approach would be to calculate the expected value of the loss for each threat as $V \times p$, where V is the monetary value of the threat and p is the probability of occurrence. Thus, a threat with a value of $100,000 but a probability of .05 would have a risk assessment of $5000.

There are numerous problems encountered in attempting to perform such a risk assessment. First, determining the precise monetary value of a threat may be very difficult. Second, most people are usually reluctant to assign a monetary measure for threats that have a social impact, such as disclosure of confidential medical information. Even if there were not such a social reluctance, it would be difficult to arrive at a value. Third, as noted in Section 3.4.1 there may be different values for a given threat to different individuals and organizations.

There is also considerable difficulty in determining the probability of occurrence. Certain physical events, such as earthquakes and floods, have been studied over a long enough period to have some reasonable probability measures, especially since these are essential to the actuarial calculations of the insurance industry. The computer threats are too diverse and recent to have allowed for the collection of statistical information.

3.4.4 Countermeasures and Costs

(For each type of threat there are usually one or more countermeasures possible.)Due to the newness of the field and the diversity of threats, it has not been possible to completely enumerate all possible threats and their countermeasures. Various attempts at such a categorization are noted in the references.

A useful categorization is presented in Table 3–1. In this table threats are divided into five categories: (a) physical security, (b) hardware security, (c) communications security, (d) operating system security, and (e) database security. Specific threats within each category are listed and appropriate countermeasures are noted. Each of the threats

TABLE 3-1

Threat	Countermeasure(s)	Section
Physical security		
Natural disaster	Site selection	4.1.1, 4.1.2
	Detection	4.1.1, 4.1.2
	Extinguishing	4.1.1, 4.1.2
	Recovery	4.1.1, 4.1.2
Intruder	Boundary protection	4.2
	Perimeter protection	4.2
	Entrance protection	4.2
	Critical-area protection	4.2
Authentication	Password	4.3
and identification	"Key"	4.3
	Physical characteristics	4.3
Electronic and	Encryption	4.4, 6.1, 6.2
electromagnetic	Intruder protection	4.2, 4.4
tampering		
Hardware security		
Memory protection	Bounds registers	5.1.1
	Locks and keys	5.1.1
	Access control bits	5.1.1
	Virtual memory	5.1.2
Execution protection	Binary states	5.2.1
	Multiple states	5.2.2
I/O protection	Microprocessors	5.3.1
	Specialized processors	5.3.2
Sequence protection	Periods processing	5.4.1
	Monitoring	5.4.2
Communications security		
Short messages	Classical cryptography	6.1.1
Long messages	Modern cryptography	6.1.2
Distributed	Terminal interface cryptographic	6.2
terminals	transformation boxes	
Network	Network cryptographic controller	6.2
communications		
Code breaking	Based on key	6.2.1
	Standard transformation	6.2.2

TABLE 3-1 (Continued)

Threat	Countermeasure(s)	Section
Operating system security		
User access	Identification and authentication	4.3
	Logging	7.1.1
Access control	Threat monitoring	7.1.2
	Access control matrix	7.2
	Capability list	7.2
	Access list	7.2
	Authority-item	7.2
Propagation of	Isolation	7.3
security breach	Multiple space method	7.3.2
	Virtual machine monitor	7.3.2
Operating	Verification	7.4.1
system flaws	Inductive assertion technique	7.4.1
	Kernel concept	7.4.2
	Penetration tests	7.4.3
Data security		
Data errors	Access restrictions	8.1.1
Value-sensitive	View mechanism	8.1.3
data	Query modification	8.1.3
History-sensitive	Prevention of inference	8.1.2
data	Keeping track of the number and type of queries asked	8.1.2
Context-dependent	Cycle detection	8.1.4
data	Directed graphs	8.1.4
Restrict actual data	Partitioning	8.2.1
accessed	Compartmentalization	8.2.2
	Security atom	8.2.2
	Improve access precision	8.2.2
Multilevel	Compartmentalization	8.2.3
security	Security molecule	8.2.3
Access authorization	Authorization hierarchies	8.3.1
and resolution	Access control procedures	8.3.2
	Resolution capability	8.3.2
Integrated security	Secure database design methodology	8.4.1
	Predicates for control	8.4.2
	Database machines	8.4.3

and countermeasures listed is discussed in this book. The principal sections to be read for further information are noted in Table 3–1.

The countermeasures are intended to decrease the risk either by (a) decreasing the probability of occurrence of the threat or (b) decreasing the impact of the threat. For example, the probability of lost information can be decreased by adding new procedures to monitor the use and location of the information. The impact of lost information can be decreased by either having duplicate copies of the information available or by setting up procedures in advance that enable rapid and inexpensive reconstruction of the information.

There are at least two major considerations for each countermeasure: (a) its effectiveness and (b) its cost. This information can provide the basis for a rational economic security plan. In particular, a countermeasure is economically reasonable if its effectiveness, in terms of decreased expected economic impact exceeds its cost. The organization can establish maximum risk levels and select one or more economically justified countermeasures, as necessary, to reduce the total risk below the maximum risk levels.

Many of the same problems that prevent precise threat and risk assessment exist in determining countermeasure effectiveness and cost. On the other hand, there have been several efforts directed at enumerating countermeasures and, at least qualitatively, rating their effectiveness and cost.

Before leaving the subject of costs, there is at least one more issue that is often studied in the context of threats by intruders, the cost of the threat. In theory an economically rational intruder will not expend more to initiate a threat than he can expect to gain from that threat (e.g., one would not reasonably spend $5000 to break into a vault that one believed only contained $10). Thus, one of the significant objectives of a security countermeasure is to increase the costs to an intruder so as to raise the price of intrusion above the value to the intruder and, thereby, reduce the risk. The intruder's costs include resources necessary, such as technology, expertise, time, and opportunity. In addition, there are penalty costs, such as the possibility of detection and the resulting economic, personal, and social penalties. For this reason countermeasures that are based upon post-facto detection rather than prevention of threats may be equally effective at reducing the risk of an intruder threat (see Section 3.5.2).

3.5 SECURITY OBJECTIVES AND ACCOUNTABILITY

As part of a meaningful security plan it is necessary to clearly consider the objectives to be accomplished and the specific organizational responsibilities necessary to carry out the plan.

As one example, it has been noted that security violations by authorized insiders may greatly outnumber those likely to occur from external intruders. Thus, a plan focusing only on the outside intruder may not provide much increase in security. Likewise, unintentional mistakes by insiders may be a major problem in many organizations. "The computer did it!" calamity has become a basic part of our culture. One has only to look at the daily newspaper to find reports such as "Correction: Stock Prices Reported Yesterday Were in Error due to Computer Mistake," "Cars Mistakenly Towed due to Computer Error," etc. (Articles with essentially these titles appeared in recent issues of the *Boston Globe*.) On a day-to-day basis computers are being blamed for almost everything from the decline in morals in the United States to changes in weather. During one week on three separate occasions one of the authors was told that the computer was at fault in (a) fouling up a membership renewal, (b) cancelling a hotel reservation, and (c) mispaying his son for his paper route. If one believed in conspiracies, this could make one quite paranoiac waiting for the lights to be cut off and the house to be foreclosed next.

Finally, in this section many of the key issues regarding auditing, authorization, and responsibility will be discussed.

3.5.1 Validation and Consistency

Techniques and procedures to validate the reasonableness and consistency of data are important in both reducing the frequency of unintentional errors as well as providing a means of detecting or preventing various forms of intentional security violations by either insiders or external intruders.

Simple format and range checks are common to most, but not all, information systems. A typical format check is verifying that the zip code of an address is five digits long. An example of a range check is verifying that an employee does not report working more than 60 hours per week. These validation checks may be set to be at the maximum possible values (such as maximum wage payment = $2000 per week) or at the maximum likely values (such as maximum wage payment = $750 per week) and require explicit manual intervention to verify the correctness of any situation that would exceed these normal limits.

More complex consistency checks can be very valuable though they are less frequently used. For example, salary range checks may be conditioned upon organizational position. For the president of the company, a wage payment of $2000 per week may not be unlikely, whereas it might be suspicious for a secretary to receive such a salary. Likewise, shipments being sent to an address different from the customer's normal address may be suspicious, etc. Such consistency checks are much more complex and time-consuming to both construct and execute than simple range checks since they require comparing several different sources of information to determine whether they appear to be consistent. For example, a property assessment of $5,000,000 is not impossible, but if you knew that it was for a 20-year-old, 7-room house on a half-acre of land, you would probably be suspicious. Such an input mistake was made in performing property reevaluation for a small town in New Jersey, resulting in the establishment of an incorrect tax rate that caused chaos and confusion for several months.

Although the specific mechanisms for actually performing validation and consistency checks are largely technical issues, the determination of the extent of validation and the specific rules and procedures to be followed require careful managerial consideration of the organization's objectives as well as the formulation of effective validation and consistency checks.

3.5.2 Surveillance

As noted in Section 3.3.3, computerized systems have often provided ways to streamline operations and greatly reduce the number of steps and amount of paperwork involved in many activities. They can also greatly increase the difficulty in detecting security violations. A simple example, based upon an actual "computer crime" may help to illustrate this point.

1. A company uses an on-line order entry system to allow salesmen in the branch offices to directly place an order to the warehouse by remote terminals.

2. An outsider who learns how to access and use the system places a large order early in the month.

3. He then rents a truck and picks up the merchandise at the warehouse (since the order was in the system, the warehouse personnel were expecting the pickup and provide help in loading the truck).

4. Accessing the system again, the thief cancels the order which removes all traces of it from the computer system before it is transferred to the billing system at the end of the month.

5. Over time the company notices that their inventory records differ from the physical inventory. In a large warehouse with annual inventory turnover of $100,000,000 or more, a $500,000 discrepancy may be attributed to breakage or normal losses. If the discrepancy is large enough to be viewed as a problem, the most obvious assumption is that the warehouse workers are stealing the equipment or that an intruder is breaking into the warehouse—thus, closed circuit televisions

and increased security guards are assigned. A thief at a remote terminal is not a likely suspect.

Using the computer's capabilities, special surveillance procedures can be incorporated into the system. There are at least two major forms: (a) audit log and (b) monitoring.

A. Audit Log

Basic to the concept of an *audit log* or *audit trail* is a permanent record of every significant action taken by the system. Thus, as in the days of quill pen journals and ledgers, a log record is made of every order placed and another log record is made if the order is cancelled —rather than merely discarding or erasing the order record. In principle, log records are accumulated and never changed.

Such an audit log can be used for several important purposes.

1. Security violation detection—as illustrated by the example above, an audit log can be used to help determine and diagnose certain security violations (there would be a permanent record of the order entry, order pickup, and order cancellation).

2. Traditional auditing—an audit log, at least in part, is essential to tracing transactions through the system as required in normal financial auditing procedures.

3. Minor and massive recovery—in an online system, an audit log of some type is essential to allow effective recovery from malfunctions caused by software or hardware during normal operations. The periodic (typically nightly or weekly) backup tapes would not yet contain records of the transactions for the current day. By use of the audit log, it would be possible to reconstruct information that may have been destroyed or invalidated due to the malfunction. In cases of minor transient malfunctions, such a recovery may be automated and accomplished in a few minutes or even seconds. In an extreme case, the audit log tapes generated over a long period of time could be used to regenerate the entire database in case the backup tapes had been destroyed or in case a backup tape procedure was not used.

4. Correction of errors—in many systems, especially on-line systems, an error may be detected by the user immediately, such as accidentally typing the wrong account number or incorrectly deleting a specific amount. The audit log can be helpful in reconstructing data that may have been incorrectly altered.

5. Deterrent—in conjunction with the first use listed, security violation detection, the mere existence of an audit log may be a deterrent to many security violations, especially by insiders. Even if one

knows how to circumvent a given system's basic security procedures and normal checks and balances, the fact that one's actions may be detected from the audit log can be a deterrent.

The concept of a post-facto security mechanism as a deterrent is often neglected in the design of many security procedures. In some situations, the system's designers may develop as complete and comprehensive a set of security procedures as they can. If an intruder manages to bypass these mechanisms, he is viewed as having "won." The important point to note is that the computer system is only one part of the security process. Just as in the case of a "successful" bank robbery, post-facto pursuit and prosecution are important elements. In a discussion with one security researcher it was suggested that "ultimately all security procedures must rely upon physical violence; I may develop elaborate passwords and other security procedures in my system, but I must also make it clearly known that if anyone manages to circumvent these procedures, I will eventually find out who it is and have his legs broken!"

A careful managerial study is necessary to determine what information should be captured in the audit log and how it should be organized for most effective use. Furthermore, a definite plan of active examination is necessary if security violations are to be detected in a timely manner. In many installations audit logs are generated and stored away—but never used. The audit logs should be used in both a systematic and nonsystematic manner. In the former case, standard reports should be developed that could be used to detect unusual situations, such as an unusually large number of invalid or incorrect log-in attempts, exceptionally large orders from certain customers, etc. An intruder who has sufficient knowledge of the standard report procedures may find a way to violate system security that does not appear on any of the standard security check reports. (It is a standard cliché in movie burglaries for one of the robbers to say "the guard makes his rounds every 30 minutes, that gives us 25 minutes to break into the safe.") A nonsystematic behavior can be accomplished by introducing an element of randomness into the examination by either having the checking programs randomly select transactions for examination or by providing on-line access to the audit log enabling security officers or management personnel to arbitrarily browse through the information.

B. Monitoring

Monitoring is a more active form of surveillance. While the system is in operation various forms of information and statistics can be gathered and displayed on special monitoring terminals. This type of facility can be used for a variety of security related and nonsecurity related purposes.

1. Security violation detection—information system monitoring facilities can be used in a manner similar to closed circuit television and intruder detector systems. They may be used in a summary mode to note any unusual situations, such as an incorrect log-in attempt, numerous data input errors, or an exceptionally large order or withdrawal. They may be used in a viewing mode to monitor in detail the actions of one or more specific terminal users.

2. Education—such monitoring facilities can be extremely instructive to both new and current managers. By actually seeing the system in operation, at both the summary and detailed level, one can gain considerable insight into the operation of the organization. Many existing and incorrect preconceived notions can be corrected and new patterns of operation can be observed.

3. System performance and utilization—by being able to monitor the system, its designers can discover and explore possible areas of improvement. In one case it was observed that the lengthy "English-like" interface to the information system, which was very popular with the infrequent management users, required excessive typing for the full-time system users and was the cause of most of the data entry errors. This was easily observed by merely monitoring any specific data entry terminal for a brief period of time. This problem had not been brought to the attention of the designers during the previous 6 months of system operation because the data entry activity was organizationally and physically quite remote from the system designers.

Many of the other points noted about the audit log apply to the use of a monitoring facility.

C. Audit and Monitor Logging

There are two additional points that must be made about surveillance facilities. First, the audit log and monitoring capability introduce additional possibilities for security violations (e.g., stealing the audit log may be easier than stealing the database itself). Thus, the security of these facilities must be carefully studied. In some installations extensive precautions may be made to secure the computer facility and the operational data while the backup and audit tapes are stored unguarded in the basement.

Second, use of the audit and monitor facilities must itself be audit logged. Otherwise, a dishonest security officer or someone who finds out how to gain access to these facilities may be able to use them to violate security and operate undetected.

D. Privacy Implications of Surveillance

Needless to say, the various surveillance mechanisms and procedures described here have definite implications for the privacy of the system's users. The monitoring facility, for example, could allow a manager to essentially "look over the shoulder" of any terminal user for as long as he wants without the employee being aware of the fact that his actions are being observed. In this regard such facilities are similar to concealed closed-circuit televisions. Thus, careful consideration should be given to their mode and purpose for use as well as the knowledge about their existence.

3.5.3 Authorization

The authorization process is an extremely important issue with numerous facets. Two specific issues will be discussed in this section: (a) authorization control and (b) rigidity of authorizations.

A. Authorization Control

The access control rules to be enforced by the system can be viewed, essentially, as merely another type of information in the system. On the other hand, this information and the ability to change it have sweeping implications. (A possible analogy is the safe that contains the combinations to all the other safes.)

There are various organizational ways to handle the changing of the access control rules (i.e., changes to authorizations). Three major categories are (1) centralized, (2) hierarchical decentralized, and (3) individual.

1. Centralized—a single individual or organizational unit, such as the security officer or database administrator, handles all authorizations.

2. Hierarchical decentralized—in this situation the central authorization organization may delegate some or all of its authority to subordinate organizations. For example, accounting files may be placed under the control of the head of accounting, etc. Authority may then be further delegated (e.g., authorization control for certain accounting files may be assigned to different managers within the accounting organization). In most implementations the higher authorities in the authorization hierarchy retain the ability to revoke or override authorization decisions made by their subordinates.

3. Individual—in this situation there is no static authorization

hierarchy. An individual may be allowed to create information (authorization to "create" may be controlled by either of the earlier two approaches). The individual who created the information is recognized as the "owner" of the information by the system. The owner may authorize others to access the information, pass ownership to someone else, or establish co-ownership arrangements.

Each of these authorization approaches has advantages and disadvantages. This has led some organizations to develop combinations or variations of these basic strategies to meet their organization's needs. Let us briefly review some of the key issues regarding each of the basic strategies.

The centralized approach, not surprisingly, is largely motivated by the military concept of "security officers." With the increasing concern over the corporate "information resource" and the establishment of a database administration function in many organizations, this approach has been adopted by some companies. Although it may be viable in small or highly structured organizations, it has been found unworkable in most large volatile or decentralized organizations. The problem is caused by the rapidly evolving functions and information, especially for test cases and development activities, as well as personnel turnover and reassignment. The net result is an extremely large number of security authorizations required every day. For example, in a study of a medium-sized but highly volatile organization (a university), it was found that authorization changes occurred at least once every 3 minutes. In summary, the centralized approach may not be desirable in situations where there is a high volume of security authorization changes or where the organizational structure is too complex or decentralized to allow effective and intelligent centralized control over authorization changes.

The hierarchical decentralized approach has been widely recommended in the literature and is basic to the security implementation on certain systems, such as the Honeywell Multics system. This approach allows the security authorization control to be delegated to the groups that can most effectively administer and monitor these controls. From an organizational point of view this may be very important. For example, if each division or function operates as a separate profit center with control over its own expenditures and plans, it probably should have security authorization control over its own data.

A major problem with most implementations of this approach is the fact that higher levels in the authorization hierarchy can revoke or override all authorization decisions. This ability is usually viewed as necessary for organizational (i.e., "the boss is the boss") and operational (i.e., to correct mistakes in authorization assignments) reasons. But, this means that there cannot be any "private" information in the system. Referring to the normal office environment, by analogy, this would mean that an employee could not have a "locked drawer" in his desk that was not accessible by his superior. In many organizational contexts this can pose serious problems. For example, in one company the vice-president of manufacturing, using real-time production data in conjunction with special programs written to his specifications, was able to track production scheduling closer and faster than the production foremen who received production summary reports at the end of the day. Previously, the reports were only made to the vice-president at the end of each week. This gave each foreman time to cope with transient problems during the week regardless of whether the problem was caused by his own scheduling mistake or an external factor, such as unusually high sickness rates. Now the vice-president was inquiring about decreases in production rates at 3 P.M., even before the foremen had received their daily summary report or could take any corrective action. A serious labor dispute resulted from this situation.

This issue of "corporate privacy" (as opposed to the more commonly accepted concept of individual "personal privacy") requires judicious management planning and procedures. It has been a major factor in the reluctance of many groups within a company to computerize their records. One salesman noted that he would rather destroy his personal notes on his client companies and the peculiarities of their purchasing agents than risk having them put into a computer system where there was any chance that this information could be seen by anyone else. In general, there are probably few of us who cannot think of some information, records, or notes regarding our organization that we keep in our offices that we would view as "private."

This problem is likely to increase significantly among white collar workers and management as advances in office automation greatly increase the scope and diversity of information stored in computerized information systems.

The approach of individual authorization control is used in many simple systems. A convenient implementation is to allow the creator of a file to designate "owner" and "user" passwords for the file. The owner password allows one to change either of the passwords, the user password allows one to access the file. Various authorization objectives can be accomplished using such a system. Private information can be kept private by not telling anyone either of the passwords. (Note: It is assumed that there is no standard way provided for anyone, whether president or systems programmer, to find the passwords for any file.) Access or ownership rights can be given out by giving the passwords. There are alternative implementation strategies that can accomplish the same results without using passwords in the above manner (one drawback to the above password strategy is that there is no way of determining all the people who know the password or of selectively revoking access).

One problem with the individual authorization approach, regardless of the implementation, is the fact that there may be occasions where it is necessary to override the security mechanism (e.g., the individual dies, becomes ill, leaves the company). In general, any security mechanism can be overcome, though some mechanisms, such as cryptographic encoding, may be very difficult to break even by the system's designers. If the mechanism is easy to break, the "privacy" assumed above will not exist; if it is very difficult to break, the organization may suffer if adverse circumstances such as those noted above, occurred.

Thus, the type of authorization control to be used in an organization requires careful consideration of many conflicting factors. For a more technical discussion of the implementation of authorization approaches, the reader may refer to Chapter 9.

B. Rigidity of Authorizations

Computer systems, lacking discretionary judgment, require a precise statement of access control rules to be enforced. This requires that very careful thought be given to the establishment of these rules and the specific authorizations assigned.

The rigidity of the authorizations have posed various problems in the past. While testing the experimental Resource Security System (RSS), IBM's Federal Systems Center (FSC) noted that "A major concern in FSC was that the use of a secure system would hamper our ability to react quickly to priority situations. . . . What this means, for purpose of system design, is that effective security overrides must be available to the installation."

Most existing security systems either do not provide any security override mechanism or it is provided in the form of a "panic" button that can be invoked by the security officer or computer operator to suspend all security enforcement. This approach is very crude, awkward to use, and may expose the system to security violations while security enforcement is suspended.

As an example, consider the situation of a doctor who desperately needs information about a patient who has been admitted in an emergency. Suppose the patient's regular doctor is currently unavailable to give the attending physician access to the patient's files. In such cases, it should be possible to use a formal procedure whereby the attending physician can request access to the patient's file. The system will record this fact and this action will be subject to later review by the patient's regular doctor.

A possible approach to this type of situation may be based upon the use of less rigid access control rules. For example, three levels of access control may be defined. The normal "access is allowed" or "access is prohibited" can be augmented by "access *may* be allowed." Thus, in an environment with high ethical standards and/or other constraints, such as post-facto prosecution, that tend to encourage ethical behavior, certain users may be assigned "access may be allowed" permission to other user's private information. In these cases, any attempted access will trigger a special action which would inform the user that he is requesting access to private information and require him to acknowledge that this is deliberate and provide a brief explanation of the reason. The final decision as to the appropriateness of the access is deferred to human review at a later time.

This type of flexible security enforcement is rare in most current security systems. Further development of these concepts and capabilities is essential in order to avoid the extremes of either impairing effective use of the system or reverting to ad-hoc emergency procedures all the time.

3.5.4 Security Responsibility

As should be clear from the preceding discussions, effective security requires the cooperation and planning of many people in an organization. Although certain aspects, such as awareness, require the active participation of almost everyone in the organization, many of the planning and decision-making issues are best resolved by a small number of people. Who should these people be?

This problem is complicated by the fact that at least three different types of issues can be identified, each implying a potentially different type of organizational responsibility. These three types are the following:

1. Policy—policy issues regarding the use and types of security procedures require the active participation, formulation, and backing of top management personnel.

2. Operational—mapping the policy decisions into practice re-

quires a detailed knowledge of the organization's information processing activities and the available security enforcement technologies. This type of activity would require the skills normally found in the database administration systems programming, and computer operations functions.

    3. Economic—it has been noted by several researchers that many security issues are essentially economic decisions, involving uncertainty or incomplete information and risks. For example, the decision to use a certain security procedure which costs X dollars and provides a certain, unquantified, degree of protection against certain types of potential security violations is very similar to the decision to expend funds on a project to develop a new product. In this context the role of "risk managers" (i.e., individuals who are experienced in making such subjective decisions) has been suggested in the literature.

    The concept of risk managers has been used in a very broad context by some researchers who have noticed that important elements of risk exist for the policy and operational as well as the economic decisions. For this reason some security experts have recommended to top management that on-going risk analysis teams be formed that include (a) EDP operations management, (b) department managers, (c) applications programmers, (d) systems programmers, (e) internal auditors, and (f) physical security personnel.

    The specific security roles and responsibilities may vary from organization to organization, but careful planning and defining of responsibilities is essential if information system security is to be attained in an effective and operationally viable fashion.

3.6 POSTSCRIPT

    Much of the literature on operational security has been primarily intended to motivate and introduce the concept of security to managers and other individuals that had little or no background or experience in this field. Introductory level references include [Hemphi 73], [Hoffma 77a], [Hoyt 73], [IBM 74a], [IBM 74b], [Parker 76a], and [Walker 77]. [Parker 76c] is an especially interesting book since it reports on Parker's studies conducted at the Stanford Research Institute (SRI) in conjunction with his Computer Abuse project since 1970. Hundreds of actual computer security violations are studied and analyzed.

    There have been many brief articles reporting on or warning about specific security violation cases, such as [Alexan 74], [Chadwi 75], [Leibho 76], and [Parker 74a]. Brief surveys can be found in various trade publications, such as [Modern 74].

One of the most comprehensive introductory references on computer security can be found in [Martin 73]. This 626-page book covers many key issues related to operational and physical computer security. This book is several years old and certain parts may be out of date but it is still an excellent reference.

Operational considerations cover a broad array of computer topics. Many of these issues are related to the problems of fraud and embezzlement [Browne 74]. Backup and recovery techniques, although important, are most often considered only in regard to system reliability. Discussion of these issues from a security point of view can be found in [Parker 74b] and [Weiss 74].

The organizational impact of security can be studied from various perspectives [IBM 74e]. Specific issues usually included within this topic include awareness and education [IBM 74c], [Meyers 75b]. [IBM 74c] is a report prepared by the Management Information Division of the State of Illinois and includes a set of nine videotapes to help stimulate security awareness among employees. The role of the auditor has been studied in computer, accounting, and management reports, such as [Nielse 75] and [Wasser 74]. The special case of trade secrets must also be considered [Honig 74].

Although there are many similarities between "computer crime" and other more conventional crimes, such as fraud and embezzlement, studies of the more than 300 security violations gathered by Donn Parker, coupled with interviews of many of the perpetrators, has resulted in the development of a profile of the typical "computer criminal" [Parker 76a], [Parker 76b], [Parker 76c].

Economic considerations of security violations and formalized approaches for performing risk assessments are important new areas of investigation. Work in this area has been reported in [Courtn 77], [Firnbe 76], [Glasem 77], and [IBM 74d]. One of the keys to a rational risk assessment is a clear understanding of the potential security threats and available countermeasures. Several organizations, such as TRW [IBM 74f], reports, such as Martin's checklists [Martin 73] and [Orceyr 78], and papers, such as [Ruder 78], have attempted to enumerate and categorize threats and countermeasures. Working with the data gathered as part of the SRI computer abuse project, the various reported crimes were placed into eight functional vulnerability categories [Parker 76b], [Parker 76c], [Parker 78]. Other interpretations of this data have been reported by [Nielse 76a] and [Nielse 76b]. Other enumerations of threats and countermeasures can be found in [Walker 77] and [Weissm 74a].

The various aspects of security objectives and accountability include considerations of surveillance policy and procedures [Hoffma

77a], [Gilson 76], legal remedies [Nycum 76], and authorization policy and procedures [IBM 74e], [IBM 74g].

The organizational role of security management, often referred to as "risk management," has received increasing attention in recent years [Clemen 74], [Datama 76], [Courtn 77], [Glasem 77], [Reed 77]. On security effectiveness, we have proposed measures in [Hoffma 78].

REFERENCES

Alexan 74

Alexander, T., "Waiting For the Great Computer Ripoff." *Fortune*, July 1974, pp. 143–150.

> Alexander has written this article to acquaint upper management level personnel with the existence of problems involving lax security in computer installations and systems. The motivation of the article is that criminal activities directed at computer systems will in most cases go undetected or if detected will go unreported. Alexander feels this has lulled many high-level managers into a false sense of security. Discussions with acknowledged experts in computer security, such as Courtney, Parker, Ware, Weissman, and Lipner, are used to argue that computer security cannot be taken for granted. Several cases of computer-related crime are reported. Additionally, certain technical parts of the system—access control, password, etc.—are explained in a readable, nontechnical manner. This article is ideal for an individual completely unfamiliar with computers wishing an introduction to the problems of computer security.

Allen 76

Allen, B. R., "Embezzlement and Automation." *Proceedings IEEE CompCon International Conference,* San Francisco, California, February 1976, pp. 187–188.

> Allen estimates that fraud and embezzlement losses that can be directly related to computers are on the order of tens of millions of dollars annually. In this short paper he lists the types of fraud and the methods used. The second section outlines the vulnerabilities of computer installations that make the fraud possible. He lists ten areas where the computer operations are vulnerable and provides brief explanations and possible safeguards for each.

Browne 74

Browne, P. S., and Cosenting, J. A., "I/O—A Logistics Challenge." *Proceedings CompCon 74 Eighth IEEE Computer Society International Conference,* February 1974, pp. 61–64.

Browne addresses the problem of securing off-line storage media. In particular he develops three categories of recommendations based on data in storage, in use, and in transit. With regard to storage, the problems of secure tape vaults and libraries are examined. With regard to data in use, the problems of allowing authorized access to these storage libraries are considered. Movement of storage media from one location to another is also discussed. Recommendations for solving these problems include inventory controls and documentation. Browne also suggests auditing should be used to guarantee correctness of procedures.

Chadwi 75

Chadwick, H. A., "Burning Down the Data Center." *Datamation*, Vol. 21, No. 10, October 1975, pp. 60–64.

Insurance in the data processing industry has become a viable means for reducing loss in the event of a disaster. Chadwick discusses the special types of insurance available to protect computer installations as well as hints on what to be aware of when choosing an insurance broker. The types of coverage examined include media, business interruption, and liability.

Clemen 74

Clements, D., and Hoffman, L. J., "Computer Assisted Security System Design." Electronics Research Laboratory, University of California, Berkeley, ERL–M468, November 1974.

Clements and Hoffman describe a software package developed at Stanford University on an IBM 370. This interactive system is designed to assist the security officer (risk manager) in developing an overall secure data processing installation.

The program accepts as input a set of threats and a set of objects. As output it provides a set of safeguards to protect the objects from the threats. This paper discusses the algorithm used as well as the actual operation of the program. Several extensions to the system are proposed that include user weighting of possible safeguards, remembering weights across runs, and a glossary defining more exactly the safeguards.

Courtn 77

Courtney, R. H., Jr., "Security Risk Assessment in Electronic Data Processing." *AFIPS Conference Proceedings, NCC*, Vol. 46, 1977, pp. 97–104.

In order to provide cost-effective safeguards to protect a computer installation from various threats, it is necessary to know where the installation is vulnerable and to what degree. Courtney offers a methodology for assessing these vulnerabilities.

Courtney asserts that the two key elements in risk assessment are determining the impact or cost of a threat occurring and the actual probability of that threat occurring. With these two parameters one can determine risk on a cost per unit time basis. The risk analysis methodology proposed by Courtney consists of enumerating the possible threats and then establishing order of magnitude estimates of the dollar impact of each event occurring, and how often the event occurs. By multiplying the cost times the number of times per year an event occurs, one obtains a rough estimate of the annual cost to the company from that threat. With these figures one can then determine whether implementing a safeguard is cost-effective. That is, if the safeguard is less expensive than the loss from the threat it is then cost-effective to implement it. Courtney details the use of this methodology and includes hints on its use. He notes that even with this formulation, risk assessment still remains largely a matter of human judgment.

Datama 76

Datamation Staff, "News in Perspective/Risk Managers Urged for Curbing Fraud." *Datamation*, Vol. 22, No. 6, June 1976, pp. 155–157.

Contained in this article is a report on a recommendation made by the General Accounting Office to establish the position of "risk manager" at all Federal data processing installations. The individual assuming the role of risk manager would be responsible for the security policies and procedures established and followed at the computing facility.

Engelm 77

Engelman, C., "Audit and Surveillance of Multi-Level Computing Systems." Mitre Corp., April 1977; MTR–3207, ESD–TR–76–369 (NTIS AD–A039 060).

This report prepared for the Air Force Electronic Systems Division pays special attention to the user behavior of the Multics kernel system. The study is based on both post-mortem and real-time analysis of the user behavior. Recommendations are sketchy.

Firnbe 76

Firnberg, D., "Your Computer in Jeopardy." *Computer Decisions*, Vol. 8, No. 7, July 1976, pp. 28–30.

Firnberg, director of Britain's National Computing Center, outlines a set of 70 security breaches. This number is obtained by combining two kinds of threats (accidental or deliberate), five unacceptable events (disclosure, destruction, etc.), and seven asset categories. For each type of breach that is relevant to particular installations (not all necessarily are) the threats that may cause that breach should be identified. If this is done correctly, then countermeasures may be taken to reduce the possible damage from these threats to an acceptably low level.

The responsibility of identifying threats and establishing cost-effective countermeasures is that of a risk manager. Other functions of the risk manager or risk management committee are also specified.

Gilson 76

Gilson, J. R., "Security and Integrity Procedures." Honeywell Information Systems, Inc., July 1976, ESD–TR–76–294 (NTIS AD–A040 328).

> This incomplete (due to project termination) report prepared for the Air Force Electronic Systems Division addresses the issues involved in the management procedures and accountability of a large design, verification, and implementation of a secure operating system. The system in consideration is the Multics kernel.

Gladne 78

Gladney, H. M., "Administrative Control of Computing Services." *IBM Systems Journal*, Vol. 17, No. 2, 1978, pp. 151–178.

> In a large system with many users, terminals, data items, and programs, it is a difficult administrative problem to control resource use. This paper describes a set of automated procedures intended to decrease the clerical burden for this control. The work described in [Gladne 75] has been extended to include batch oriented systems, general-purpose interactive systems (TSO, APL), and a transaction-oriented system (IMS).
>
> Controls can be applied to resources such as data sets, terminals, accounts, groups, storage volumes, transaction executions, or program library members; to services such as an application subsystem, a batch class, a security class, or an administrative status; and to commodities such as processor time, processor time weighted according to time of day, storage space, or session elapsed time.
>
> Since this complete system has not been implemented, no performance statistics are available. However, the author reports that the prototype system has had less than a 1% consumption of system resources.

Glasem 77

Glaseman, S., Turn, R., and Gaines, R. S., "Problem Areas in Computer Security Assessment." *AFIPS Conference Proceedings*, NCC Vol. 46, 1977, pp. 105–112.

> The problem of providing adequate computer security at a reasonable cost has prompted study of what has come to be called risk assessment. The authors provide an overview of topics and specify where they feel research in risk assessment should be directed. Recent work such as Courtney's [Courtn 77] is briefly critiqued, and the problems of risk assessment are pointed out.
>
> The subjects the authors feel are worthy of further research include methods for specifying assets and their value, identification of vulnerabilities and the degree to which they may be exploited, identifica-

tion of resources needed for successful intrusion, and identifying and specifying explicit threats.

Hemphi 73

Hemphill, C. F., Jr., and Hemphill, J. M., *Security Procedures for Computer Systems.* Dow Jones–Irwin, Homewood, Illinois, 1973. (See Chapter 2.)

Hoffma 77a

Hoffman, L. J., *Modern Methods for Computer Security and Privacy.* Prentice-Hall, Inc., Englewood Cliffs, New Jersey, 1977. (See Chapter 2.)

Hoffma 78

Hoffman, L. J., Michelman, E. H., and Clements, D., "SECURATE— Security Evaluation and Analysis Using Fuzzy Metrics." *AFIPS Conference Proceedings—1978 NCC,* Vol. 47, 1978, pp. 531–540.

A procedure for helping to evaluate security effectiveness is described. Security is described in terms of FEATURES which reduce THREATS to OBJECTS. The procedure first requires a set of object–threat–feature triples with each component described by a word such as high, low, or not high. "Fuzzy" set theory provides a means for combining these objectives, say, into a "fuzzy" mean. Objects are divided into sections. Security can be viewed at the level of the overall system, all subsections of a section, or an individual section based on several outlooks such as weakest link or fuzzy mean.

An APL based implementation has been used to assist in a risk analysis of several installations. It is reported that the users felt they had achieved an increased understanding of installation security.

Honig 74

Honig, J., "Company Security and Individual Freedom." *Datamation,* Vol. 20, No. 1, January 1974, p. 131.

A problem which has been with other industries for some time and is now beginning to surface in the data processing industry is that of employees leaving a company to take a job elsewhere and taking with them trade secrets. Honig comments on the various facets of this problem and suggests establishment of a code of ethics to alleviate some of the difficulties.

Hoyt 73

Computer Security Research Group—Hoyt, D. B. (Chairman), *Computer Security Handbook.* Macmillan, New York, 1973. (See Chapter 2.)

IBM 74a

IBM, *Data Security and Data Processing Volume 1: Introduction and Overview.* International Business Machines Corporation, Data Processing Division, White Plains, New York, Form Number G320–1370, 1974.

In May 1972, IBM announced the formation of four study sites for the purpose of gaining more information about data security and identifying user requirements in this subject. External study sites were the Massachusetts Institute of Technology, TRW Systems, Inc., and the Management Information Division of the State of Illinois. The internal study site was IBM's Federal Systems Division.

This brief 20-page report, written primarily for top management, discusses data security in general and capsulizes the study site findings. The findings are summarized in Volume 2 and presented in detail in Volumes 3 through 6.

IBM 74b

IBM, *Data Security and Data Processing Volume 2: Study Summary.* International Business Machines Corporation, Data Processing Division, White Plains, New York, Form Number G320–1371, 1974.

This 25-page report presents a brief summary of the study site finding in major areas of interest and is primarily directed toward data processing management.

The primary reasons for the data security studies were (a) to build a body of knowledge, and (b) to gain practical experience with data security in an actual data processing operation. In this latter regard, the Resource Security System (RSS), an experimental modification of OS/360 Release 21.0, was installed at each of the study sites. This system provided enhanced integrity and an access control mechanism. The experience with this system was used to evaluate the techniques developed by the study site participants.

The study sites addressed themselves primarily to that part of data security which deals with the computing system's approach to protecting potential threats to data. Toward this end, the sites were asked specifically to investigate the economic and procedural effects of using a secure system (State of Illinois), to determine whether and to what extent the degree of data security of a computing system can be measured (TRW), to do research on how a system can best authorize access to data (M.I.T.), and to gauge the impact on existing operations of the process of converting to a secure system (IBM FSC).

A reader directory and abstracts of each paper in the following volumes are included in this volume.

84 COMPUTER SECURITY

IBM 74c

IBM, *Data Security and Data Processing Volume 3: Part 1 State of Illinois Executive Overview.* International Business Machines Corporation, Data Processing Division, White Plains, New York, Form Number G320–1372, 1974.

The Management Information Division (MID) of the Department of Finance of the State of Illinois formed the Secure Automated Facility Environment (Project SAFE) to conduct its part of the study.

The MID study team wrote this document to assist executive management in achieving privacy and security awareness among employees in the organization. This report's full title is "What Every Executive Should Know About Privacy in Information Systems." The report notes that a well-defined plan of action is necessary. An example, 10-step action plan, is presented and discussed. A checklist of considerations is summarized in a compact 2-page privacy executive action chart.

IBM 74d

IBM, *Data Security and Data Processing Volume 3: Part 2 Study Results State of Illinois.* International Business Machines Corporation, Data Processing Division, White Plains, New York, Form Number G320–1373, 1974.

The State of Illinois studied the economic impact of imposing data security objectives on an existing installation, and the ease of use of certain security features. In summary, it concluded: (a) there is a need for increased privacy and data security awareness in most organizations, especially at the executive level; (b) to achieve greater security, many organizations will have to raise their level of physical security and introduce new administrative procedures; and (c) the cost and difficulty of achieving an increased level of security depend upon the nature of the organization and the degree of its past emphasis on security.

In addition to the two written reports [IBM 74c] and [IBM 74d], nine educational videotapes were produced by the State of Illinois and made available to organizations to help stimulate security awareness among employees.

IBM 74e

IBM, *Data Security and Data Processing Volume 4: Study Results Massachusetts Institute of Technology.* International Business Machines Corporation, Data Processing Division, White Plains, New York, Form Number G320–1374, 1974.

M.I.T. evaluated the needs of several industries and studied the technical aspects of authorizing user access to data in computer systems. M.I.T. found that (a) different industries perceive both the need for, and the problem of, data security in different terms, and (b) security responsibility needs to be decentralized to be effective in large multiuser computer system environments.

Individual papers contained in this 300-page report include (a) surveys of the financial, medical, educational and service bureau industries, (b) technical papers on authorization and a variety of topics that pertain to computer system data security, and (c) a comprehensive annotated bibliography of over 1000 references on "Computer and Data Security."

IBM 74f

IBM, *Data Security and Data Processing Volume 5: Study Results TRW Systems, Inc.* International Business Machines Corporation, Data Processing Division, White Plains, New York, Form Number G320–1375, 1974.

TRW studied the means of certifying a computer system as secure. It also documented what features and functions computer systems require to counteract potential vulnerabilities. Some of the TRW findings are (a) no existing computer system is completely secure (b) the certification of a computer system for security is not within the current state of the art, and (c) 187 requirements are identified and techniques are proposed to counteract a system's vulnerabilities.

IBM 74g

IBM, *Data Security and Data Processing Volume 6: Evaluations and Study Experiences with the Resource Security System.* International Business Machines Corporation, Data Processing Division, White Plains, New York, Form Number G320–1376, 1974.

IBM's Federal Systems Center (FSC) in Gaithersburg, Maryland, studied problems related to installing a secure operating system in an ongoing data processing environment. In addition, FSC functioned as the technical control site for the installation of RSS at the other study sites.

Some of FSC's major findings were (a) special security procedures are needed at installations where operators or other production personnel, rather than programmers or end users, control computer operations, and (b) owners of data rather than a central security officer should control the authorization of access to their data.

Leibho 76

Leibholz, S. W., and Wilson, L. D., *User's Guide to Computer Crime: Its Commission, Detection and Prevention.* Chilton, Radnor, Pennsylvania, 1976. (See Chapter 2.)

Martin 73

Martin, J., *Security, Accuracy, and Privacy in Computer Systems.* Prentice-Hall, Inc., Englewood Cliffs, New Jersey, 1973. (See Chapter 2.)

Meyers 74a

Meyers, E., "News in Perspective/The Benefits of a Year Old Scandal: 'Everybody's Teaching EDP Auditing.'" *Datamation,* Vol. 20, No. 3, March 1974, pp. 116–118.

> The value of internal auditing in a data processing environment is being realized as a result of the Equity Funding Scandal. This brief report includes comments from EDP auditing experts on the problems involved with internal auditing.

Meyers 75b

Meyers, E., "News in Perspective/Computer Criminals Beware." *Datamation,* Vol. 21, No. 12, December 1975, p. 105.

> Contained in this article is a brief look at training being done at the FBI and Los Angeles District Attorney's Fraud Section to better educate their agents in the methods used for detection and prevention of computer crime.

Modern 74

Modern Data Staff, "A Computer Security Survey." *Modern Data,* Vol. 7, No. 7, July 1974, p. 52.

> Partial results of a computer security survey made by *Modern Data* magazine are reported in this article. Over 2000 questionnaires were sent out to medium- and large-scale computer installations with 300 replies in at the time this article was published. Findings of the survey reported include security category considered most important, fire protection devices now employed, and use of uninterruptable power supplies.

Nielse 75

Nielsen, N. R., "Computers, Security and the Audit Function." *AFIPS Conference Proceedings,* NCC Vol. 44, 1975, pp. 941–946.

> With businesses and organizations depending on computers more and more as an integrated part of their daily operation, the role of the internal auditor must be adjusted. Nielsen explains that the auditor, who is partially responsible for protecting the company's assets, must become increasingly involved in computer security procedures since the computer facility usually represents a large asset of the company. This implies that the role of risk manager must become part of the auditor's duties.
> In addition, the actual function of auditing has changed with computers now being included among the auditor's tools. Methods for using the computer in this way are covered.
> Prospective changes in computer technology and their impact on auditing practices are examined. These changes will further modify the

role of the auditor while providing him with better tools to perform his job.

Nielse 76a

Nielsen, N. R., Ruder, B., and Brandin, D. H., "Effective Safeguards for Computer System Security." *AFIPS Conference Proceedings,* NCC Vol. 45, 1976, pp. 75–84.

This paper contains the preliminary results of a research project underway at the Stanford Research Institute reported at the 1976 National Computer Conference. The final results are reported in [Nielse 76b].

Nielse 76b

Nielsen, N. R., Brandin, D. H., Madden, J. D., Ruder, B., and Wallace, G. F., "Computer System Integrity Safeguards System Integrity Maintenance." Stanford Research Institute, Menlo Park, California, October 1976.

The 291 security violations compiled by Donn Parker (see [Parker 76b]) of the Stanford Research Institute were studied as the first phase of a three-part Computer System Integrity project. This first part titled "System Integrity Maintenance" isolates techniques effective against the types of threats being faced by computer facilities today. The security violation cases were placed into seven categories each with subcategories based on the source of the violations. Based on this categorization, a set of four generic safeguards was developed and broken down into more specific safeguards. The security violations were then placed into these security categories if the safeguard would have helped prevent the violation.

An evaluation of the safeguards was then undertaken to determine (a) the cost and (b) the effectiveness of each safeguard. The methodology used is explained and qualifications made as to the subjectiveness of the cost/effectiveness rating. One result the authors found disturbing was the lack of broad applicability of specific safeguards implying a computer facility must employ a set of safeguards to protect against particular types of threats.

Based on the results of the above evaluation, several areas of security safeguards that need further research are specified, providing a basis for the next two phases of the project—Security Comparison Methodology and Detection Tool Development.

Several useful tables and appendices are included in the report. These are organized to provide the reader with information on the cost, applicabilities, and effectiveness of the safeguards rather than actually recommending specific ones to use. Included within the appendices is a detailed explanation of the methodology used for the cost/effectiveness ratings.

Nycum 76

Nycum, S. H., "Legal Aspects of Computer Abuse." *Proceedings IEEE CompCon International Conference,* San Francisco, California, February 24–26, 1976, pp. 181–183.

> Within the context of the four categories of computer abuse developed at the Stanford Research Institute [Parker 76b], Nycum discusses the laws affecting perpetrators of computer crime. Of the four areas (acts directed at the computer, those directed at computerized assets, those acts using the computer as a tool, and those using the computer as a symbol—fraudulent programming schools), she finds that the second is most lacking in legal safeguards. Illustrative of this is that perpetrators who destroy or steal such intangible objects as data files or computer time may be prosecuted at times only under such obscure laws as those prohibiting obscene or harassing telephone calls. The author mentions other legal precedents relating to various forms of computer crime.

Orceyr 78

Orceyre, M. J., and Courtney, R. H., Jr., "Considerations in the Selection of Security Measures for Automatic Data Processing Systems." *National Bureau of Standards,* June 1978, NBS SP 500–33.

> Prepared for the Federal Information Processing Task Group 15 (Computer Systems Security) by two of IBM's security specialists, this document discusses the following types of security measures: authentication, authorization, surveillance, cryptography, and system integrity. In addition, certain other concerns such as performance, testing and auditing are discussed. The authors urge that these measures be considered only after a risk analysis [Reed 77].

Parker 74a

Parker, D. B., and Nycum, S. H., "The New Criminal." *Datamation,* Vol. 20, No. 1, January 1974, pp. 56–58.

> Several stories of various computer related crimes are told with a short section on the vulnerabilities of computer facilities including a profile of the computer criminal. See [Parker 76c] for a detailed treatment of the subjects.

Parker 74b

Parker, D. B., "Computer Security: Some Easy Things to Do." *Computer Decisions,* Vol. 6, No. 1, January 1974, pp. 17–18.

> Protecting a computer installation through the use of such things as signs, messages sent to terminals, and employee agreements is outlined in this article. Among other safeguards Parker feels are easy to implement are backup copies of valuable tapes and offsite storage of those.

Parker 76a

Parker, D. B., "Computer and Data Abuse." *Proceedings IEEE Comp-Con International Conference,* San Francisco, California, February 1976, pp. 184–186.

Based on the computer abuse research project headed by Parker at the Stanford Research Institute this 3-page paper presents the basic results obtained so far. Parker describes the four roles that computers play in computer abuse: as the object of the act, providing the environment, as a tool for carrying out the act, and as a symbol. Additionally, a profile of the typical computer criminal is presented. While this paper provides a good summary of the results of the study, the reader is directed to [Parker 76c] for a more detailed treatment of the material along with actual case studies.

Parker 76b

Parker, D. B., "Computer Abuse Perpetrators and Vulnerabilities of Computer Systems." *AFIPS Conference Proceedings,* NCC Vol. 45, 1976, pp. 65–73.

A computer abuse study undertaken at the Stanford Research Institute is concerned with establishing sources of threats to computer facilities. Additionally, the study is meant to establish where the computer facilities are vulnerable to computer abuse violations.

Parker, who has been leading this study for many years [Parker 76c], reports on interviews with 17 computer abuse perpetrators selected from his case file of 375 known violations. From these interviews a profile of the typical "computer criminal" is developed and the results reported in the first part of the paper.

The second portion of the paper deals with the vulnerabilities which made the violations possible. Over 300 violations from the file are placed into 8 functional vulnerability categories and 9 general locations in the computer facility operations where the violations occurred. The results of a similar study which categorized computer abuse violations from the same file are reported in [Nielse 76a], [Nielse 76b].

An appendix is included which contains short descriptions of the typical violations that were examined. This appendix is organized around the functional vulnerability categories mentioned earlier.

Parker 76c

Parker, D. B., *Crime by Computer.* Charles Scribner's Sons, New York, 1976. (See Chapter 2.)

Parker 78

Parker, D. B., "Computer Security Differences for Accidental and Intentionally Caused Losses." *AFIPS Conference Proceedings–1978 NCC,* Vol. 47, 1978, pp. 1145–1149.

It is argued that accidental and intentionally caused losses are different and therefore a security assessment procedure should be aware of this difference. For example, accidental losses are more frequent and may therefore be subject to statistical analysis; accidental errors and omissions can be effectively treated in an isolated manner whereas all potentials for intentional losses must be covered.

A combined strategy for reducing the probability of loss is suggested. First apply safeguards to reduce the probability of the most likely intentional act. Identify the accidental acts also reduced in probability. Repeat these steps until the probability of intentional loss is sufficiently low. Then apply safeguards to reduce the probability of accidental loss still possible to an acceptable level.

Reed 77

Reed, S. K., "Automatic Data Processing Risk Assessment." *National Bureau of Standards,* March 1977, NBS–IR 77–1228.

A technique for conducting a risk analysis of a computer facility is presented. The method is based on the work of several members of the Federal Information Processing Standards Task Group 15 (Computer Systems Security). The method involves the assessment of possible damage from an unfavorable event and the likelihood of that event occurring. A small hypothetical example is discussed.

Ruder 78

Ruder, B., and Madden, J. D., "An Analysis of Computer Security Safeguards for Detecting and Preventing Computer Misuse." *National Bureau of Standards,* January 1978, NBS SP 500–25.

Based on a file of computer misuse cases [Parker 76c], SRI has developed a list of computer safeguards that would have prevented or detected the misuses. The resources to be protected include data and programs, equipment and supplies, and computer services. The possible safeguards are also categorized. Then the vulnerabilities and safeguards are compared.

Shanka 77

Shankar, K. S., "The Total Computer Security Problem: An Overview." *Computer,* Vol. 10, No. 6, June 1977, pp. 50–73.

Shankar provides a good survey of the problems in providing computer security. He first discusses the user environment and the requirements for security. This involves noting that at times these requirements include that the system be verifiably secure. Within this context he reviews certain research efforts undertaken for this purpose.

The second portion of the paper discusses the external controls for protecting the computer resources including operational and physical security.

The protection mechanisms within the computer system are then outlined. These internal mechanisms are discussed in detail in a section which focuses on the requirements placed on these mechanisms including completeness, integrity, and certifiability. The paper also includes sections on the reliability aspects of computer systems and how they relate to security.

The paper includes an excellent set of 120 references to related papers.

Walker 77

Walker, B. J., and Blake, I. F., *Computer Security and Protection Structures.* Dowden, Hutchinson and Ross, Inc., Stroudsburg, Pennsylvania, 1977. (See Chapter 2.)

Wasser 74

Wasserman, J., "Selecting a Computer Audit Package." *The Journal of Accountancy,* April 1974, pp. 30–34.

Wasserman explains why, with businesses relying more and more on computers in their daily operations, the internal auditor must work through the computer rather than around it. The author, president of Computer Audit Systems, Inc., advocates the use of generalized audit packages. In this paper he outlines the benefits to be gained from the use of such programs. Several criteria for comparing the various audit packages on the market today are listed. These include time and storage requirements, vendor support, and his reputation in addition to the actual auditing capabilities of the package.

Weiss 74

Weiss, H., "Computer Security: An Overview." *Datamation,* Vol. 20, No. 1, January 1974, pp. 42–47.

In order to help management investigate the security features of a facility, Weiss reviews typical disasters which may befall a computer center and then presents various recovery and prevention techniques.

Weissm 74a

Weissman, A., "Security—The Analyst's Concern." *Modern Data,* Vol. 7, No. 4, April 1974, p. 28.

In this short article Weissman points out that security should be the concern of the system analyst in conjunction with the internal auditor and department manager. He outlines four categories into which threats to computer installations fall: unauthorized inquiry, unauthorized data manipulation, denial of computer services, and computer professional crimes.

Chapter 4

PHYSICAL SECURITY

An important aspect of any total security plan is *physical security,* which can be considered in two categories: protection against natural disasters, such as fire and floods; and protection against intruders by restricting physical access. If the major threat is of natural origin, then fire and flood protection is warranted. If the threat is of man-made origin, physical security must restrict access and support internal access controls via security officer, authorization control tables, and audit and surveillance functions. This chapter will survey some of the problems and solutions in physical security. The reader should refer to the references for further information.

4.1 AGAINST NATURAL DISASTERS

4.1.1 Fire Control

For computer facilities, fire is the most common natural disaster. A fire safety plan should include the following elements:

1. Site selection and preparation—Location, design, construction, and maintenance of the computer facility must minimize the exposure to fire damage.

2. Detection procedure—Measures to insure prompt detection of and response to a fire emergency must be available.

3. Extinguishing means—Adequate means to extinguish fires and for quick human intervention must be devised.

4. Recovery routine—Adequate means and personnel to limit damage and effect prompt recovery must be provided.

5. A human evacuation plan.

There are two aspects affecting the site selection and preparation. First is the *adjacent check*, i.e., the nature of the occupancy of the building and adjacent buildings. Is there a high risk activity involved such as chemical processing nearby? Based on the materials involved, how hot would an adjacent fire get? The second aspect is the *material check*, i.e., the actual type of building construction. Some materials are much more susceptible to fire than others. In addition, the actual

TABLE 4-1 Comparison of Sprinklers and Halon

	Automatic sprinklers (water)	Monobromotrifluoromethane (Halon–1301 gas)
Extinguishment mechanism	Water cooling and smothering of fire site	Chemical interference with combustion process
Reliability	Very high; limited by reliability of water supply	Very high; limited by reliability of detection system
Effectiveness	Very high	Very high if effective concentration is achieved at fire site
Life safety hazard	None	Some danger if concentration greater than 10%
Side effects	Prompt cooling and cleaning of air by water spray with attendant damage to contents	No side effects if effective; otherwise corrosive toxic decomposition products
Approximate cost to install	$1.00/ft² new building, $3.00+/ft² retrofit	$0.50/ft³ of protected volume
Discharge controlled by	Air temperature (or automatic recycle)	Detection system or manual
Time and cost to refurbish after fire	Minutes and $5 to $20	Hours and 40% of installed cost

SOURCE: Guidelines for Automatic Data Processing Physical Security and Risk Management (NBS 74), p. 19.

design details, such as the use of firewalls and low-flame-spread materials, will limit the danger of fire loss.

It is also important to have fire detection facilities. A fire goes through three stages. First after ignition there is usually *smoldering* which can be detected by smoke detectors. Then the fire can spread through the *direct contact* of an open flame. Finally, when the temperature is sufficiently high, the fire can spread through *heat radiation*. Heat detectors are only effective at the last stage. However, by this time, a fire is very hard to control. Thus, we need not only heat detectors, but also smoke detectors and careful arrangement of flammable material to avoid direct contacts.

After a fire is detected, there are four approaches to its control: *hand extinguishers, hose systems* to be used by professional fire fighters, *automatic sprinklers,* and *automatic gas extinguishers.* Two types of gas systems have been used: carbon dioxide and monobromotrifluoromethane, known as Halon. Carbon dioxide is no longer recommended because of its extreme danger to humans. A comparison of automatic sprinklers and Halon is given in Table 4–1.

The final aspect of fire control is to limit the damage and then to be able to recover if a fire does occur. In order to limit the damage, it may be desirable to have a local fire brigade that is trained to act, until the arrival of the professional fire fighters. As for all forms of natural disaster, there should be a recovery plan.

4.1.2 Other Controls

In addition to fire, there are other possible natural disasters. Flooding is very possible in a building lying on a river flood plain or on a coastal plain. Computers should not be in a low-lying area of a building if it is susceptible to flooding. A supply of nonflammable plastic sheeting has been found to be invaluable for protecting computer equipment in several instances, for example, to protect against water leakage from a higher level.

Damage may also be caused by earthquakes, wind, lightning, explosion, gases, airplanes, etc. In addition, there may be a general disruption, such as to the power supply, or to physical access due to either of these threats.

4.2 AGAINST INTRUDERS

In order to protect the physical facilities against intruders—common criminals, so-called activists, espionage or sabotage agents, vandals, and trusted persons engaged in any unauthorized acts—physical access must be restricted. Physical protection can be broken down into four parts: *boundary protection* (the area outside a building), *perimeter protection* (the building itself or barrier around it), *entrance protection*, and *critical-area protection*. The boundary can be protected using fencing, intrusion detectors (infrared or microwave), or closed-circuit television.

To protect the building perimeter, the building itself must be made of sturdy material. It is surprisingly easy to make a hole through some kinds of building materials. Many buildings have thick walls. For example, the IBM Building which houses the IBM Advanced Administrative System has 13-inch reinforced concrete walls. Some of the results of a recent penetration study are shown in Table 4–2.

For entrance protection, each possible entry point must be secured including both legitimate entrances and other possible entrances, such as windows and air conditioning vents. An *electromechanical intruder detection device* can also be attached to the alarm system.

Legitimate entrances can be controlled by personal recognition of the entrant by a guard or by some mechanism such as a key or a key card. The latter mechanisms are discussed more fully in Section 4.3.

Sophisticated alarm systems are available for intruder detection in a critical area. *Photometric systems* detect a change in light level. *Sonic, ultrasonic, or microwave motion detection systems* are sensitive to a change in signal frequency received off the reflection of a moving

TABLE 4-2 Comparison of Penetration Times to Make an 8-in X 12-in Hole

Wall construction	Tools used	Penetration time
2-in × 4-in studs with 1-in siding both sides	Hand brace and electric sabre saw	1.55 minutes
8-in cinder block wall	Sledgehammer	1.52 minutes[a]
8-in cinder block wall with brick veneer on one side	Sledgehammer	2.12 minutes[a]
5½-in reinforced concrete	Rotohammer drill and sledgehammer	5.44 minutes[a]
8-in reinforced concrete	Rotohammer drill and sledgehammer	10 minutes approximately[a]

SOURCE: Guidelines for Automatic Data Processing Physical Security and Risk Management (NBS 74), p. 50.

[a]Add approximately 1 minute for each reinforcing rod encountered.

TABLE 4-3 Comparison of Common Interior Surveillance Systems

Sensor type	Approximate cost	Limitations	Resistance to defeat
Photometric	$500	Extraneous light must be excluded from area; limited to interior rooms	High
Motion ultrasonic	$250	Air motion may cause false alarms	Moderate to High
Motion micro- wave	$500	Energy can penetrate walls, etc., causing nuisance alarms	High
Accoustical- seismic, sound	$250	Extraneous noises will generate nuisance alarms	High
Accoustical- seismic, vibration	$100	Localizing the source of nuisance alarms could be difficult	High
Proximity, capacitive	$350	Susceptible to nuisance alarms; require backup	High

SOURCE: Guidelines for Automatic Data Processing Physical Security and Risk Management (NBS 74), p. 52.

body. *Audio* and *seismic systems* detect noise and vibration, respectively. Finally, *proximity systems* detect a disturbance to an electromagnetic or electrostatic field. In Table 4-3, we compare some of the more common interior surveillance systems.

4.3 IDENTIFICATION AND AUTHENTICATION

Since all software and hardware security mechanisms are based on the assumption that a user has a given identity, there must be some mechanism to authenticate this identity. Such a mechanism may be based on something the person knows, carries, or is.

A "combination" may be used in a lock or an electrical or mechanical push-button system. For computer access, such a system is called a *password system*. Problems with passwords are that they may be stolen without the user becoming aware of the loss, forgotten, or given away. In order to decrease the danger from stolen passwords, they must be changed frequently, thus leading to problems of creation and distribution. A similar method, called *handshaking*, involves the successful execution of some algorithm by the user. The user must provide a series of passwords to the algorithm even though the user does not know the algorithm. The algorithm, i.e., the handshaking algorithm, may be implemented in the computer system either by software or hardware means. Because of its simplicity, password authentication is most commonly used in computer systems.

Something carried may be a standard key or some kind of card. Cards may contain optical bar codes or a Holerith code. *Plastic cards* with a magnetic strip or implanted magnetic slugs may also be used. Many such systems are now commercially available.

Several systems based on what a user is are available. In small installations, a guard may know and recognize all users. In a larger installation, a guard may compare a photocard with the actual face. Recently, *computerized facsimile systems* utilize this technique to store a photo of the user so that a guard can compare a live TV image with the stored image. At least one *signature system* is available to examine a signature, which must be written with the known motion and style. *Fingerprint systems* are available which compare a fingerprint with a stored fingerprint. Other systems have been developed, based on *hand geometry* and *voiceprints*. These systems based on what a person is are much more complex than those based on something known or carried, since they involve a sophisticated pattern-matching operation. In addition to their expense, they have a second disadvantage in that they are much more likely to reject a legitimate user by mistake than is a system based on something known or something carried. In addition to being required for controlling access to the critical area of a computer facility, the computer system must be able to identify and authenticate a user before it can generate a unique user ID for subsequent use.

4.4 AGAINST ELECTRONIC AND ELECTROMAGNETIC TAMPERING

With increased use of remote facilities, additional threats to physical security are possible.

4.4.1 Wire Tapping

Wire taps may be used in two ways. In a *passive* tap the intruder only listens to transmission; whereas in an *active* tap the intruder actually sends some of his own data either at the end of the legitimate data or in its place. The chief countermeasure to wire tapping is *encryption*, which is discussed fully in Chapter 6. In addition, since the only locations where it would be easy to install a wire tap are inside the sending or receiving building, the communication lines and junction boxes should be secured. Due to the high degree of multiplexing involved, wire tapping of external lines or microwave transmissions is expensive.

4.4.2 Electromagnetic Radiation

It is also possible to pick up electromagnetic radiation from a computer or a terminal. Due to the multiprogramming involved, the data from most computer systems would be very hard to decipher. However, there is a real possibility of eavesdropping on a terminal, especially within 20 feet. The difficulty does increase rapidly with distance so that eavesdropping from more than 150 feet becomes expensive. With more expensive equipment, it is possible to augment a weak signal. For example, most CRT terminals regenerate their display at frequent intervals. Thus, sophisticated techniques can be used to combine the data from several generations. No instances of this type of eavesdropping from commercial installations have been reported.

4.5 POSTSCRIPT

The material on protection against natural disaster and against intruders is based on [NBS 74]. Other sources are [Bauer 74], [Caffer 75], [Honeyw 74], and [NBS 75b]. The particular problems of terminal security are discussed in [Jeffer 74a].

Identification and authentication are basic problems of computer security, both for physical site access and software access. A survey of methods is given in [Meissn 76]. [Bowers 74] has a rather complete discussion of devices available for physical access control. A system using key cards with modifiable magnetic strips is described in [Masson 74]. Signature analysis systems [Herbst 77] and fingerprint analyzers [Swonge 76] are also used. A general discussion of passwords, the method used in most software systems, is given in [Wood 77a] and [Wood 77b]. The storage of encrypted passwords is suggested by [Evans 74b] and [Purdy 74]. The generation of pronounceable-word passwords is discussed in [Gasser 76a]. Problems from the use of pseudorandom number generators are described in [Johnso 74].

Methods to control wire tapping and electromagnetic radiation are described in [Martin 73], which, along with [Hemphi 73], provide extensive checklists for physical security.

REFERENCES

Bauer 74

Bauer, G. M., "User's Needs—Space Conditioning, Fire Protection, Data Processing, Life Support and Life Safety Systems, Communication Systems." *IEEE Transactions on Industry Applications,* Vol. 10, No. 2, 1974, pp. 202–204.

> The important systems to be considered when evaluating the need, size and type of backup power sources are outlined. These include fire protection, life support, air conditioning and circulation, and support for volatile computer memory devices. While not specific to data processing facilities, the paper covers subjects certainly applicable to them.

Bowers 74

Bowers, D. M., "Access Control and Personal Identification Systems: Guide and A State-of-the-Art Report." Bowers Engineering Co., 1214 Post Road, Fairfield, Connecticut, 1974.

> Bowers, in this excellent report, discusses four types of personal identification systems used for access control. The four types of systems examined are
> (a) pushbutton systems,
> (b) coded card systems,
> (c) coded card plus pushbutton systems, and
> (d) physical attribute systems.
> The general attributes of each type of system are outlined followed by informative descriptions of commercially available systems. Each of the four sections ends with a helpful table-like summary of the characteristics and features of the systems. This report is recommended for anyone interested in becoming familiar with what is currently available in sophisticated physical access control systems.

Caffer 75

Caffery, J. J., "Protecting Computers," *Datamation,* Vol. 19, No. 10, October 1975, pp. 94–95.

> A brief overview of fire and intrusion detectors is presented in this paper.

Evans 74b

Evans, A., Jr., Kantrowitz, W., and Weiss, E., "A User Authentication Scheme Not Requiring Secrecy in the Computer." *Communications of the ACM,* Vol. 17, No. 8, August 1974, pp. 437–442.

> Passwords are used by many computer systems to authenticate a user's identity. Passwords, in some form, must be stored in the computer

so that a comparison can be made. The authors suggest that instead of storing the password itself, the result of some noninvertible function performed on the password should be stored. Thus, if someone obtained the password file they would find it of little value.

Any system of this type depends on the noninvertibility of the function for security. Rather than depending on mathematical analysis to establish the difficulty of inverting the function [Purdy 74], the authors take the approach of making the function computationally difficult to invert. They use a family of functions and select the specific function based on the password itself. Proposed functions include permutation based on the password, exclusive-or, addition, etc.

Gasser 76a

Gasser, M., "A Random Word Generator for Pronounceable Passwords." Mitre Corp., Bedford, Massachusetts, MTR–3006, November 1976 (NTIS AD–A017 676).

Gasser outlines a method for randomly generating pronounceable passwords in this report. This work was prompted by three considerations: (a) it is convenient to allow users to change their own passwords, (b) when users choose their own passwords it is fairly easy to guess what it is, and (c) users tend to forget their passwords if they are not pronounceable. Thus, Gasser states, the requirements for a random password generator are that it generates easily remembered words and the words would be difficult to guess.

The scheme described by Gasser is to have a set of units where a unit may be one letter or a specified combination of two letters. Subject to various rules outlined in the report, units are randomly chosen and concatenated to form a pronounceable word. This has been implemented for use on Multics.

Approximately one-fourth of the report is the description while the rest is appendices that include tables of the units, the random word algorithm, source code in PL/I, and the documentation from the Multics Programmers Manual.

Hemphi 73

Hemphill, C. F., Jr., and Hemphill, J. M., *Security Procedures for Computer Systems.* Dow Jones–Irwin, Homewood, Illinois, 1973. (See Chapter 2.)

Herbst 77

Herbst, N. M., and Liu, C. N., "Automatic Signature Verification Based on Accelerometry." *IBM Journal of Research and Development,* Vol. 21, No. 3, May 1977, pp. 245–253.

An automatic, on-line signature verification system developed at IBM's Thomas J. Watson Research Center, Yorktown Heights, New York, is discussed in this paper. This system is based on accelerometry or the time it takes to make each stroke of the signature. For reasons explained in detail in the paper this acceleration-time function of an individual's signature remains nearly constant relative to the size of the signature. This allows comparisons to be made on this basis.

The paper is broken into three major sections. The first discusses the model of the signature described briefly above. The second section discusses the actual system they developed in somewhat technical detail. Experiments were run in April 1975, and the results are presented in the final section. The system appears to perform well in terms of not accepting forged signatures, but less so in terms of rejecting valid signatures. This latter problem is reduced when the signers were allowed up to three trials. The authors feel that the failures of the system were due to imperfections in measurement design and instrumentation rather than a flaw in the model itself. It is felt that this type of signature verification system provides a feasible means for personal identification.

Honeyw 74

Honeywell Commercial Division, "Building Security Systems: Applications and Functions—General Concepts," Form No. 74-2803(1–69).

In this report Honeywell outlines various types of security systems. While specifically presenting the systems that Honeywell offers, the report does contain material of general interest which is presented in more detail than usually found in other sources. Intruder detection systems discussed are photoelectric, audio, vibration detectors, motion detectors, as well as others. The systems are presented in a manner that facilitates comparison between them adding to the value of the report.

Also included in this report is a section on equipment monitoring and the typical systems that are used for that purpose.

Jeffer 74a

Jeffery, S., Branstad, D. K., and Branstad, M. A., "Terminals—Out of Sight but Under Control." *Proceedings CompCon 74, Eighth IEEE Computer Society International Conference,* February 1974, pp. 53–55.

Noting that terminal security is but one aspect of the total computer security problem, the authors describe three types of terminals along with their individual and common security needs. The types of terminals discussed are general-purpose, unattended terminals (cash dispensing), and attended terminals (point-of-sale).

The security techniques for terminals in general include terminal identification, protection from electromagnetic radiation eavesdropping and encryption of data before transmission.

The authors outline the following seven categories of security needs for point-of-sale terminals:

1. Attendant identification.
2. Journal tape protection.
3. Cash drawer protection.
4. Credit authorization.
5. Emergency standalone operation.
6. Data entry error detection.
7. Application dependent security.

Methods for filling these needs are mentioned.

Johnso 74

Johnson, S. M., "Certain Number Theoretic Questions in Access Control." Rand Corp., R–1474–NSF, January 1974.

The use of passwords for authentication of a user's identity at remote terminals is examined in this paper. In particular, systems that use pseudorandom number generators to generate the passwords which are given to each user are discussed by Johnson. Generators such as: $X(n + 1) = aX(n) + b$ (mod M), where M is large, a and b are constants, and $X(n)$ is the nth password generated are the type actually studied by Johnson. The author shows how in systems where there are N users receiving passwords and each user receives every Nth password when a set is generated, then two users cooperating can discover the parameters of the generating sequence. This can be done using number theoretic techniques explained in the paper. By doing this they can generate the passwords themselves thereby compromising the security of the system.

The solution to this problem suggested by Johnson is to permute the assignment order of passwords each time a new set is generated.

Martin 73

Martin, J., *Security, Accuracy, and Privacy in Computer Systems.* Prentice-Hall, Inc., Englewood Cliffs, New Jersey, 1973. (See Chapter 2.)

Masson 74

Masson, A. L., "Computer Access Utilizing Magnetic Cards with Modifiable Codes," Air Force Electronic Systems Division, Hanscom Field, Massachusetts, January 1974 (NTIS AD–775 150).

In this report, Masson outlines the use of key cards with modifiable magnetic strips for accessing computer terminals. In this system, a user would place his card in a reader device connected to the computer. The code or "password" on the magnetic strip would then be checked for validity. Furthermore, at each access a new password is written on the card thereby enhancing security. The major portion of the report discusses a demonstration of such a system utilizing a PDP–11/20 computer.

Meissn 76

Meissner, P., "Evaluation of Techniques for Verifying Personal Identity." Proceedings ACM–NBS Fifteenth Annual Technical Symposium, Gaitherburg, Maryland, June 1976, pp. 119–127 (NTIS PB–255 200).

In this brief report, Meissner first explains the three means for authenticating an individual's identity: something known by the individual, something carried by the individual, and something observed about the individual. The author describes the various methods within each category that are employed. He explains that there are generally two types of errors that may occur: failing to recognize authorized individuals and failing to reject unauthorized ones. The report contains a valuable set of criteria for evaluating personal identification and authentication systems.

NBS 74

National Bureau of Standards, "Guidelines for Automatic Data Processing Physical Security and Risk Management." FIPS–PUB–31, June 1974 (NTIS COM–74–51062).

NBS 75b

National Bureau of Standards, "Computer Security Guidelines for Implementing the Privacy Act of 1974." May 1975 (NTIS NBS–FIPS PUB 41).

Purdy 74

Purdy, G. B., "A High Security Log-In Procedure." *Communications of the ACM,* Vol. 17, No. 8, August 1974, pp 442–445.

Purdy proposed the use of a password system in which the value of a function performed on the password rather than the password itself is stored in the computer system. In order for this system to be secure the function must be noninvertible or what is known as a one-way cipher. Additionally, the function should be as close to one-to-one as possible to reduce the possibility of trial-and-error intrusion.

Purdy discusses the selection of suitable noninvertible functions and concludes that polynomials over a prime modulus are superior to those derived from Shannon codes. Purdy mathematically analyzes the use of polynomials over a prime modulus.

Swonge 76

Swonger, C. W., "Access Control by Fingerprint Identification." Presented at the IEEE International Convention, Boston, Massachusetts, May 1976.

An interesting review of fingerprint characteristics and why fingerprints are unique human identifiers is included in the first part of this paper. In the second half of the paper, Swonger describes the features of an actual access control mechanism using automatic fingerprint comparison. This is the FINGERSCAN system developed by Calspan Technology Products, Inc. Essentially, an ID number and digital description of a user's fingerprint are entered under the auspices of a security officer. Once this is done the user obtains access by typing in his ID number on an access terminal and placing one finger on a scanner. After the fingerprint has been analyzed and put in digital form, it is compared to the original entry for that user.

Errors such as accepting false fingerprints and rejecting valid ones are described with figures given showing a low error rate when FINGERSCAN is used.

Wood 77a

Wood, H. W., "The Use of Passwords for Controlling Access to Remote Computer Systems and Services." *AFIPS Conference Proceedings–1977 NCC,* Vol. 46, 1977, pp. 27–33.

In an easily readable fashion this paper presents a good review of passwords and their use in authenticating a user's identity. Different password schemes and their associated problems are described. The final two sections on password protection and cost consideration are particularly worth reading.

Wood 77b

Wood, H. M., "The Use of Passwords for Controlled Access to Computer Resources." *National Bureau of Standards,* May 1977, NBS SP 500–9.

Chapter 5

HARDWARE SECURITY

The chief components of computer hardware are primary memory, central processing units (CPUs), peripheral devices, and secondary memory. Hardware security is therefore concerned with the incorporation of protection mechanisms into the primary memory, in the CPUs, in the peripheral devices, and in the secondary memory. The sophistication of these mechanisms varies greatly. The variety is influenced by cost, information needs, the designer's understanding of the security requirements, and his ability to meet the requirements.

Most computer manufacturers consider any hardware protection mechanism as an "overhead." Obviously, they intend to introduce as little overhead as possible. It is therefore not surprising that when the computer systems of the IBM 360 series were first introduced, there was no read protection in the primary memory. In other words, the user program being executed in one part of the primary memory can read another user program being run in other parts of the same primary memory.

The ultimate goal of hardware security is, of course, to protect information. Since information is represented in the hardware as data and programs, the protection of the data and programs must be facilitated. However, depending on the needs, data aggregates may be large (say, files) or small (words). Furthermore, programs may be executed serially or concurrently. One of the difficulties encountered by the hardware security designers is to determine the "ideal" aggregate size of memory (or device storage) units for incorporating the protection mechanisms. Should the designer build the mechanisms at the word level (thus incurring more cost) or at the block level? Similarly, should the designer allow many execution states for concurrent running of several programs or limit the execution states to one or two for batch processing only? One of the issues here is cost versus security. However, little research is available to address this issue. What the designers would like to have is some security–cost formulas which can yield the hardware implementation cost required for a given degree of security specifications. With the availability of these formulas, the designer can then perform trade-off studies and determine how much protection mechanisms are to be incorporated into the hardware. Furthermore, the possibility of developing a flexible hardware architecture which can be configured easily for desired cost–security ratio is not in sight.

There are two important factors which underlie the cost–security ratio of the hardware protection mechanisms. The first factor is technology. In other words, protection mechanisms must be built with existing and emerging technology at a cost which is commensurate with the security requirements. Fortunately, advances in microprocessors, minicomputers, storage technology, I/O controllers, and microprogrammable devices have enhanced the work on hardware security considerably. We shall mention some specific examples in the following sections.

The other factor is the designs that one can discover for the implementation of hardware security. Conceptual breakthroughs are necessary in order to provide effective and efficient solutions to old and anticipated security problems in hardware. Effectiveness is necessary because we want the mechanism to work well. Efficiency is important since we like to incur minimal cost. Not only do we need clever implementors who know how to "cut" corners, but also researchers who can devise elegant (and therefore simple) schemes for design and implementation. Both of these require active interfaces between the researchers and the implementors. We will elaborate some interesting solutions proposed by the researchers in the following sections.

5.1 MEMORY PROTECTION

The address space is the memory used by the (user and system) programs for making references during the course of program executions. Memory references are necessary since an executing program may fetch and store its data in the memory, may follow or alter the execution sequence of its instructions, and may jump to other programs.

However, there are two types of address spaces: the real memory and the virtual memory. The traditional file space which resides on the secondary storage has a different addressing scheme. Furthermore, its addresses are not interrogated by the CPU. Therefore, in this section we shall restrict our survey of memory protection to the real and virtual memories. The discussion of file-space security and the supporting hardware will be covered in Chapter 8.

Basic hardware *protection attributes* are read-only and read/write. However, for more elaborate hardware, additional attributes such as execute-only, not-accessible, and journal-taking are possible. The *execute-only attribute* enables a (proprietary or secret) program to be executed for either accounting, monitoring, or other purposes without having its program logic revealed. The *not-accessible attribute* is an active security provision which, if violated, may cause a hardware alarm or interrupt. The alarm may ring a bell; the interrupt may alert an operator (or a system program) of the computer system. The *journal-taking attribute* enables the hardware to record the source, time, and target of the reference. Such information is usually recorded on system tapes and may provide post-mortem analysis of the reference patterns.

5.1.1 Real-Memory Protection

In real-memory protection, the real memory is divided into mutually exclusive areas. Protection is facilitated in real-time by controlling access to these areas. Whenever an instruction is to be interpreted by the CPU, the instruction is, of course, in the instruction register (IR). By examining the IR, the CPU can determine the effective addresses necessary for carrying out the instruction. These addresses are memory locations. Authorized memory locations are those which are confined within the areas and are those whose protection attributes are the same as the ones assigned to the executing program. The hardware protection mechanism verifies whether the memory locations needed for the instruction are legitimate and whether the requested instruction meets the protection attributes associated with the areas. Unless the mechanism authorizes the use of these locations, the CPU will not complete its interpretation of the instruction in the IR. Incomplete interpretations by the CPU will result in a hardware illegal instruction interrupt (or trap). Consequently, the program in execution will be aborted.

A. The Use of Bounds Registers

A way to assign protection attributes to a memory area and to keep track of a protected area is by the use of a set of CPU registers, known as *bounds registers*, for the area. Most medium to large computer systems utilize one form or another of bounds registers. For example, the Control Data 6000 series computers use one register to note the beginning of an area and another register to note the length of the area. With these two registers, the CPU can effectively determine the lower and upper bounds of the protected area (see Fig. 5–1). Unless the referenced address lies within the bounds, access to the memory cannot take place.

Although simple, this type of memory protection mechanism has several limitations.

1. For multiprogramming or multiprocessing of programs, the hardware may have to provide a set of bounds registers. Otherwise, loading and unloading of a single set of registers for different user programs will incur considerable execution delay. The number of bounds–registers pairs will determine the degree of multiprogramming and multiprocessing.

2. In addition to bounds registers, there is the need of attribute registers—one for each pair of bounds registers. Otherwise, more elaborate protections such as preventing a program to modify itself (i.e., read-only) cannot be facilitated in the hardware.

3. Bounds registers are useful to restrict program references within bounded areas. However, continuous memory areas must be used, so

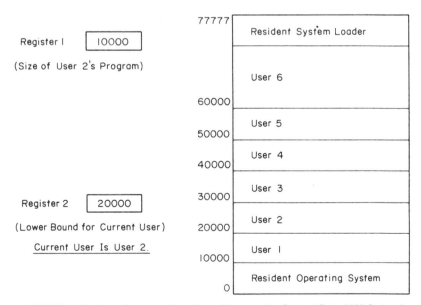

FIGURE 5-1. Use of memory bounds registers on the Control Data 6000 Series Computers.

that making reference to other areas with different protection attributes is not possible.

B. The Use of Locks and Keys

Locks are identification numbers assigned to areas of a real memory for security purposes. Unlike the bounds registers, the same number may be assigned to one or more areas (in a time period), allowing several scattered areas in the real memory to be used by the same program. In order to make proper references (thus, authorized accesses) to these areas, the user program must provide a key. The keys can be used by the CPU either to identify the locks or to override the locks. Normally, the key is loaded into a specific location by the operating system prior to the program execution. Furthermore, the assignment of the key to the program is done by the system operator, administrator or the operating system itself. An example of lock and key mechanisms can be found in the IBM 360 series computers as depicted in Fig. 5–2.

The lock and key protection mechanism has the advantage over the bounds-registers mechanism in that different memory areas can be secured for the same program. It also allows some overriding hierar-

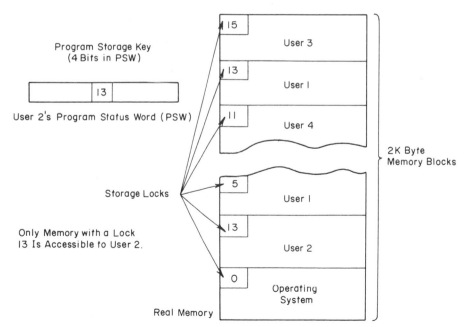

FIGURE 5-2. Use of storage locks and keys on IBM System/360.

chies to be established among the locks and keys. Say, key zero can open all the locks and no nonzero key can open lock zero. In this case, the operating system may reside in the real memory area with lock zero. Furthermore, the operating system may serve as a "big brother" by possessing the key zero so it may open every lock. Finally, protection attributes may be stored along with keys to indicate the authorized use of the locked areas. Nevertheless, there are limitations.

1. The number of locks is determined by the precision of their identification numbers. If the precision is short (say, 4 bits), there can only be few locks (16 locks, since $2^4 = 16$).

2. If the real memory is large and the number of locks is small, then the locked areas must be large and the scattered areas must be few. This allows neither finer protection of the memory areas nor flexible allocation of the memory areas.

C. The Use of Access Control Bits in Memory

One means to make the incorporation of memory protection easier is to "tag" each memory location (usually, a word) with some extra storage for description. This descriptive information is used by the CPU to interpret the mode (say, data word instead of instruction word), the type (say, floating-point number instead of fixed-point number), and other properties of information in a given location. Proper interpretations of tagged information by the CPU can avoid arithmetic operations in the mixed mode, confusion of data for instruction in execution, and other pitfalls. By extending the descriptive information to include protection attributes, reference to the location (i.e., access to the word) can be facilitated by the CPU at the time of interpreting the descriptive information.

A tagged architecture provides a very fine-grain memory protection down to the word level at the expense of the extra storage at each memory location. It can also be used to implement the lock and key mechanism by placing the key in a data word, by tagging the word with key-attribute bit, by storing the lock in the tag of another word, and by modifying the CPU to read the key in one word, compare it with the tag in another word, and determine the results. Such an extension, although promising, is not yet in sight (see Fig. 5–3) due perhaps to the cost of introducing protection at the word level.

5.1.2 Virtual-Memory Protection

There is a universal limitation associated with real memory protection. For accessing a common area, it is difficult to carry out different

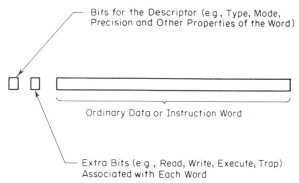

FIGURE 5-3. Tagged architecture.

security requirements for different users (programs). This is particularly acute when several programs make references to the same area at the same time. For example, with a common data area, we may place more secure requirements such as read-only for one program and less secure requirements such as read/write for another program. We would also like such requirements to be recorded within the data area. In the case of the lock and key protection mechanism, we would like the lock to distinguish who could only read and who could both read and write. This may be accomplished in the lock and key mechanism by placing the security requirements as protection attributes along with the keys. Furthermore, modification of the CPU must be made so that even if the key opens a lock, subsequent accesses to the unlocked areas must still be dictated by the associated protection attributes. Thus, two different programs with two different sets of protection attributes (in their respective PSWs; see Fig. 5–2) may have different access to the common data areas. Similarly, the same program whose key opens two or more locked areas may be regulated by two or more different sets of protection attributes—one for each area. This is not possible in the present lock and key mechanisms. However, it is easy to accommodate in a virtual memory.

By definition, *virtual memory* requires the hardware to have an *address translation table*. Addresses in user programs are always (either absolute or relocatable) virtual addresses. Addresses of an instruction (in the IR) are then translated by the CPU into real memory locations for the completion of the instruction. Translation tables are therefore a permanent addition to the system data. If the size of all the virtual memories of a computer system is the same as the size of its real memory, then the translation tables are usually stored in a fast random-access memory. If the virtual memories of a computer system are larger than the real memory, there is the need of an auxiliary storage device

(such as disk, drum, or bulk core) for accommodating the extra programs and data segments in the virtual memory and the additional
translation tables. Nevertheless, there is some fast random-access
memory for the present translation table. Although the translation
table is mainly a convention for relating virtual addresses to real
memory locations, it can easily be expanded to include additional bits
for protection attributes. In fact, in translation tables, more bits are
used for other purposes than for address translation. Suppose, for ex-

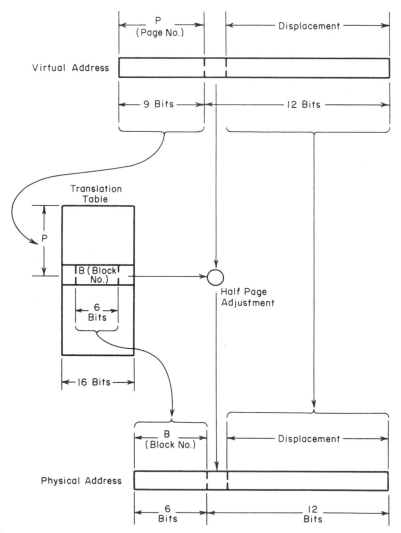

FIGURE 5-4. The Univac Spectra 70/46 virtual address and memory translation.

ample, that an instruction (in the IR) involves the writing of data into a virtual address as depicted in Fig. 5-4. The CPU will consult the translation table, calculate the page number (high-order bits of the virtual address), locate the block number (using the page number as an offset to the translation table) of the real memory block (i.e., the block containing the page) into which the data should be written, and determine the exact real memory location. We note that there are ten bits of control information associated with the block which is identified by a mere six bits. Some of these ten bits can be used to specify protection attributes of the block. By enlarging the translation table column-wise, we may have more control bits. Thus, the real memory blocks can be protected in a variety of ways. These extensions can easily be accomplished in a "two-dimensional" virtual memory system where two levels of translation tables known as *segment tables* and *page tables* are employed. Not only can we have more gross security over larger virtual areas such as *segments* by placing protection attributes in the segment table entries, but we can also have finer security at smaller virtual areas such as *pages*, *half-pages*, or *quarter-pages*, by placing protection attributes and page size controls in the page table entries (see Fig. 5-5).

5.2 MULTIPLE EXECUTION STATES

The memory protection mechanisms discussed in the previous section have very limited overriding hierarchies (see the discussion on lock and key mechanisms in Section 5.1.2). Overriding hierarchies are important since in a computer system:

1. There are instructions whose use is privileged (only highly secure programs can override the limitations of their use). For example, physical I/O instructions; instructions for the storage, retrieval and modification of page and segment tables; instructions for changing locks, keys, and protection attributes; and the instruction to set the timer.

2. There are critical programs such as the supervisory programs which call other programs, oversee the completion of these other programs, and override their completion.

We note that neither the privileged instructions nor the supervisory programs are necessarily tied down to a fixed area, making the security of those instructions and programs by memory protections alone inadequate. In other words, without additional measures, any user can write

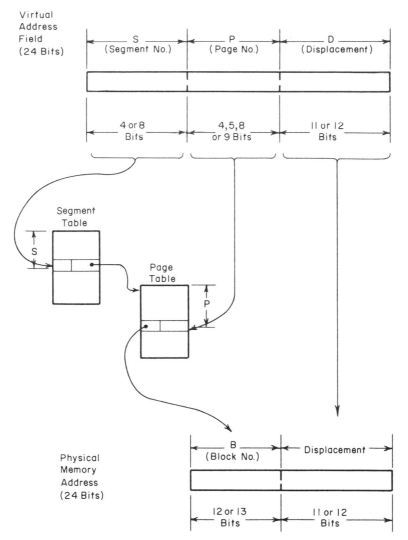

FIGURE 5-5. The IBM 370 virtual address and memory translation.

a supervisory program and also issue privileged instructions. What the computer system must therefore know is the source environment (i.e., the *state*) in which either the critical program is being executed or the privileged instruction is being interpreted by the CPU. If the state indicates that the program is being executed for, say, the system administrator and the instruction is being interpreted for the same, then the program can be executed and the instruction can be completed.

5.2.1 Binary States—The Supervisor and User States

The simplest way to create states is to have two different states—
one for privileged users such as the system administrator, and one for
all others. By placing a program in the privileged state, the program
can issue privileged instructions and supervise those programs in the
other state. Thus, in addition to the interpretation of instructions of a
program, the CPU must also determine the state by interpreting a flip-
flop, say. In this way, a given program executing in one state may issue
privileged instructions and in the other state may not, although the program code is exactly the same.

5.2.2 Multiple States—Different Levels of Execution

Multiple states allow an overriding hierarchy to have many levels
of protection. For example, it is possible to have a "hard-core" supervisor program for handling hardware and software interrupts and data
for keeping track of users' virtual space origins (pointers to the segment
tables). At the second level of the hierarchy, supervisory programs for
job initiation, accounting and termination may be facilitated. At the
next level, we may have programming language subsystems such as the
PL/1 compiler system. At still another level, we may have a user supervisor program (say, written in PL/1). Finally, the user application programs being called and monitored by the user supervisor program may
be run in the highest level. In this example (see Fig. 5–6), we have five
levels of hierarchy. The basic overriding strategy is as follows:

1. The program executing in a lower level has free use of instructions at a higher level.
2. The program executing in a higher level has only limited use of
those instructions at a lower level.

The implications of 1. and 2. are many. With multiple execution
states, for each instruction in a computer system, if the instruction requires an address for reference, the address must also be associated
with a level number (see Fig. 5–6 again). At instruction interpretation
time, the CPU not only must know the level number of the memory
location from which the instruction was fetched (this information is
available in the Program Counter), but also must know the level
number(s) of memory location(s) involved in this instruction (this information is available in the Instruction Register). If the level numbers of
the memory locations are smaller than the level number of the fetched
instruction, then the instruction is not considered. An illegal instruction

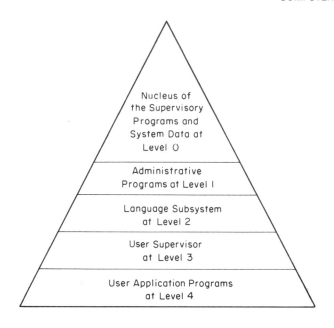

The Address Parameter of an Instruction	Level Number	Virtual Address

FIGURE 5-6. Multiple execution states.

trap (or interrupt) will occur. In addition, execution of the instruction may be restricted if it is not one of the instruction set assigned to the level in which the instruction is issued. The most complicated implication is when an instruction with high level number attempts to execute an instruction (to reference a piece of data, or to call a program) which can only be available in a lower level. In this case, the hardware must make certain that only a limited set of instructions, data entries, and program names can be made available. The limited set of instructions is managed by the CPU and therefore known to the CPU directly; the data entries and program names are managed by the file subsystem (a part of the operating system) and made known to the CPU by the operating system. Obviously, for the less privileged programs to make reference to more privileged programs in the hierarchy, it is a time-consuming and cost-consuming undertaking.

An ambitious multiple execution state mechanism which is slightly different and somewhat specialized from the above discussion was conceived and designed in the M.I.T. Multics Project. A hardware version

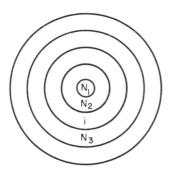
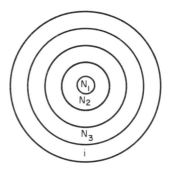

P Is in Ring i,Where $N_2 \leq i \leq N_3$.   P Is in Ring i, $i > N_3$.
Call Is Allowed to Only Certain   Call Not Permitted at All.
Entry Points.

Parameters in a Call Instruction	Segment No.	Length	Access Indicator	N_1	N_2	N_3

FIGURE 5-7. Honeywell-Multics rings.

has since been made available in Honeywell 6000 series computers with some modification of original concept (see Fig. 5–7). In this implementation, the term "ring" is used to replace the term "level."

5.3 MICROPROCESSORS AS SECURITY AIDS

As mentioned in the previous sections, the physical I/O instructions and the file subsystem operations are privileged operations which require particular scrutiny by the CPU. This scrutiny, involving both the software and the hardware, requires processing cycles from the CPU and main memory resulting in some degradation of performance for other tasks.

5.3.1 Between I/O Channels and the Main Memory

The use of additional processors and memories for I/O and local processing may alleviate this degradation. Since these processor and memory pairs are physically separated, they enhance security by *isolation* (see the CDC 6600 System in Fig. 5–8). The isolation approach has the disadvantage of duplication of physical resources. However, where

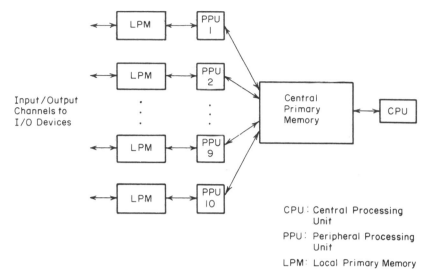

FIGURE 5-8. Control Data 6600 computer system architecture.

system utilization is high, where peripheral processing requirements are diverse, and where security requirements are overwhelming, the cost of redundant hardware in terms of processors and memories may well be justified.

5.3.2 Specialized Processors

Technological advances in memories and processors make the microprocessors exceptionally attractive as a security aid. These advances have reduced the cost of microprocessors and have facilitated their use. In particular, microprogrammable microprocessors allow a baseline of microprocessors to be designed and configured for various applications.

A. Database Processors

For example, microprocessors may be designed and configured for content-addressable search of a database stored on magnetic and electronic disks. For small databases, there could be one content-addressable microprocessor for each disk track. This notion of *logic-per-(all)-track* in which content-addressable logic is applied to every track of the on-line magnetic or electronic disks can be implemented in the hardware by incorporating the microprocessor (therefore, the logic) in the read–write heads of the disks. Security is assured in data

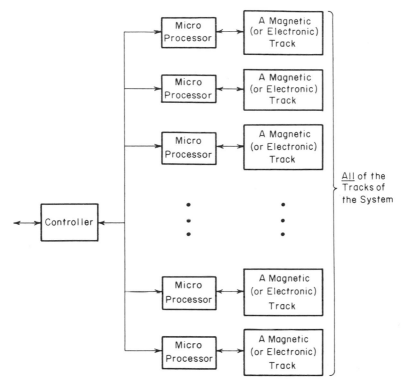

FIGURE 5-9. Logic-per-(all)-track approach.

retrieval when the microprocessors search in parallel all those tracks and output only those whose content does not violate the security specification (see Fig. 5–9). For large databases, the notion of *logic-per-(some)-track* can be implemented in the hardware where a small number of microprocessors is incorporated in the disk controller. At any given time, only one disk cylinder (say, 40 tracks) is being content-searched by the set of microprocessors. Other cylinders, if needed, will be searched in sequence. This approach has the advantage of lower cost (see Fig. 5–10). In addition, performance will not be degraded since at most 5 to 10% of the database will be involved in the typical database search.

Security performed where the data resides is a most desirable form of protection. In this way, unauthorized data will never need to be routed to the main memory for subsequent processing by the CPU. In fact, all the data routed to the main memory are indeed authorized. The data traffic among the main memory, CPU, and the I/O channels is drastically reduced. Any accidental spillage of secure data due to

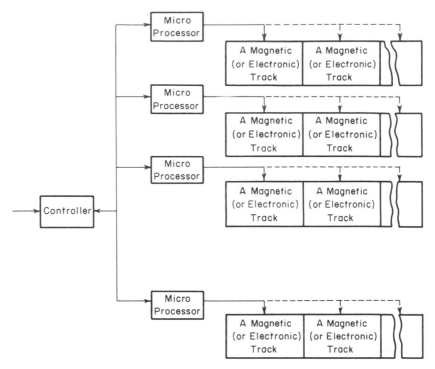

FIGURE 5-10. Logic-per-(some)-track approach.

system malfunction and user penetration will be confined to the
content-addressable disks and will not be scattered all over the computer system.

B. Post-Processing

Specialized microprocessors are necessary for *post-processing* of
data for security reasons. For example, a doctor may authorize a
medical researcher to access all his patient records in the computer
system provided that the names and other personal data of the patients
are masked out of the records. For another example, consider the protection of statistical data in which an entire record set should not be
output if the average salary of the retrieved records is greater than a
predetermined number.

In general, field-level protection of large data aggregates requires
post-processing for the purpose of checking the fields, computing the
field values, and removing either the field names or the field values or
both. Furthermore, it may cause the entire data aggregate to be protected from access. In this case, the *post processor* prevents the CPU

and the main memory from receiving data whose overall data attributes may satisfy the request but whose particular field-level protection attributes require more stringent control and monitoring (see Fig. 5–11).

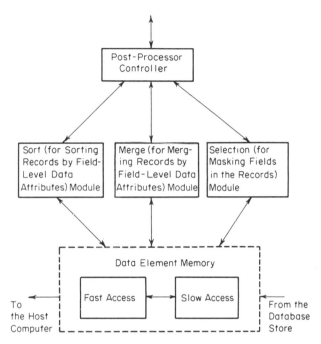

FIGURE 5-11.   The organization of a post-processor.

5.4 MINICOMPUTERS AS SECURITY CONTROLLERS

Minicomputers are needed when the volume of secure information processing is too high to be relegated to the microprocessors. They are also needed when security enforcement by the hardware requires complex computations and elaborate management of data and resources.

5.4.1 Periods Processing

The notion of *periods processing* has been practiced in the Department of Defense (DOD) environment. Whenever a class of secure processing is required, the minicomputer treats the entire processing session as a stand-alone period. It executes the following steps:

1. Instruct the CPU to erase the main memory, to initiate a clean copy of the operating system, to reset the channels, controllers, and registers. In other words, return the main computer to its initial state.

2. Switch the I/O controllers to the appropriate I/O devices which contain the information for the class. These switches are *not* alterable by the main computer system.

3. Upon completion of the initiation and switching, control is passed to the CPU of the main computer system.

4. Requests for the class (say, A) processing are always stacked on the tapes (or disks), known as *input tapes* (or *disks*) which are, of course, switched on for the period. Processing requests for other classes (say, B and X) are deferred.

5. When the period for this class is over, a period for another class may begin. Steps 1. through 5. will be repeated again.

An improvement of the aforementioned procedure for periods processing has been suggested. Instead of manual performance of steps 1. through 5. by the operator, the operating system is modified to perform the steps automatically. More specifically, jobs of different security classes can be batched in a job stream with *job separators*. These job separators are indeed JCL statements (i.e., job control language statements or job control cards) and are inserted into the job stream by the operating system for the purpose of performing steps 1. through 5.

Users of conventional batch operating systems may recall that device switching, memory erasure, system state reset, and job start and termination have been the functions typically provided by the JCL statements of these systems. By making certain that only the operating system can issue these statements (instead of the users), the operating system can assure secure batch processing of jobs with different classes. One way to prevent the user from using these statements is to "hardwire" them. As hardware and privileged instructions, they can only be executed by the operating system.

There are several limitations related to periods processing. Most severe is that it is good for batch processing but does not allow time-sharing. The second limitation is the considerable duplications of physical resources such as disks and tape drives. Although removable tapes and disk packs may be used on the same drives, the security of the system in this case depends on the operator's integrity in changing tapes and packs. Many periods processing installations do not want to trade hardware switching reliability for human integrity. In other words, the removable medium, no matter how cost-saving and flexible, is not a good security risk if human effort is involved (see Fig. 5–12).

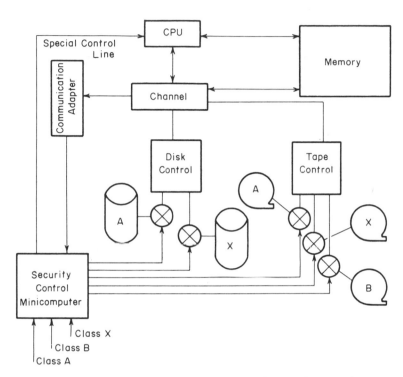

FIGURE 5-12. Minicomputer security control system for periods processing.

5.4.2 Monitoring

One of the main reasons that a minicomputer is used for monitoring is the large amount of information that may be collected by the minicomputer. Potentially, every hardware main memory access, I/O activity, and terminal activity can be collected, stamped with a system clock, and logged on a tape dedicated to the minicomputer. The tape, known as the *journal tape*, can be used for post-mortem security analysis. However, the minicomputer is most likely used to perform some computation on the basis of collected information. The result of the computation may trigger an alarm, print a message at the security officer's console, and cause the main computer to go into an "infinite" loop. The exact alarm and detection algorithm may vary with the security requirements. For example, a request for reading a secure file may merely cause the request, the requester's ID, and other information to be entered in the log. On the other hand, an attempt to insert information into the file may cause a message alert to be sent to the officer's console, whereas any effort to modify the file may cause a physical alarm to be rung (see Fig. 5–13).

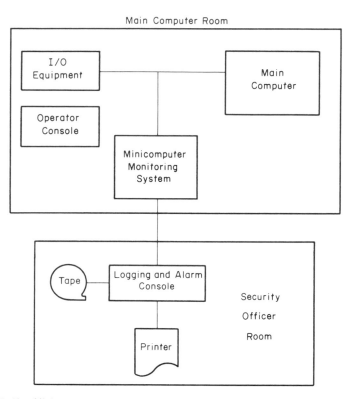

FIGURE 5-13.   Minicomputer security monitoring system.

5.5 HARDWARE REALIZATION OF
OPERATING SYSTEM FEATURES

As mentioned in the previous section the JCL statements of the operating system may be hardwired for periods processing. There are also more ambitious efforts in introducing some of the known operating system features into hardware for performance gain and security enhancement. Consider the notion of capability and capability-oriented systems (for a discussion on operating system security, the reader may refer to Chapter 7). In these systems, all resources (such as programs, data sets, channels, devices, and memory block) are considered as *objects* which are identifiable by the operating system. For a user to perform some operations (via a program, say) on an object, the user must have a copy of a *capability*. The capability thus dictates all the permissible operations (which may be performed on the object). It was originally created by the owner of the object and is subsequently authorized for the user. However, the user may not modify the (copy of the) capability. The capability is used by the operating system to determine for the user whether the requested operations are indeed authorized and whether the object is in fact the right one. Furthermore, the operating system must provide mechanisms to create and remove capabilities for the object owners, to make copies of the capabilities for the users, to interpret the capabilities against pending operations and objects, and to safeguard the capabilities from tampering. For a system with a large number of objects and capabilities, the task to provide the aforementioned mechanisms in the operating system may be overbearing. Thus, efforts have been directed toward implementing these mechanisms in hardware and achieving "hardwired" operating systems known as *capability computers*.

Another example in realizing the operating system features in hardware can be found in the Honeywell 6000 series computers as discussed in Section 5.2.2. The original MIT Multics ring mechanism was mostly implemented in the software Multics operating system and finally realized in the hardware of the Honeywell computers. In this development, we may also refer to the Honeywell 6000 series computers as the *Multics Computers*.

5.6 SUMMARY REMARKS

Computer hardware contains information: data and programs. The hardware units, whether they are memory units or storage devices, are containers of the information. Hardware security is therefore concerned with how to develop secure containers, how to regulate the transmission of information from one container to another, and how to monitor the transmission activities. Memory protection ranges from simple and primitive protection of real memory units using bounds registers to complex and elaborate protection of virtual memory units using page and segment tables. Protection of memory units provides access control to memory units at the time of the address reference and memory access.

When programs must call each other and when memory access involves shared data, the address references and memory accesses require control of both the target and source memory locations. They also have to do with the issuer of the references and accesses. To determine whether the issuer has the authorization, the hardware must know not just the memory units in which the issuer is present (the program is being executed) and the memory units that will be affected, but also the state of the hardware. Multiple states allow issuers (programs) to have a hierarchy of authorities and privileges. The hierarchy of security control is particularly useful where there is the need of layers of supervisory programs and software systems.

To monitor system activities, process on-going information, and perform security checking, both microprocessors and minicomputers may be utilized. The former are for the development of special-purpose security hardware; the latter are for high-volume processing and monitoring—both have found their way into hardware security. In addition, efforts at realizing operating system security features in hardware have become in vogue.

Hardware solutions for secure networks are included in Chapter 6. Both the secure front-ends (see Fig. 6–4) and the privacy controller (see Fig. 6–6) are discussed there.

5.7 POSTSCRIPT

For an introduction to tagged architecture and its security capability, the reader is urged to refer to [Feusta 73]. Hardware implementation of the Multics ring mechanism is detailed in [Schroe 72] and Multics kernel in [Adlema 76c]. Hardware implementation of the capability-list approach (see Chapter 7 for a discussion of capability-list oriented operating system) is expounded in [Fabry 74], [Englan 74], and [Saal 78]. Periods processing is argued in [Lipner 74a]. Hardware monitoring is proposed in [Smith 75]and [Anders 78]. I/O device security is emphasized in [Weissm 74b] and also in [Anders 78]. A system using encryption is discussed in [Sindel 74]. Military requirements for secure computer systems are covered in [Burr 77]and [Strauss 77] and for communications processor in [Kilgor 76]. All the references on secure database machines and processors are included in Chapter 8. Here, we merely cite the references of all those hardware-related articles included in other chapters. For operational and physical security, see [Hemphi 73], [Martin 73], in Chapter 1, and [Jeffer 74a] in Chapter

4. For identification and authentication (Chapter 4), see [Herbst 77] and [Swonge 76]. On data encryption (Chapter 6), see [Bartek 74], [Burris 76a], [Carson 77], [Diffie 77], [Feista 75], [Ingema 74], [Keys 74], [NBS 77], [Pless 75], [SICGS 77], [Stahl 74], [Tuchma 77], and [Yasaki 76].

On operating systems related references (in Chapter 7), see [Bisbey 74j, [Hoffma 73], [Hoffma 77a], [Hsu 76], [Linden 76b], [NBS 76a], [Redell 74b], [Rotenb 74], [Saltze 75], [Shanka 77], [Wagues 75], and [White 75b]; also see [Walker 77] in Chapter 1.

On database machines, database processors, and post-processing (Chapter 8), see [Banerj 78a], [Banerj 79a], [Banerj 78b], [Baum 76a], [Baum 76b], [Baum 76c], [Hsiao 76b], [Hsiao 76c], [Hsiao 77b], [Hsiao 77c], [Hsiao 77d], [Hsiao 77e], [Lorie 76], and [Vonbue 74].

REFERENCES

Adlema 76c

Adleman, N., "Engineering Investigations in Support of Multics Security Kernel Software Development." Honeywell Information Systems, Inc., October 1976; ESD–TR–77–17 (NTIS AD–A040329).

> This incomplete (due to project termination) report prepared for the Air Force Electronic Systems Division examines the software and hardware implementation problems related to the new Multics secure kernel in the context of the existing Honeywell Multics structure and mechanisms. In other words, it attempts to size up the complexity and difficulty in introducing the new kernel if it were being incorporated into existing Honeywell Multics operating system and hardware by way of modifications.

Anders 78

Anders, F., Mall, W., McGill, R., McLaughlin, J., and Thompson, B., "Intelligence Security Subsystem." Harris Corp., March 1978, RADC–TR–78–33 (NTIS AD–A054508).

> This report prepared for Rome Air Development Center emphasizes the use of disk controller, microprocessors, and minicomputers for security checking, logging monitoring, and encryption of incoming and outgoing data. Although the methods discussed such as database guard, red–black multiprocessing, record encipherment, and secret record tags have been known perhaps, in somewhat different terminology, to workers in the security field, the contribution of this report is in its estimation of the hardware cost and use of off-the-shelf hardware for such methods.

Burr 77

Burr, W. E., Coleman, A. H., and Smith, W. R., "Overview of Military Computer Family Architecture Selection." *AFIPS Conference Proceedings–1977 NCC,* Vol. 46, 1977, pp. 131–137.

A combined Army/Navy Selection Committee was formed to select a Computer Family Architecture for use in a new Military Computer Family (MCF). They were to study existing architectures to determine if any was appropriate for use in the MCF. The authors explain the criteria used and then detail the selection process. The committee studied nine potential candidate architectures and narrowed this down to three after initial study. These were the IBM S/370, DEC PDP–11, and Interdata 8/32. Results of the final evaluation are provided and the authors explain why the PDP–11 was selected as the best possible candidate for the MCF.

Englan 74

England, D. M., "Capability Concept Mechanism and Structure in System 250." *Proceedings of IRIA International Conference on Protection in Operating Systems,* Rocquencourt, France, August 1974, pp. 63–82.

Fabry 74

Fabry, R. S., "Capability Based Addressing." *Communications of the ACM,* Vol. 17, No. 7, July 1974, pp. 403–412.

Fabry, in his much referenced paper, examines the use of capabilities as a part of addressing most resources in the computer system. In the first part of the paper he discusses the problems of sharing segments and then compares four solutions: Uniform Addressing Solution, Indirect Evaluation Solution, Multiple Segment Table Solution, and the Capability Addressing Solution. In the next portion of the paper, Fabry examines several aspects of hardware implementation of capabilities. The discussions cover integrity of capabilities, address translation, paging, instruction sets, and stacks.

The integrity of capabilities is done through one of two methods known as the tagged approach and the partition approach. The author explains that the tagged approach [Feusta 73] involves adding one or more bits to each word of memory to designate whether they contain capabilities or not. The partition approach separates memory into segments of either capabilities or data. For reasons explained in the paper, Fabry feels the partition approach is best.

Fabry next reviews several methods for address translation used on previous machines using capability addressing. He then suggests several improvements that could be made with recent advancements in technology. The major one is assigning all objects unique codes which are kept in a hash table maintained in primary memory. The hardware then finds the resource via this hash table.

Feusta 73

Feustal, E. A., "On the Advantages of Tagged Architecture." *IEEE Transactions on Computers,* Vol. C–22, No. 7, July 1973, pp. 644–656.

The paper asserts that for today's general-purpose computers the von Neumann type design is not optimal. Instead of program and data being indistinguishable, it is suggested that self-identifying representation at all levels of storage within the computer system would be more useful. The paper contains a short review of previous architectures using this philosophy. The most notable of these being the IBM 360's use of a hardware lock–key mechanism for main storage and the GE 645 (Multics) lock-out of writes through interpretation of bits in segment table.

In the next two sections Feustal explains how a tagged architecture would simplify programming. The general advantage is that data types in a program may be mapped in a better manner to their actual physical representation.

The ways in which a tagged architecture would contribute to the performance of operating systems are discussed in the next section. Feustal examines tagged architecture with respect to naming, protection and sharing, resource management, and debugging and instrumentation. Within protection and sharing, the author explains how capability or access lists could be implemented through the use of tagged architecture.

The next section establishes the advantages of tags as they affect computer architecture. Register allocation, stream (pipeline) processing, cache memories, and specialized processors are considered in this portion of the paper.

The final section concerns itself with methods for implementing tagged architecture. Feustal suggests using ten-bit bytes with one bit for parity, one for a tag and eight for data. He feels the necessary hardware would add 2 to 3% to the system cost.

Kilgor 76

Kilgore, G. A., "Probabilistic Measures of Compromise." Honeywell Information Systems, Inc., January 1976, ESD–TR–76–160 (NTIS AD–A037302).

This report prepared for the Air Force Electronic Systems Division is aimed to develop probabilistic measures of security breaches due to hardware failure and methods for certifying hardware in meeting the design specifications. Both the security measures and the certification methods are specifically applied to a computer-communications front-end of Multics, known as the Secure Communications Processor (SCOMP).

Lipner 74a

Lipner, S. B., "A Minicomputer Security Control System." Mitre Corp. MTP–151, February 1974, *Proceedings of Compcon 74,* San Francisco, California, February 1974, pp. 57–60.

A computer organization scheme in which a minicomputer is placed between the main computer and secondary storage devices is described in this paper. In this system information of different security classifications would be placed on different storage devices. When jobs of a certain category were to be processed the minicomputer would lock all the devices of different security level so no access would be allowed. Lipner justifies the development of this system and explores some of its possible applications.

Saal 78

Saal, H. J., and Gat, I., "A Hardware Architecture for Controlling Information Flow." *Proceedings 5th Symposium on Computer Architecture, SIGARCH Newsletter,* Vol. 6, No. 7, April 1978, pp. 73–77.

Capability-based systems are able to enforce certain restrictions on information flow. Suppose a process has the following access rights to segments A, B, C, and D: (A, READ), (B, WRITE), (C, READ), (D, WRITE). There is no way to allow the transfer of data from A to B and from C to D while preventing the transfer of data from A to D. This paper proposes extending the capability concept to a capability vector concept such as < (A, READ), (B, WRITE) > .

Schroe 72

Schroeder, M. D., and Saltzer, J. H., "A Hardware Architecture for Implementing Protection Rings." *Communications of the ACM,* Vol. 15, No. 3, March 1972, pp. 157–170.

Sindel 74

Sindelar, F., and Hoffman, L. J., "A Two Level Disk Protection System." Technical Report, Electronic Research Laboratory, University of California, Berkeley, ERL–M452, 1974.

The authors introduce a hardware mechanism for protecting data stored on disks. The method involves a password scheme for file protection and the use of a hardware encryption device located in the disk controller to encipher the data on the disk.

The password scheme is a fairly simple one. The authors explain the file owner provides a password to be associated with the file. When an individual wishes to access the file he provides the file name and password which is then matched to that kept in the disk file directory. Details of the necessary hardware support are given. The encryption method uses the exclusive OR technique with the key being generated from a linear shift register.

This system has been implemented by the authors and a discussion of the cost and performance of the system is included in the paper.

Smith 75

Smith, L., "Architecture for Secure Computing Systems." Mitre Corp., Bedford, Massachusetts, MTR–2772, April 1975 (NTIS AD–A009 221).

Smith attempts to define the architectural features of a computer that would permit implementation of a secure system. He notes that, although a secure system could be designed for any machine, certain features help implement "the three characteristics of a secure operating system: (a) each access to memory must be checked for correctness by a reference monitor, (b) the reference monitor is self protecting, and (c) the reference monitor is provably correct."

The author outlines problems of providing protection and approaches to solving these problems. He then describes a mathematical model of secure systems [Bell 73], [Bell 74a] using it to characterize desirable architectural features. These features are then compared to those of five commercially available systems: Burroughs B6700, XDS Sigma 9, IBM 370, DEC–KI–70, and the Honeywell 6180 (Multics), with the latter being judged as the best available for implementing a secure system.

Straus 77

Strauss, J. C., and Thurber, K. J., "Considerations for New Tactical Computer Systems." *Proceedings of 4th Annual Symposium on Computer Architecture,* March 1977, pp. 135–140.

A prototype of a new computer system known as Advanced Real-Time Processing System (ARPS) is being developed by the Moore School of Engineering at the University of Pennsylvania in conjunction with Sperry Univac. This paper discusses the features of the new system with respect to the following areas: Cost/Power Balance, General Registers, Addressing, Memory Management, Sharing and Protection, Interrupts, Input/Output, Instruction Set, and Data Representation, Micro Architecture, Maintenance, and other features. The paper describes the features for file protection and the sharing of memory. Protection at the file level is done by a check of an access rights list associated with the file owner. The ARPS computer uses a virtual memory type of addressing scheme to facilitate sharing and protection.

Weissm 74b

Weissman, C., "Security—The Responsibility of the Peripherals Industry." *Proceedings of CompCon 74, IEEE Computer Society,* February 1974, pp. 33–35.

Weissman observes some of the typical vulnerabilities of today's computer systems. These are insecure I/O channels, side effects of parallelism, and memory residue. He suggests that virtual memory systems through hardware may provide the solutions to these and other problems. Bringing I/O into the domain of virtual memory may alleviate many problems according to the author. He feels that addressing peripherals as memory similar to the DEC PDP–11's UNIBUS in conjunction with making the peripheral devices smarter will help improve security.

Chapter 6

CRYPTOGRAPHIC TRANSFORMATIONS

Whether it is geographically centralized or distributed, a computer system may be viewed as a network of terminals, storage devices, and processing units. Thus, we have communications among the terminals, devices, and units. *Cryptographic transformations* are techniques for encoding data to hide their content in the course of communications in the network.

6.1 CRYPTOGRAPHY

Since data are handled as messages in communications, classical cryptographic techniques have been used for these transformations. Consider cases where there are communications between terminal and processing units. The data are enciphered at the time and place of the entry. The encipherment involves the data (known as the *plaintext*), a *key*, and an *operation*. By performing the operation on the data digits and key digits, the data entry terminal produces cipher messages (known as the *ciphertext*), which will then be sent to the central processing unit. A cipher message returned by the processing unit is deciphered at the data exit terminal. Decipherment involves the cipher message, a related key and a similar operation. By performing the operation on the cipher digits and the key digits, the data exit terminal produces the original data (i.e., *plaintexts*). Because both of the operations performed and the keys used at the data entry and the data exit terminals are similar, it is possible to use a single terminal for both data entry and data exit. Furthermore, the same operation may be built into hardware, in lieu of software, for more rapid and reliable communications. However, the key (say, on a card with magnetic stripes) must be guarded by the user and changed often.

6.1.1 Message-Oriented Systems

In Fig. 6–1, a typical cryptographic system is depicted. Cryptographic systems are primarily used for the communication of messages, implying that the plaintexts (therefore, ciphertexts) must be short and transient. For such messages, the classical *ciphers* are applicable. These ciphers can be considered in two classes, those that deal with *transpositions*—interchanging of characters—and those that deal with *substitutions*—replacing one character with another. Because certain common words (therefore, letters) appear more frequently than others in messages, *monographic substitutions* may not be adequate. In this case, *polyalphabetic substitutions* may be used where for each letter in the plaintext a list of distinct letters is used in sequence to replace the occurrences of the same letter.

Frequent changes of keys require a way to produce random patterns of keys. The use of pseudorandom generators for producing keys has been noted.

6.1.2 Information-Oriented Systems

In the information system environment where the databases are large and messages are long, there is the need of longer keys. The use of multiple short key tapes to produce a long compounded key have been used. Because certain information such as numerical data is critical in some data operations, and because errors in this information cannot be

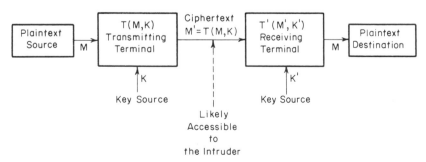

FIGURE 6-1. Cryptographic systems used in communications.

detected by context, there is the need of a type of transformation whose ciphertexts are rich in bits and sensitive to any change of a single digit position. Such transformations not only can provide high message confidentiality, but also can provide for error detection. The classical substitution ciphers are not adequate for this purpose. Instead, a type of transformation, known as *confusion techniques,* is used. For a binary plaintext of few ones, there are more ones generated in the ciphertext, for example. Actually, confusion is a form of nonlinear substitution. In Fig. 6–2, we depict a transformation which employs both the transposition technique (the P boxes) and the confusion technique (the S boxes). Both the P boxes and the S boxes are implemented in the hardware. Furthermore, the level of transpositions is determined by the number of P boxes stacked and the degree of confusion is determined by the number of S boxes juxtaposed. Together, the P and the S boxes can form very flexible and modular transmitting and receiving terminals for cryptographic transformations.

When data is required at the central site, the database may have to be deciphered either in part or in whole for subsequent data operations. To decipher a database either in part or in whole for data operational purposes, the central processing unit must have access to keys. A fundamental problem is therefore the capability of the processing unit to protect the keys.

When data operations are heavy, direct processing of the ciphertext may be desirable. Cryptographic transformations, which ''preserve'' certain data operations (say, order-preseving operations such as ' > ' or ' < '), enable the system to perform those operations on an enciphered database without the need of deciphering the data-

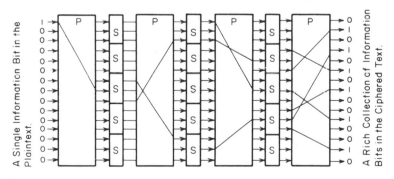

P Box for Transposition : Hardwired

S Box for Non-Linear Substitutions: Set by Keys

FIGURE 6-2. The ''building'' boxes of the IBM's Lucifer system.

base. For such data operations, the system needs no key. The problem of key protection, therefore, does not exist. Since preservation of data operations may reveal certain patterns of operations, these transformations tend to aid the revelation of the key. An open question is whether there are strong cryptographic transformations which preserve certain data operations and which also provide little aid to the revelation of the transformations.

6.2 CRYPTOGRAPHIC TRANSFORMATION SYSTEMS

6.2.1 System Is No Secret, Only Keys Are

One of the fundamental assumptions about the cryptographic transformation is that the transformation will soon be known to the intruder. In terms of a cryptographic transformation system built with P and S boxes as depicted in Fig. 6–2, there is a good possibility that someone may steal the boxes and thus figure out the transposition and confusion techniques used in the boxes. The underlying assumption of any cryptographic transformation system is that someone may steal the system. The only protection of a system is therefore the safeguard of its keys.

The second assumption about the transformation is that once in possession of the system, the intruder would want to determine the keys. Thus, an important exercise for the designers of a cryptographic transformation system is to estimate the amount of effort and cost needed to determine the keys. Prohibitive cost tends to discourage the intruder. During the time needed to determine a key, the user may have switched to a new key. Since high-performance computers with great computation capability can hasten the effort with moderate cost, the estimation of "code-breaking" effort should also be considered in terms of the intruder's computer access and capability.

6.2.2 Federal Standard

If we assume that the intruder will get hold of a transformation (or a system), we may as well reveal the transformation to the public. Furthermore, for the ease of hardware and software implementation of the transformation, such revelation may encourage common adoption of the transformation as a *standard*. In this way, plaintexts can be received and transmitted as ciphertexts among different units, devices, and terminals, making communications among heterogeneous computer systems possible. The only requirement is that each user of the network safeguard his own key.

The National Bureau of Standards has provided an encryption standard (for all those federal agencies which are not exempted) for handling a data block of 64 bits, (Fig. 6–3). The transformation consists of a series of transpositions (i.e., right half of the block becomes the left half of the "next" block), confusions, (i.e., the 32-bit right half is generated into a 48-bit code, and each key bit is generated into a 48-bit subkey), and logical operations (first the 48-bit code is exclusively "or"ed with 48-bit subkey, then 32 bits are selected from the resulting

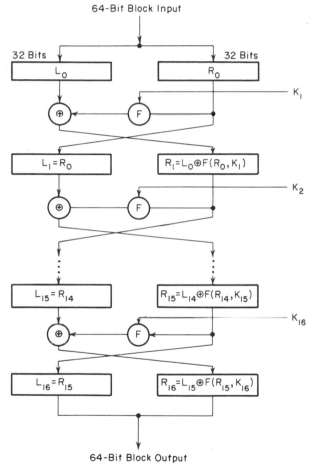

FIGURE 6-3. Standard cryptographic transformation algorithm by the National Bureau of Standards—the Data Encryption Standard (DES).

48 bits, and finally the selected 32 bits are exclusively "or"ed again with the 32-bit left half). This process of half-block transposition, repetitive confusion, and multiple logical operations is performed 16 times, since the key is of 16 bits, each of which generates 16 subkeys (through confusion).

Despite such an elaborate transformation, the NBS standard has met with criticisms. One criticism is that the block size of 64 bits is too small as a unit for data transmission, since some of the bits are used for parity check and other purposes. Another criticism is that the key is too short, and the subkeys should not depend on each other, making it easier for the intruder to exhaustively try all those possible keys and subkeys.

Suggestions are made in two directions: either use single keys that are long, or use, in sequence, several keys (or subkeys) which are short and independent. In the latter case, the idea is to encipher the plaintext with the first short key, the ciphertext with the second short key, and the next ciphertext with the next short key. The only problem with the multiple short key approach is the delay in transmitting and receiving of the information.

6.2.3 Terminal and Device Communications with the Central Computer

The application of cryptographic transformations in the computer system ranges widely. Consider the devices 1 through 4 where each device has its own cryptographic transformation as shown in Fig. 6–4. This is necessary if the devices are geographically situated away from the central processing unit and if communication between the devices and the controller (i.e., controller 2) are *via common carriers*. Furthermore, this application allows different cryptographic transformation boxes to be used in different devices to reflect the degree of security associated with the devices. Nevertheless, such an undertaking is most expensive and requires hardwiring of the transformation boxes. If the controller (in this case, it is controller 3) is close to the devices (i.e., devices 9 through 12), and is far away from the central processing unit, then a more economical way to have security in communication is to include a common cryptographic transformation box in the controller. Since some of the controllers are microprogrammable, the box can also be microprogrammed. Although several devices may use the same box, this application does not preclude the use of tailor-made boxes for individual devices. The least expensive application is to implement the transformation in software and to execute it in the main memory (as

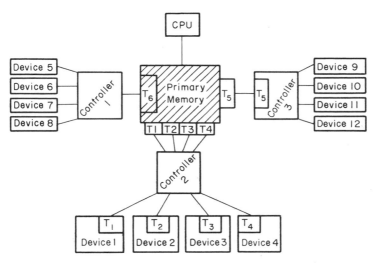

FIGURE 6-4. Cryptographic transformation boxes (shown as T_i) incorporated into computer components.

depicted by T_6 in Fig. 6–4). This application is only viable if the devices (5 through 8) and controller (i.e., controller 1) are being serviced with well-secured communication lines and channels.

In general, devices 1 through 4 are likely remote stations such as the bank stations for electronic fund transfer. Devices 5 through 8 are likely to be local I/O devices such as disks and tapes. Devices 9 through 12 are likely to be slow terminals such as teletypewriters.

6.2.4 Network Communications

In a computer network environment with n nodes, every pair of nodes may have some communications. Instead of building a cryptographic transformation system for each node-to-node communication which will result in $\binom{n}{2}$ such systems (see Fig. 6–5), we invest in a *network cryptographic controller*. The controller needs only n such systems and also the capability to identify and authenticate the source and target nodes as depicted in Fig. 6–6. In this way, the controller not only saves a factor of $\frac{1}{2}(n-1)$ cryptographic transformation systems, but also can serve as a central site for maintenance and replacement of existing transformation systems.

A second method for alleviating the need for $\binom{n}{2}$ systems in a network environment is the *public key system*. In this system, each user has two keys, one of which is made public. To send a message to an individual, the *public key* is used for encryption. The message can then only be decrypted using the *private key*. Several techniques have been

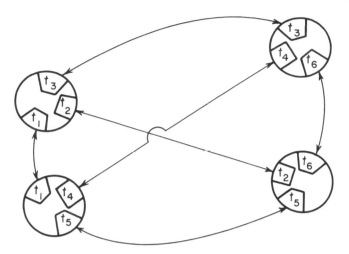

FIGURE 6-5. Node-to-node cryptographic transformations.

created for easily determining the public key given the private key, while requiring a very large amount of work for determining the private key given the public key.

Since the public key system is particularly suitable for different users to transmit data through the network with different sets of public–private keys, there is the problem of *public key distribution and management* (i.e., how to safely get the right public key to the right person and to keep track of who has what keys) and *data signature* (i.e., how can the data be securely identified with the sender's ID).

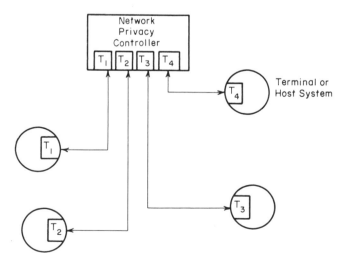

FIGURE 6-6. The use of a cryptographic controller.

6.3 POSTSCRIPT

Although fascinating stories about cryptography have been written for leisure reading in book form such as *The Codebreakers* (by D. Kahn, McMillan Co., 1967), we restrict our references to articles since 1973. Modern use of cryptographic techniques in information system environments is different from its classical use. General treatments can be found on cryptographic transformations in computer systems [Feista 73], in computer networks [Heinri 76], [Heinri 78], [Kent 77], [Sykes 76], in databanks [Turn 73], in man–computer communications [Feista 75], and in message handling [Ames 77], [Ames 78]. The implementation of cryptographic transformation in hardware for removable storage media such as disk packs is motivated in [Bartek 74], and prompted with the advent of LSI technology [Keys 74]. Hardware implementations of cryptographic transformations for terminal and data communication are many. Notable ones include IBM's early start on a terminal system [Feista 73] and subsequent applications in block transfer [Feista 75]. Other proposals for hardware implementation can be found in [Ingema 74] and [Pless 75], and for validating correct implementation in [Gait 77].

A hardware implementation standard known as the DES for the federal agencies is available [Branst 77], [Branst 78], [NBS 77]. Controversies around the DES are many. The cons attempt to show that the DES may well be an extension of the IBM work [SIGCS 77] and under the influence of the National Security Agency (NSA) [Kolata 77a] (e.g., citing other influence exerted by NSA [Shaple 77], can be broken by exhaustive search [Diffie 77] due to short key length, can show the dependence between bits of the plaintext and key after five tries [Meyers 78], and should definitely be boycotted [Rotenb 77]. The pros argue the absence of any influence of NSA and cooperation from IBM [Tuchma 77], and justify it as a federal standard due to its practicality [Ingema 76a] and its intended short lifetime (5 years) utilization [Yasaki 76].

Software implementations of transformations have been advanced. The use of a microprocessor to execute software transformations for terminals can be found in [Carson 77] and [Flynn 78]. The use of large digital computers to execute various transformations is studied and measured in [Friedm 74]and [Bright 76]. The application of software means to operating system environment can be found in [Benedi 74], to database environment in [Gudes 76] and [Culpep 77]. The use of random number generator software for providing keys is emphasized in [Matyas 78], [McCart 75], and [Payne 78].

Network requirements for utilizing cryptographic transformations are outlined in [Burris 76a], [Cole 78], [Karger 77], and [Karger 78]. Specific requirements for DES in a network environment are found in [Abene 77] and [Stepha 78]. Specific requirements for IBM network to use cryptographic transformation are proposed in [Lennon 78]. The problem of key distribution involving many nodes is studied in [Diffie 76a], [Ehrsam 78], [Everto 78], [Gait 78], and [Sendro 78]. On data signature, see [Saltze 78] and [Hellman 78]. The advantage of using both public and private keys in a network is suggested in [Diffie 76b], [Hellman 78], [Gardne 77], [Merkle 78], and [Rivest 77].

There are also some controversies around the public key systems. A number of "attacks," [Simmon 77] and [Tuchma 78], is aimed at the public key systems, in particular, the MIT Public-Key Cryptosystem [Rivest 78b]. However, the attacks do not seem to have any mathematical foundations [Rivest 78a].

Theoretical treatments of cryptographic transformations center on extensions of classical homophonic techniques [Stahl 74], on the introduction of nonlinear substitution technique [Fiesta 73], on the use of short keys to generate the long key [Payne 78], and on information-theoretic extensions of Shannon's concept of unicity distance [Hellma 74].

The relationship between cryptographic transformations and both operational and physical security can be found in Chapters 3 and 4 under the references [Clemen 74], [Martin 73], [Nielse 76a], [Nielse 76b], [Shanka 77], [Evans 74b], and [Purdy 74]. The relationship between cryptographic transformations and hardware security can be found in Chapter 5 under [Sindel 74], and data security in Chapter 8 under [AFIPS 75] and [Bayer 76]. The relationship between cryptographic transformations and operating system security can be found in Chapter 7 under the references [Hoffma 77a], [NBS 76a], and [Rotenb 74]. The relations between cryptographic transformations with the privacy requirements can be found here [Turn 77] with load utilization on a network [Lientz 78]. In Chapter 1, see [Hoffma 73], [Katzan 73], and [Walker 77].

REFERENCES

Abene 77

Abene, P. V., "Secure Commercial Digital Communications." M. S. thesis, University of Colorado, Boulder, Colorado, July 1977, (NTIS AD-A-046 887).

After reviewing digital communication and cryptographic techniques this thesis examines the application of the Data Encryption Standard [NBS 77] to existing asynchronous and synchronous communications protocols.

Ames 77

Ames, S. R., Jr., "User Interface Multilevel Security Issues in a Transaction-Oriented Data Base Management System." *Data Base Engineering*, Vol. 1, No. 3, September 1977, pp. 7–14.

This paper presents a general description of the system more fully described in [Ames 78].

Ames 78

Ames, S.R., Jr., and Oestreicher, D.R., "Design of a Message Processing System for a Multilevel Secure Environment." *AFIPS Conference Proceedings - 1978 NCC*, Vol. 47, 1978, pp. 765–771.

The Department of Defense Advanced Research Projects Agency (DARPA) and the Navy are sponsors of several prototype secure computer/aided message handling services for the receipt, filing, retrieval, creation, and coordination of military messages. The SIGMA system developed at the Information Science Institute of the University of Southern California and MITRE to operate on a DEC PDP–10 computer is described. The system is based on the security kernel and the *-property of [Bell 74a]. The unique problems of a message system include (a) the dynamic nature of the user's "working security level;" (b) the desire to present to the user information at more than a single security level; (c) the desire to accurately inform the user of the security level of all information being read or written; and (d) the ability of users to extract text information and place it in a message of a lower classification than the source.

Bartek 74

Bartek, D. J., Encryption for Data Security." *The Honeywell Computer Journal*, Vol. 8, No. 2, 1974, pp. 86–89.

Bartek examines the value of cryptography and how its use would prevent several types of security violations related to computer systems. He lists several features of good encryption techniques that include simplicity, easily changeable keys, transparency to users, and most importantly that only the keys need be kept secret and not the method.

Bartek then describes several methods for communication cryptography and techniques for encrypting removable storage media. Problems of key storage and distribution are mentioned. The paper also includes descriptions of the way cryptography is used to enhance the security of Honeywell's Multics system.

Benedi 74

Benedict, G. C., "An Enciphering Module for Multics." Massachusetts Institute of Technology, MAC TM–50, July 1976 (NTIS AD–782 658).

Branst 77

Branstad, D., Gait, J., and Katze, S., "Report of the Workshop on Cryptography in Support of Computer Security." National Bureau of Standards, September 1977, NBS 77–1291.

> A workshop was held in September, 1976, at the National Bureau of Standards to discuss the mathematical and statistical characteristics of the then proposed NBS Data Encryption Standard (DES) [NBS 77]. Problems discussed included potential weaknesses of the DES, potential attack by exhaustive search [Diffie 77], choice of the S-boxes used, and the acceptability of a standard based on classified material. It was also determined that the greatest potential for reduction of security was in the areas of key generation and distribution.

Branst 78

Branstad, D. K., ed., *Computer Security and the Data Encryption Standard.* Proceedings of the Conference, National Bureau of Standards, February 1978, NBS SP 500–27.

> Applications and implementation of the Data Encryption Standard (DES) were discussed at a NBS Workshop in February 1977. Topics discussed included the relationship of encryption to the general computer security problem, problems of procurement and use of the DES, applications of the DES, and the implementation of the DES. This report should be read by anyone who is thinking of using data encryption.

Bright 76

Bright, H. S., and Enison, R. L., "Cryptography Using Modular Software Elements." *AFIPS Conference Proceedings–1976 NCC,* Vol. 45, 1976, pp. 113–123.

> Two types of encryption schemes (strong algorithm and long key systems) are discussed in this paper. Strong algorithm encryption schemes are those that depend on computational complexity for their strength such as the NBS data encryption standard. Long key systems are those that use the nonpredictability of a long key in conjunction with a relatively trivial algorithm for their security. The authors detail these two types of systems and present results of experiments using software emulations of example schemes of each.
>
> The authors outline their successful emulation of the NBS Data Encryption Standard as a software package. They feel it has several applications that include testing and debugging of programs and ideas before its hardware implementation becomes available, validating and mainte-

nance of hardware, preparation and evaluation by manufacturers of hardware test data. Results of tests using the emulator are given in the paper.

A software package for a long key encryption system is also described. The system uses the well-known Vernam or exclusive OR function. The discussion in the paper centers around the generation of the long key and methods such as pseudorandom number generators for doing so. The technique used by the authors is known as the Tausworthe–Lewis–Payne bitwise linear recurrence modulo 2 type, which is described in detail in an appendix. Test results from using this long key encryption system are provided.

Burris 76a

Burris, H. R., "Computer Network Cryptography Engineering." *AFIPS Conference Proceedings–1976 NCC,* Vol. 45, 1976, pp. 91–96.

Several design considerations relating to the use of cryptographic techniques are outlined in this paper. Burris first defines security objectives as follows:

1. Restriction of information to authorized persons.
2. Protection of system performance.
3. Restriction of system resources to authorized persons.

He then discusses three types of enciphering methods: transposition, substitution, and additive encoding. Transposition involves reordering the characters of the plaintext. Substitution is the technique of replacing the characters of the plaintext. Lastly, additive encoding is the use of the exclusive OR function to encrypt the plaintext.

Cost, in terms of actual hardware purchase price and performance parameters, and efficiency (security achieved) are used to compare alternatives for five design decisions relating to network use of cryptography. Synchronization, implementation, keying methods, key distribution, and extent encryption are the topics discussed. The authors note that in almost all cases the trade-offs involved increasing security from one attack while sacrificing security from another.

Carson 77

Carson, J. H., Summers, J. K., and Welch, J. S., "A Microprocessor Selective Encryption Terminal for Privacy Protection." *AFIPS Conference Proceedings–1977, NCC,* Vol. 46, 1977, pp. 35–38.

The results of an experiment, performed by the NETREK division of The Mitre Corporation are reported in this paper. The experiment involved the use of a Digital Equipment Corporation LSI–11 microcomputer which allowed the user to selectively encrypt any information before transmission to the host computer. By doing this at the terminal, through the LSI–11, data protection was provided independent of the host computer.

The LSI–11 could operate in either plaintext or encryption mode. In plaintext mode it simply relayed information sent from the terminal and vice versa. The user, by surrounding a string of characters with square brackets, indicates the string is to be encrypted before transmission. The encryption is done via software implementation of the NBS data encryption standard. Details of the encryption process and variations are outlined in the paper. Costs for the experimental system along with projected costs for a production version are also presented.

Cole 78

Cole, G. D., "Design Alternatives for Computer Network Security." National Bureau of Standards, January 1978, NBS SP 500–1, Vol. 1.

The use of network security center(s) [Heinri 76], [Henri 78] for network security is discussed in the framework of the NBS Data Encryption Standard [NBS 77]. Implementation options involving the access control data structures, the I/O structure, the control structure, and size and performance limitations are given.

Culpep 77

Cullpepper, L. M., "The Feasibility of a Method of Processing Encrypted Data." Naval Ship Research and Development Center, Bethesda, Maryland, January 1977 (NTIS AD–A036 713).

Culpepper describes a system for encrypting a database in which the responsibility for encryption would be placed at intelligent terminals. The database organization would be that of B-trees proposed for encryption by Bayer and McCreight [Bayer 76].

Diffie 76a

Diffie, W., and Hellman, M. E., "Multiuser Cryptographic Techniques." *AFIPS Conference Proceedings–1976, NCC,* Vol. 45. 1976, pp. 109–112.

New problems evolving from the use of cryptography in computer communication systems are the topic of this paper. In particular the problem of key distribution within a network of a large number of users is studied. The problem is that for two users to communicate in a secure manner only they should know the key used to encrypt a message. This can be solved by each of n users having n-1 keys—one to communicate with each of the other n-1 users. This would require distribution of $n^{(n-1)}$ pairs of keys which the authors feel is infeasible. The next method is to have the users trust the network. This allows them to only have to remember one key. With this key a message is encrypted and sent to a node, reencrypted, and sent to the next node. This process continues until the message finally reaches its destination. Since only one node needs to be subverted to compromise the security of the network, the authors do not advocate this approach either and suggest two methods that will solve the problems.

The first method requires a small number (m) of the networks nodes to act as key distribution nodes. Each user remembers m keys, one to be used for communicating with each node. When two users wish to communicate they contact all of the m nodes and receive a random key from each. These are exclusively ORed together by the user to become the actual key used for encryption of any m messages. This method is discussed in detail in the paper. Its advantages are a reduced number of keys to be distributed and yet requiring subversion of all key distribution nodes in the network.

The second method is based on the use of one way ciphers [Evans 74], [Purdy 74] and allows even the keys to be public. That is, the user has a pair of keys E and D, where E is used for encrypting messages sent to the user and D is used for decrypting messages received by the user. The necessary feature is that the E–D pairs must be easy to generate and yet it must be infeasible to compute D from E. Possible ways of doing this are presented in the paper. The authors also show how this might be used to authenticate messages eliminating forged messages.

The ideas put forth by the authors in this paper are quite interesting and demonstrate practical applications of advanced cryptographic techniques.

Diffie 76b

Diffie, W., and Hellman, M. E., "New Directions in Cryptography." *IEEE Transactions on Information Theory*, Vol. IT–22, No. 6, Nov. 1976, pp. 644–654.

The use of cryptography in communication systems has always suffered from the burden of secure key distribution. In this paper the authors explain two methods developed that do not require secrecy of keys. In the first method, known as a public key crypto system, each user owns two distinct keys, E and D. E is used by others to encrypt messages sent to its owner and is therefore public. D is used by the owner to decrypt messages he has received. While D and E are related, it is obviously necessary that deducing D from E must be computationally infeasible. Several techniques for implementing a public key cryptosystem are discussed. An interesting method based on these ideas is reported in [Rivest 77].

The second method, public key distribution, consists of having two users who wish to communicate over an insecure channel exchange keys until an agreed upon one is found. This was developed in [Merkle 78]. The authors suggest another method which is less costly.

Authentication of messages and ways this may be accomplished is also considered. The authors also discuss the relationship of cryptography to the problem of computational complexity.

Diffie 77

Diffie, W., and Hellman, M. E., "Exhaustive Cryptanalysis of the NBS Data Encryption Standard." *Computer,* Vol. 10, No. 6, June 1977, pp. 74–84.

The National Bureau of Standards has adopted a data encryption standard for commercial and public use. Diffie and Hellman argue that the standard is weak since it is economically feasible to build a machine which can break it. This machine could be built for $20 million using today's technology and would need only 12 hours of computation time to actually break the standard using an exhaustive trial and error method. The cost of building this machine will be reduced to $200,000 in 10 years.

The basis for the authors' criticism of the standard is the size of the key used for encryption. The key is 56 bits in length yielding 2^{56} or 10^7 possible keys. A machine with a million devices searching in parallel, each trying a possible solution once every microsecond, would take only one day to try every possible solution and one-half day on the average to discover the correct key. The authors show why they feel such a machine can be built and justify their placing the cost of this machine at $20 million.

Diffie and Hellman answer several objections made by the NBS to their basic criticisms of the standard. Most of these objections center around the cost and time estimates to break the standard made by the authors. A fairly detailed description of how the machine could be built and why it would work is then presented. In its normal operating mode the machine would take a block of ciphertext and corresponding block of plaintext and then test all possible keys until the correct one was discovered. The authors also show how it would be possible to break the standard by using only a block of ciphertext.

A fairly convincing argument that the standard can be broken is made by the authors of this paper. They suggest that the standard be changed with the key size increased to 128 or 256 bits. They note this will not guarantee the security of the standard, but only prevent a successful attack from exhaustive search techniques.

Downey 74

Downey, P. J., "Multics Security Evaluation: Password and File Encryption Techniques." Air Force Electronics Systems Division, Hanscomb AFB, Massachusetts, June 1974, ESD–TR–74–193, Vol. III (NTIS AD–A001 120).

Ehrsam 78

Ehrsam, W. F. Matyas, S. M., Meyer, C. H., and Tuchman, W. L., "A Cryptographic Key Management Scheme for Implementing the Data Encryption Standard." *IBM Systems Journal,* Vol. 17, No. 2, 1978, pp. 106–125.

An important problem in the use of any data encryption method is the management of the many keys that are needed. This paper proposes a technique that is applicable to communication security in single host-multiple terminal systems. This technique is also shown to be adaptable to data storage security and to network communication security.

Assume that each terminal has a unique terminal master key known by the terminal and the host. That key may be protected by the host using a host master key which is unavailable to any user program. For any session the host generates a session key which is transmitted to the terminal after encryption using the terminal master key. This key is then used throughout the session by both the host and the terminal. A method for generating the session key on the host processor without allowing the key to appear in clear form is proposed.

The types of keys needed can be divided into data-encrypting and key-encrypting keys. The key-encrypting keys must be very secure so that a real random process should be used in their generation. Data-encrypting keys are much more numerous and are changed much more frequently. Thus they must be generated by some mechanical process. Specific key generation methods are discussed in [Matyas 78]. These papers should be read by anyone about to set up an encrypting system.

Everto 78

Everton, J. K., "A Hierarchical Basis for Encryption Key Management in a Computer Communications Network." *Proceedings Symposium on Distributed Processing—Trends and Applications*, Gaithersburg, Maryland, May 1978, pp. 25–32.

The large number of keys required in a network means there must be a key management system. In particular, there may be (a) "sessionkeys" used during one session for data transmission, (b) "submasterkeys" used to protect the sessionkeys when stored or transmitted, and (c) "master keys" to protect the submaster keys that are stored. The paper discusses the generation of keys, the transportation of keys, and the protection of keys.

Feista 73

Feistal, H., "Cryptography and Computer Privacy." *Scientific American*, Vol. 228, No. 5, May 1973, pp. 15–24.

In this much referenced paper, Feistal provides a good introduction to cryptography and its uses within computer systems. He first explains the difference between codes and ciphers and introduces methods for the latter. These include Ceasar ciphers and a complete explanation of using the exclusive OR (Vernam ciphers) function for encryption purposes. Methods using permutation and substitution including their use in IBM's Lucipher system are also described.

Feistal concludes with details of a complete system utilising cryptography to authenticate messages sent from remote terminals.

Feista 75

Feistal, H., Notz, W. A., and Smith, J. L., "Some Cryptographic Techniques for Machine-to-Machine Data Communications." *Proceedings of the IEEE*, Vol. 63, No. 11, November 1975, pp. 1545–1554.

Cryptography provides a viable means for protecting data in a multiuser computer environment. The authors point out several ways in which cryptography may be used to protect information being transmitted between hardware devices in a computer system. The authors first discuss a stream cipher technique in which a long string of bits called the key is generated and exclusively "or"ed with the plaintext to obtain the ciphertext. The second technique is the block cipher method in which the bits of plaintext are permuted and substituted obtaining ciphertext. The block cipher method is the method preferred by the authors. Details and variations of it are included in the paper.

Sections are included on the use of the block cipher method for authenticating the user's identity, implementation choices, an experimental system, and cost and performance measures.

This paper, while relatively complicated at times, is nevertheless suggested reading for the individual desiring details of modern uses of cryptography.

Flynn 78

Flynn, R., and Campasano, A. S., "Data Dependent Keys for a Selective Encryption Terminal." *AFIPS Conference Proceedings–1978 NCC*, Vol. 47, 1978, pp. 1127–1129.

Applications of the selective encryption terminal of [Carson 77] are discussed.

Friedm 74

Friedman, T. D., and Hoffman, L. J., "Execution Time Requirements for Encipherment Programs," *Communications of the ACM*, Vol. 17, No. 8, August 1974, pp. 445–449.

Friedman and Hoffman feel that while encipherment has often been discussed as a technique for security its costs have never really been measured. To this extent they conducted experiments to gather data on the execution time of various encipherment programs. The tests were conducted on a CDC 6400 computer and the general encipherment technique used was that of exclusively oring plaintext with a key to produce ciphertext. Tests were run with programs written in both Fortran and assembly language.

Five different tests were made:

1. A null transformation to provide a standard for comparison.
2. A one word key cipher.

3. A long key cipher.
4. A double key cipher.
5. A pseudorandom key cipher of "infinite" length.

Results of these tests are given in the paper.

Gait 77

Gait, J., "Validating the Correctness of Hardware Implementations of the NBS Data Encryption Standard." National Bureau of Standards, November 1977, NBS SP 500–20.

> The National Bureau of Standards has implemented a test procedure for certifying that a hardware implementation of the NBS Data Encryption Standard is correct. The procedure consists of running the hardware to be certified in parallel with a standard implementation. A set of 291 test cases are first used. Then a Monte-Carlo test using 8×10^6 encryptions and 4×10^6 decryptions is performed. If the device performs correctly for these tests, then it is certified.

Gait 78

Gait, J., "Easy Entry: The Password Encryption Problem." *Operating Systems Review*, Vol. 12, No. 3, Jul. 1978, pp. 54–60.

> A summary of implemented and proposed methods for protecting passwords.

Gardne 77

Gardner, M., "Mathematical Games." *Scientific American*, Vol. 237, No. 2, August 1977, pp. 120–124.

Gudes 76

Gudes, E., Koch, H. S., and Stahl, F. A., "The Application of Cryptography for Data Base Security." *AFIPS Conference Proceedings–1976 NCC*, Vol. 45, 1976, pp. 97–107.

> The applications of cryptographic transformations for securing information stored within database systems is discussed in this chapter. The authors state that a major reason behind the limited study of this topic is the lack of a suitable database model. Such a model is presented in this paper to provide an understanding of the connection between the database structure and cryptography as applied to the database. This model consists of four levels: user-logical, system-logical, access level, and storage level. User-logical refers to the concept of a user view. System-logical is the logical structure of the entire database. The access level refers to the directories, indices, and access paths to the database. Finally, the storage level is the actual structure of the database on secondary storage. The authors show how encryption can be applied between the various levels of the model and discuss possible encryption methods which could be used. The authors feel this model provides a framework

for further research into the area of cryptography and its applications for database protection.

The multilevel model concept is due originally to M. E. Senko's Data Independent Accessing Model (DIAM) which appeared first in *IBM Syst. J.*, Vol. 12, No. 1, 1973.

Heinri 78

Heinrich, F., "The Network Security Center: A System Level Approach to Computer Network Security." National Bureau of Standards, January 1978, NBS SP 500–21, Vol. 2.

> Originally prepared for the Department of Defense by the System Development Corporation in 1974, this report examines the issues and trade-offs related to network security for a range of applications, topologies, and communication technologies. The issues examined are identification and authentication, access request and authorization, establishment of network connections, use of network connections, security monitoring, and assurance of secure operation.
>
> A four-level design based on host systems, security controllers, cryptographic devices, and communications nets is proposed. Each of the identified issues is then discussed for each of these levels. [Cole 78] extends this approach.

Hellma 74

Hellman, M. E., "The Information-Theoretic Approach to Cryptography." Technical Report, Information Systems Laboratory, Stanford University, Stanford, California, April 1974. (Also in [AFIPS 75].)

> In this fairly technical paper Hellman explores and extends Shannon's well-known information-theoretic approach to cryptography. Shannon's idea, known as unicity distance, is that there is a certain critical amount of text required to break a cipher is reexamined. Hellman introduces the idea of matching an encryption method to a language. Also the topic of a work factor, or amount of work necessary to break a cipher is discussed. In this context he explores the complexity of various encryption techniques.

Hellman 78

Hellman, M. E., "Security in Communication Networks." *AFIPS Conference Proceedings–1978 NCC*, Vol. 47, 1978, pp. 1131–1134.

> Research on public key systems and digital signatures reported in [Diffie 76b], [Rivest 78], and [Merkle 78] is summarized.

Ingema 74

Ingemarsson, I., Blom, R., and Forchheimer, R., "A System for Data Security Based on Data Encryption." Report LiH–ISY–R0032, April 1974, Dept. Electrical Engineering, Linkoping University, Linkoping, Sweden.

This report gives the details of a data encryption scheme for use in computer systems. The report states the scheme is based on four principles:

1. Data shall be stored in encrypted form.

2. No information about a user's authority shall be stored in the computer.

3. Each user shall possess a key, physical, or in the form of a password, or a combination of both. This key is able to encrypt or decrypt data belonging only to those categories to which the user is authorized.

4. The information on the keys shall be necessary and sufficient for successful encryption or decryption.

The encryption method is detailed in the report. Its most interesting feature is that different keys may allow access to the same category of data. A hardware prototype incorporating the method has been developed and the report describes the use of this device.

Ingema 76a

Ingemarsson, I., "Analysis of Secret Functions with Application to Computer Cryptography." *AFIPS Conference Proceedings–1976 NCC,* Vol. 45, 1976, pp. 125–127.

Data stored within a computer system, whether protected by cryptography or not, is usually accessed more than once and usually by several users. The author asserts that an individual may have a copy of the plaintext, ciphertext, and knowledge of the encryption algorithm. If that user can somehow deduce the key from this information, he will then be able to transform any other ciphertext into plaintext for which the same critical amount of text and knowledge of the encryption algorithm. If that user can somehow deduce the key from this information, he will then be able to transform any other ciphertext into plaintext for which the same key was used for encryption. In this paper, Ingemarsson uses an information-theoretic approach to investigate the possibility of determining the key from observations of the plaintext and ciphertext. That an individual may identify the key after only a few observations is shown to be theoretically possible in most cases. Avoiding this in actual practice can be done through the use of a computationally complex process to derive the key. The NBS Data Encryption Standard [NBS 77] is used as an example of an encryption process that theoretically is possible to break after a few observations but in reality would prove to be extremely difficult.

Karger 77

Karger, P. A., "Non-Discretionary Access Control for Decentralized Computing Systems." S.M. thesis, Massachusetts Institute of Technology, 1977, MIT/LCS/TR–179, ESD–TR–77–142 (NTIS AD A040 808).

Karger 78

Karger, P. A., "Non-Discretionary Security for Decentralized Computing Systems." *Proceedings Symposium on Distributed Process-*

ing—Trends and Applications, Gaithersburg, Maryland, May 1978, pp. 33–39.

> In addition to discussing general problems of security in a computer network, this paper considers methods for allowing a computer at one security level to transfer data to a comptuer at a higher level. This problem is complex since the higher level computer must also send messages to the lower level computer for acknowledgement and error detection. A more detailed discussion is available in [Karger 77].

Kent 77

Kent, S. T., "Encryption-based Protection for Interactive User/Computer Communication." *Proceedings 5th Data Communications Symposium,* 1977, pp. 5.7–5.13.

> Communications between a terminal and a host over an insecure connection are subject to five types of attack: (a) release of message content, (b) traffic analysis (for example to determine identity or location of communicating parties), (c) message modification, (d) denial of service, and (e) spurious connection initiation. Data encryption has been applied to prevent attacks a and b. This paper suggests a combination of communication protocols and data encryption to allow detection of attacks c, d, and e.

Keys 74

Keys, R. R., and Clamons, E. H., "File Encryption as a Security Tool." *The Honeywell Computer Journal,* Vol. 8, No. 2, 1974, pp. 90–93.

> Hardware devices for encrypting stored data are discussed in this paper. The authors explain that current technology would allow the use of these devices in conjunction with tape or disks. The advantages and disadvantages of placing the devices in the channel, device controller, or device itself are examined.
>
> Possible means for protection of data in main storage by encryption is described. While doing so is not currently feasible, the authors feel that developments in large scale integration (LSI) technology may eventually allow hardware encryption at all levels of memory.

Kolata 77a

Kolata, G. B., "Computer Encryption and the National Security Agency." *Science,* Vol. 197, 29, July 1977, pp. 438–440.

> This article provides an excellent report on controversy surrounding the National Bureau of Standards Data Encryption Standard [NBS 77]. This controversy involves the length of the key used in the standard (56 bits). Critics feel that it is too small and that a machine could be built to break the standard [Diffie 77]. Some feel that the National Security Agency, which was involved in the development of the NBS work may

have wanted the standard to be breakable. This is refuted in [Tuchma 77]. The article does a thorough job of explaining views of critics and proponents of the standard.

Kolata 77b

Kolata, G. B. "Cryptography: On the Brink of a Revolution." *Science*, Vol. 197, 19, August 1977, pp. 747–748.

> This article, similar to [Gardne 77], reports on recent developments in cryptography [Diffie 76b] which would allow keys for encryption to be public.

Lennon 78

Lennon, R. E., "Cryptography Architecture for Information Security." *IBM Systems Journal*, Vol. 17, No. 2, 1978, pp. 138–150.

> Extensions to IBM's Systems Network Architecture to allow data encryption are discussed. The methods used are based on those discussed in [Ehrsam 78].

Lientz 78

Lientz, B. P., and Weiss, I. R., "Trade-Offs of Secure Processing in Centralized vs. Distributed Networks." *Computer Networks*, vol. 2, 1978, pp. 35–43 (NTIS AD–A053 344).

> Assuming that secure processing degrades system performance, the authors built a simulation model to study how to distribute a workload in a network. Parameters include what network structure is used, how many computers use secure processing, and the percent degradation caused by the security processing. It is shown that the preferred network structure can be sensitive to the amount of degradation.

Matyas 78

Matyas, S. M., and Meyer, C. H., "Generation, Distribution, and Installation of Cryptographic Keys." *IBM Systems Journal*, Vol. 17, No. 2, 1978, pp. 126–137.

> Key generation is an essential part of any cryptographic system. This paper discusses key generation methods based on the hardware used in the key management scheme in [Ehrsam 78]. Specific algorithms are proposed for the generation of both key-encrypting keys and data-encrypting keys.

McCart 75

McCarthy, J., "Proposed Criterion for a Cipher to be Probable-Word Proof," *Communications of the ACM*, Vol. 18, No. 2, February 1975, pp. 131–132.

> In this note McCarthy points out that the encryption used by Friedman and Hoffman [Friedm 74] is not necessarily secure. Their system

used a random number generator to produce a long key [Bright 76] which is exclusively ORed with plaintext to come up with the ciphertext. McCarthy feels that the key can be discovered if an attacker knows the method used by the random number generator, a small amount of plaintext, and has the encrypted message. McCarthy suggests that a second random number generator be used to select bits from the output of the first which are then used for the key.

McCarthy then proposes the following criterion for a cipher to be "probable word-proof": Even if all the plaintext but one character were known, it should still require an unacceptable amount of work to learn more about the character than is suggested by the known remainder of the message and statistics of the assumed message population.

Along with this note is a reply by Hoffman and Friedman. They agree that it is possible to break their cipher the way McCarthy suggests, although they feel it will be in most cases impractical to do so.

Merkle 78

Merkle, R. C., "Secure Communications over Insecure Channels." *Communications of the ACM,* Vol. 21, No. 4, April 1978, pp. 294–299.

Classical data encryption methods assume that a key is transmitted in a completely secure manner, preventing its interception or modification. This paper proposes a technique where the two parties can agree on a key of length N utilizing only work of order N on their parts, but requiring work of other N^2 for an enemy. It is hypothesized that other methods can be found that require an exponential amount of work for an enemy. The ideas presented are similar to the public key system suggested in [Diffie 76b].

Meyer 78

Meyer, C. H., "Ciphertext/Plaintext and Ciphertext/Key Dependence vs. Number of Rounds for the Data Encryption Standard." *AFIPS Conference Proceedings–1978 NCC,* Vol. 47, 1978, pp. 1119–1126.

The National Bureau of Standards data encryption algorithm consists of 16 repetitions of the same basic transformation. This paper shows that after five repetitions each bit of the ciphertext is dependent on all bits of the plaintext and on all bits of the key.

NBS 77

"Data Encryption Standard." *National Bureau of Standards,* January 1977 (NTIS NBS–FIPS PUB 46).

This document contains a complete description of The National Bureau of Standards' Data Encryption Standard. The algorithm, which must be implemented in hardware to completely comply with the standard, is based on a 64–bit key of which 8 bits are used for parity checking. The method is a specialized block enciphering scheme utilizing the exclusive-or technique along with a specialized function. Although this algorithm has not been challenged in terms of the security it provides, the size of the key has received a certain amount of criticism [Diffie 77], [Rotenb 77].

Payne 78

Payne, W. H., and McMillen, K. L., "Orderly Enumeration of Non-singular Binary Matrices Applied to Text Encryption." *Communications of the ACM,* Vol. 21, No. 4, April 1978, pp. 259–263.

One method to obtain a long key is to use a short key as a seed in a pseudorandom number generator. On such an algorithm, the generalized feedback shift register method requires a nonsingular binary matrix for a seed. In order to use this method for data encryption, it is necessary to associate the user key, in the form of an integer, with a unique matrix. This paper shows a way to make this association.

Pless 75

Pless, V. S., "Encryption Schemes for Computer Confidentiality." Massachusetts Institute of Technology, Project MAC Technical Report, MAC–7M–63, May 1975 (NTIS AD–A010 217).

In this report Pless describes a stream ciphering technique for encrypting data and the hardware necessary to implement it. Essentially the scheme uses a linear shift register in combination with J–K flip-flops to obtain a random stream of bits. Several variations of the method are proposed and a discussion of the strengths and weaknesses of each is included.

Pless 77

Pless, V. S., "Encryption Schemes for Computer Confidentiality." *IEEE Transactions on Computers,* Vol. C–26, No. 11, November 1977, pp. 1133–1136.

See [Pless 75].

Rivest 77

Rivest, R., Shamir, A., and Adleman, L., "A Method for Obtaining Digital Signatures and Public Key Cryptosystems." Technical report, Laboratory for Computer Science, Massachusetts Institute of Technology, (MIT/LCS/82) April 1977.

Given impetus by Hellman's and Diffie's work [Diffie 76b], Rivest *et al.* have developed a public key encryption system. This interesting system, specifically designed for use on computer systems, is based upon the difficulty in factoring large (200 digit) integers. This scheme may be used to establish private communication and eliminate worry over loss of information when the encryption key is transmitted over a "public" line.

Also, it may be used for providing "unforgeable" signatures on electronic mail. This scheme is also discussed in [Gardne 77].

Rivest 78a

Rivest, R. L., "Remarks on a Proposed Cryptanalytic Attack on the M.I.T. Public-Key Cryptosystem." *Cryptologia*, Vol. 2, No. 1, January 1978, pp. 62–65.

It is shown that the attack proposed in [Simmon 77] to the M.I.T. Public-Key Cryptosystem [Rivest 78b] is no more likely to succeed than trying to factor the large integer given as part of the public key.

Rivest 78b

Rivest, R. L., Shamir, A., and Adleman, L., "A Method for Obtaining Digital Signatures and Public-Key Cryptosystems." *Communications of the ACM*, Vol. 21, No. 2, February 1978, pp. 120–126.

Rotenb 77

Rotenberg, L. J., "NBS Data Encryption Standard Considered Weak and Unfit." *ACM SIGCS: Computers and Society*. Vol. 8, No. 2, Summer 1977, p. 1.

A brief description of the NBS Data Encryption Standard [NBS 77] and the criticisms of it [Diffie 77] are included in this letter calling for a boycott of the proposed standard.

Saltze 78

Saltzer, J. H., "On Digital Signatures." *Operating Systems Review*, Vol. 12, No. 2, April 1978, pp. 12–14.

It is pointed out that there are two problems in the use of a cryptographic system for a digital signature [Diffie 76a]). First, authenticating information must be added to any message. Second, there is no solution proposed to prevent the possible loss of the enciphering key.

Sendro 78

Sendrow, M., "Key Management in EFT Networks." *Proceedings Fall COMPCON 78*, Washington, D.C., September 1978, pp. 351–354.

The problems of secure key generation, transmission, use, storage, and destruction in an electronic fund transfer system are discussed.

Shaple 77

Shapley, D., and Kolata, G. B., "Cryptology: Scientists Puzzle Over Threat to Open Research Publication." *Science*, Vol. 197, September 30, 1977, pp. 1345–1349.

This article outlines efforts by the National Security Agency (NSA) to discourage the IEEE's Information Theory Group from sending preprints of talks to be presented at a cryptology symposium to the Soviet Union. The NSA feels the publication abroad of certain material to be presented at the symposium would violate national security regulations, specifically the Arms Export Control Act. In particular the work by Diffie and Hellman [Diffie 76a], [Diffie 76b] along with that of Rivest and his associates [Rivest 77] is being examined by the NSA.

SIGCS 77

ACM SIGCS Staff, "Federal Data Encryption Standard Approved by Commerce Department." *ACM SIGCS,* Vol. 8, No. 1, Spring 1977, pp. 14–15.

This short note is on the Commerce Department's approval of the National Bureau of Standards Data Encryption Algorithm [NBS 77]. The report comments on the algorithm's applications, strengths, and that it was originally designed by IBM.

Simmon 77

Simmons, G. J., and Norris, M. J., "Preliminary Comments on the M.I.T. Public-Key Cryptosystem." *Cryptologia,* Vol. 1, No. 4, 1977, pp. 406–414.

A possible attack on the M.I.T. public key cryptosystem [Rivest 78b] is proposed. This attack consists of reencrypting the ciphertext until the ciphertext is reobtained. The original clear text must then be the last text encyphered. A response is given in [Rivest 78a].

Stahl 74

Stahl, F. A., "On Computational Security." Ph.D. dissertation, University of Illinois at Urbana-Champaign, 1974 (NTIS AD–775 451).

Stahl, in his dissertation, investigates the use of cryptography to protect information transmitted to and stored within the computer system. The two areas that Stahl's research focused on were first a "generalized homophonic cryptographic ciphering device," and second a software cryptographic technique that encodes a database by the use of statistical phrases that occur.

The technique used by Stahl's homophonic enciphering device requires the key, 256 characters in length, to be loaded in memory each character individually addressable. Stahl explains that to encipher a character, say "A," an address into this 256 word table is generated randomly. The table is then searched sequentially until the first occurrence of "A" is found. The address of this second "A" is then taken as the cipher text symbol. Deciphering simply requires looking up the contents of the appropriate memory location. Stahl details this system and analyzes its characteristics.

The second system is based on finding the longest statistical phrase occurring in some text. Stahl explains that a statistical phrase is a pattern of words that repeats itself. The details of discovering these phrases is presented in the thesis. Once these have been determined and placed in a dictionary, their occurrence in the text may be replaced with a pointer to the dictionary. Not only is the text encrypted, but it also requires less storage.

Stepha 78

Stephan, E., "Communications Standards for Using the DES." *Proceedings of Fall COMPCON 78*, Washington, D.C., September 1978, pp. 348–350.

> The special problems and security in the use of the NBS Data Encryption Standard in a communications environment are discussed. The objectives of compatibility are (a) to allow substitution of one supplier's product for another's and (b) to allow information transfer between products of different suppliers. Thus there must be a standardization of the modes of operation and of the methods of establishing synchronization between devices. The objectives of security are to prevent (a) inadvertent transmission of plaintext, (b) emanation of the key, (c) theft of the key, and (d) theft of the device containing the key.

Sykes 76

Sykes, D. J., "Protecting Data by Encryption." *Datamation*, Vol. 22, No. 8, August 1976, pp. 81–85.

> Sykes feels that encryption, if used together with adequate physical security, can become a powerful tool for protecting data. This is felt to be true for networks and in communication links between computers and remote terminals. Furthermore, data files may also be made more secure from unauthorized access by encryption.
>
> Sykes explains three types of encryption techniques: link, end-to-end, and media. Link encryption involves placing the actual encryption devices at modem interfaces, thus making the process transparent to the sender and receiver stations. In a network environment end-to-end encryption is necessary. This is similar to link, only the sender and receiver actually perform the encryption and decrypting. The fact, that the key must be remembered for a longer period of time since files are more permanent, makes media encryption different than the others. Also, the higher transfer rates to disk than to communication lines makes a faster encryption device necessary. Techniques for media encryption are not given, although Sykes notes their existence.
>
> A reasonably complete description of the proposed NBS encryption standard is included in the paper.

Tuchma 77

Tuchman, W. L., "Computer Security and IBM." Letter, *Science*, Vol. 197, 2, September 1977, p. 938.

Tuchman was one of the developers at IBM of what was to become the National Bureau of Standards Data Encryption Standard. In this letter he refutes statements in [Kolata 77a] that alleges cooperation between IBM and the National Security Agency in designing the algorithm used in the standard. Comments pertaining to other criticisms are also included.

Tuchma 78

Tuchman, W. L., and Meyer, C. H., "Efficacy of the Data Encryption Standard in Data Processing." *Proceedings of Fall COMPCON 78,* Washington, D.C., September 1978, pp. 340–347.

This paper reviews the origin and strength of the NBS Data Encryption Standard (DES) [NBS 77]. It also argues that the public key system of [Rivest 78] has not yet been shown to have the strength of the DES.

Turn 73a

Turn, R., "Privacy Transformations for Databank Systems." *AFIPS Conference Proceedings–1973 NCC,* Vol. 42, 1973, pp. 589–601.

Turn 77

Turn, R., "Implementation of Privacy Protection Requirements." *IFIP Congress Proceedings,* 1977, North-Holland Publishing Co., Amsterdam, pp. 957–962.

This paper reviews privacy protection in North America and Western Europe.

Yasaki 76

Yasaki, E. K., "News in Perspective/Encryption Algorithm: Key Size is the Thing." *Datamation,* Vol. 22, No. 3, March 1976, pp. 164–166.

The controversy surrounding the National Bureau of Standards encryption algorithm is reported in this article. A brief explanation of the reasons behind the creation of such an algorithm is given. The article then describes the center of the controversy—the 56-bit key used by the algorithm. The article includes statements by Hellman [Diffie 77] that the key is too small to ensure that it could not be discovered by exhaustive search techniques. Dr. Ruth Davis, then Director of the Institute of Computer Sciences and Technology at the National Bureau of Standards, states that the key is large enough to thwart any such attack. She feels this will be true for at least five years given the current rate of changes in technology and that five years is an acceptable lifetime for a standard.

Chapter 7

OPERATING SYSTEM SECURITY

An operating system is part of a large amount of software that runs on a computer system. Thus, the issues of operating system security are a part of the software security issues. Because the operating system manages and controls the computer hardware resources whereas the other software (e.g., application programs) merely makes requests for resources, the issues involved in the operating system are more critical and far-reaching. Therefore, solutions to operating system security will not only be timely and welcomed but will also lead to more general solutions of software security.

To properly identify the user, to process program requests, and to supervise the granting and the denying process, the operating system relies on *surveillance*. The surveillance is carried out in two areas: At the time of user identification, known as *logging*; and at the moment of granting or denying the request, *threat monitoring*.

7.1 SURVEILLANCE

To manage and control the hardware resources, the operating system must be able to uniquely identify the resources. This represents no difficulty, since devices and CPUs are always furnished with hardware identifications. Memory units can be identified by bounds registers, locks, or translation table entries. Stored programs and files can be identified by program names, program entries (or entry points), and

165

file names. However, to provide security to the user of the resources, the operating systems must also identify the user. It must associate the user with the IDs of those resources which were authorized for him. Furthermore, it must provide various protection attributes to be assigned to the resources during authorization. Finally, when requests are received during the course of a program execution, the operating system must identify the ID of the user who initiates the program and the IDs of the resources requested, locate the protection attributes assigned to the resources, determine whether the request should be granted or denied, and carry out the granting or denying process.

7.1.1 Logging

Whether in an interactive or batched processing system, logging at the beginning and end or each interactive or batched processing session is mandatory. Through logging, the operating system can activate the identification and authentication mechanisms (see Section 4.3 for a discussion of these mechanisms) to positively identify the user. With proper identification, the operating system can then maintain an entry in the *system log* for the user throughout the entire session. The entry records his ID; the source device(s) from which his commands, programs, and data are entered; the status of the device(s); the starting time; the status of his present processing state (e.g., program-in-execution, command-pending, etc.), and pointers to other system data which are unique to this user (e.g., general registers contents, the real memory bounds, the locks, or the location of the virtual memory translation table).

The system log entries are important data, which must be well protected. Although system log entries may be purged when the user–system session is over, the user ID is not a piece of temporary information (see the next section for explanation). In other words, the logging mechanism of the operating system must be able to generate and maintain a permanent ID for each active user of the system.

7.1.2 Threat Monitoring

After requests are verified and granted, the operating system is still responsible for monitoring the requested operations in progress. For example, if the user is allowed to access a file, it is one thing to allow him to access the file with his own file processing routine and another thing to force him to access the file with the system routine. The latter requirement enables the operating system to control the manner with which the resources are utilized. *Threat monitoring* is a means for achieving such control. Each resource may be associated with a *surveillance (system) program* which will be activated by the operating system for the purpose of accessing the resource on behalf of the user (program) and monitoring the use of the resource on behalf of the system. In Fig. 7–1, we depict such an environment.

The notion of threat monitoring can be extended to allow the surveillance program to have greater access rights in order to facilitate more effective control. This extended notion is known as *amplification*. For example, if we want the user (program) to learn the average of many data values in a file without letting the user receive the individual data values, then the way for the operating system to carry out such control without violating the security of the data is to provide a system program to do the average. The program can be executed by the user but cannot be read or modified by the user. Furthermore, direct file access (such as read) is not allowed for the user. Statistical inference, a problem associated with this type of application, can be minimized by having the surveillance program monitor the number of requests put forward by the user, the overlapping characteristics (such as attributes) of the requested data among the successive requests, and the ranges (such as maximum and minimum) of the data collection.

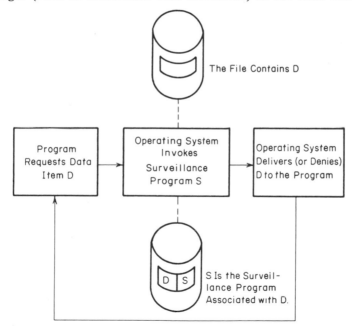

FIGURE 7-1. Threat monitoring.

(For a more detailed discussion of statistical inference, the reader may refer to Section 8.1.2.) Without amplification, the only way to safeguard the data values is to deny any access to these values. Obviously, such a crude way of protection eliminates some methods of utilizing resources in an authorized manner.

7.2 ACCESS CONTROL

When a program is being executed in the computer system, the program may make (a) real or virtual memory references, (b) calls for other programs, and (c) requests for files. Item (a) can be taken care of by the hardware in real-time since the CPU must interpret the referenced addresses. Hardware security discussed in Chapter 5 applies to (a). Items (b) and (c) cannot be handled by the hardware alone. They must be handled first by the operating system. Conceptually, the operating system maintains a table, known as the *access control matrix*, where the row headings are user IDs and the column headings are resource IDs, program names, program entries, and file names. The matrix entry of row *i* and column *j* represents the protection attributes of the resource identified in the *j*th column for the user recorded in the *i*th row. In Fig. 7-2 we depict an access control matrix where for example user U_4 may execute program D_3 and read or append to the file D_4.

Legend: A for Append
R for Read
E for Execute
O for Delete

	D_1	D_2	D_3	D_4	D_5	D_6	$\cdots$
U_1	R		E	R,A	R,A		
U_2				O	O		
U_3				R	R	R,A	
U_4	R		E	R,A	R,A		
⋮							

FIGURE 7-2. An access control Matrix. A = append, R = Read, E = execute, D = delete.

Because the number of potential users and available resources, programs, and files is large, it is not possible for the operating system to keep the entire access control matrix in the primary memory. Furthermore, the sheer size of access control information requires careful management by the operating system. The part of the operating system which manages the access control information is the *file subsystem*. During the user–system session, only portions of the access control matrix are brought in by the file subsystem for actual use. The rest of the matrix remains on secondary storages.

We note in Fig. 7–2 that the first and fourth rows have identical protection attributes. Likewise, the fourth and fifth columns have identical protection attributes. Furthermore, there are many empty entries. For implementation of the access matrix, consideration has been given to consolidating identical protection attributes by merging either rows or columns. Furthermore, there is no need to keep track of the resources and users which are not assigned any protection attribute. A *capability-list oriented operating system* organizes the access control information by user IDs. In other words, its file subsystem creates, for each unique user ID, a *capability list* of authorized resource IDs and program and file names and their associated protection attributes. Whenever a user logs on and is authenticated, the operating system enters the user ID into the system log. The file subsystem then retrieves the user's *capability list*. A pointer is generated by the operating system to refer to the location of the list and is inserted in the system log entry. This approach has the advantage that all known resources, programs, and files which are authorized to the user will have their IDs and names in the newly retrieved list, making it easy for subsequent verifications of users' requests for resources, programs, and data.

An *access-list oriented operating system* organizes the access control information by the resource IDs. Thus, for each resource (stored program, or file), the file subsystem creates a list of user IDs and their associated protection attributes. Whenever a request for some resource is received by the operating system during the course of executing a user's program, the ID of the resource is used by the file subsystem for retrieving the list, known as the *access list*. With the access list, the operating system can verify whether the user's ID is on the list and if this is indeed an authorized user, whether the requested operation satisfies the assigned protection attributes. The access list approach has the advantage that once a resource is requested, subsequent requests for the same resource by the same or other users can be verified and processed readily.

Both capability-list and access-list approaches have shortcomings.

When a resource is removed from the system or its protection attributes have been changed uniformly, such removals and changes must be reflected in the file subsystem through update. To update this information in the capability-list oriented operating system, an exhaustive search of every capability is required. This is time consuming. On the other hand, if an existing user is to be barred from the system or his access to all resources are temporarily suspended without being specific about the naming of the resources, these changes should be readily recorded. To record this information in the access-list oriented operating system, an exhaustive search of every access list is required. This is also time consuming. The *authority-item approach* attempts to overcome these deficiencies by organizing the access control information into authority items, each of which corresponds to a user. Furthermore, every resource (program name, program entry, and file name) in an authority item is linked with the same resources (program name, entry, and file name) in other authority items. Thus, the authority-item approach supports capability lists directly and access lists indirectly through linkages. In this way, search of authority items due to removal, changes, and suspension need not be exhaustive.

7.3 ISOLATION

The purpose of *isolation* is to contain any security breach so that violation in one part of the system will not affect the other parts of the system. With multiplicity of software requirements for logging, access control and threat monitoring, the task of a modern operating system is quite complex. Such complexity and multiplicity can create system crashes and data spillages, which can lead to breaching of security. To reduce complexity and multiplicity of the tasks, approaches are used to partition the computer hardware and software into mutually exclusive parts, each of which may carry out its tasks in isolation. The underlying assumption is of course that, for the same amount of work, several independent small systems may create fewer security breaches than an all-embracing large system.

7.3.1 Security versus Cost

Whether the aforementioned assumption is true (or false) depends considerably on the ability (or inability) of the system designer to partition the hardware and software into mutually exclusive small systems. Hardware and program modules seem to lend themselves more easily to partitioning since we can always use duplicate modules and redundant hardware. The data, especially the shared data, are difficult to handle. Multiple copies of the data may create *integrity problems* in data update (e.g., for an update, some copies may have been completed; other copies may have not yet begun). They may also create *inconsistency problems* in data security (e.g., security requirements for different copies may negate or contradict each other). In addition to problems in update integrity and security inconsistency, there are also the cost and the performance to consider. Duplicate hardware units and program modules require additional costs. Duplication of a resource tends to eliminate fierce competition for the resource. Consequently, there is the likelihood of resource underutilization. The trade-off between cost and security is still an art which has eluded serious scientific study. The performance issue is even more difficult to grasp. No definitive studies have been conducted which allow one to compare the throughput of a collection of small systems versus the throughput of a large simple system for the same amount of work.

7.3.2 Methods

There are two isolation methods in use. In the first method, all user programs are monitored by the same operating system. However, each group of user programs (therefore, each user group) is run in a separate primary memory partition. Furthermore, if a program module is to be used by two or more user groups, duplicate copies of the module will have to be included in the separate partitions. In this method, known as *multiple space method*, the redundancy of the hardware and modules consists of the primary memory and user programs. On the other hand, the operating system and its system modules are not duplicated. Furthermore, secondary storage and communication terminals which are under the operating system's control are also not duplicated. Thus, the shared data and system resources are still monitored by the central operating system. This method is particularly viable for a computer system with multiple virtual spaces. In this case, each user group occupies a part of a virtual space. The remaining parts of every virtual space are taken up by the operating system. In Fig. 7–3, we illustrate an implementation of the method. The interesting effect is that the operating system appears (virtually) in every virtual space and is situated at the same positions relative to each user program. Yet, there is only one copy of the operating system. In other words, the operating system appears in every virtual space without duplication itself. The only penalty incurred on the part of the user is that the part of virtual

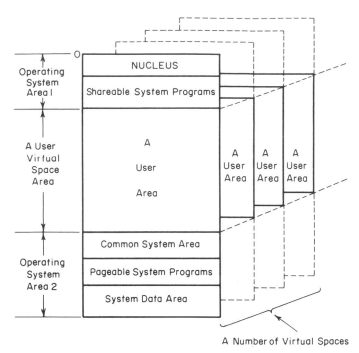

A Number of Virtual Spaces

FIGURE 7-3. The IBM 370 OS/VS2-2 virtual spaces layout. Both operating system areas 1 and 2 are not available to the user. These areas are for the operating system to execute its own programs and collect system data about the users and itself. Some of the shareable system programs are intended for amplification and threat monitoring. They are therefore indirectly activated by the user programs.

space occupied by the operating system is not available to the user programs. The use of a central operating system enables the computer system to have a unified logging, access control, and monitoring mechanism for security purposes. However, the complexity and multiplicity of the operating system has not been reduced. Furthermore, if the "big brother" is penetrated, all the user virtual spaces and isolations will be breached.

The second method differs from the first in that each user group may have its own operating system and several operating systems may exist on the same computer system. Thus, the user has the illusion that he has the entire machine for his software. This concept is known as the *virtual machine concept.* A computer system with virtual machine capability is usually a large system endowed with considerable hardware facilities, such as a high-performance CPU and primary and secondary memories. In addition, it consists of a control program, known as a *virtual machine monitor (VMM).* The VMM can emulate a computer system environment for a partition so that the operating system and its associated user programs running in the partition may consider the emulated environment as if it is a stand-alone computer system. Normally, the VMM of a large computer system may emulate several small computer systems, each of which is a member of the computer family or series (see Fig. 7–4). For example, an IBM 370/168 with VMM capability may create three virtual machines on it which resemble IBM 370/135, IBM 360/50, and IBM 360/30, respectively. Essentially, the VMM works closely with the CPU of the host machine (i.e., IBM 370/168 in this case), keeps track of the virtual machines being emulated on the host computer (e.g., by having three program counters), and translates instructions of the virtual machines into equivalent instructions of the host machine for execution. In this way, the host machine may run the MFT (multiprogramming with fixed number of tasks) operating system for the 370/135 virtual machine, the TOS/DOS (tape and disk-oriented operating system) for the 360/50, and the BOS (basic operating system) for the 360/30. It is interesting to note that, in this example, the 370/168 is a machine with virtual memory (do not confuse with the term machine) capability. In order to support either 360/30 or 360/50 (neither of which has virtual memory capability), the host machine is actually using its virtual addresses to emulate physical locations of the real memory of the 360/30 or 360/50. Thus, the address spaces of different virtual machines are also separated (by virtue of being supported in different virtual spaces of the host machine).

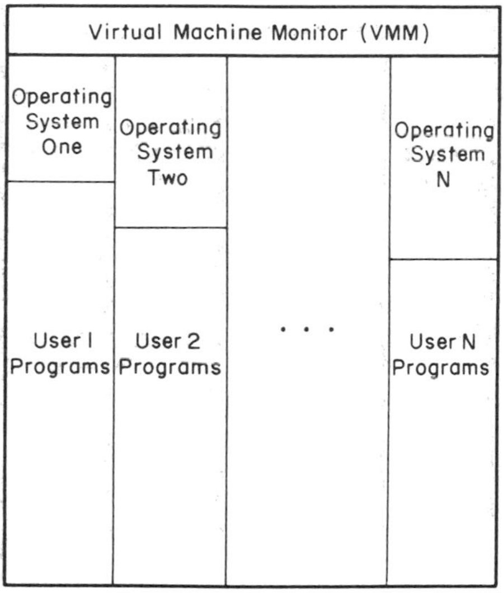

Virtual Machine Monitor (VMM)			
Operating System One	Operating System Two		Operating System N
User I Programs	User 2 Programs	· · ·	User N Programs

FIGURE 7-4. The virtual machine concept.

This isolation techniques has several advantages. (a) It allows different operating systems to be used for different security and processing requirements. (b) Any security breach of one operating system will not affect the other operating systems and their corresponding user programs. (c) The virtual machine monitor (VMM) is small, making it difficult to penetrate and less likely to malfunction. There are, nevertheless, some fundamental limitations. One of the most important limitations is that the host machine can only emulate compatible (lesser or equal) machines within the family or series. Another important limitation is that no two virtual machines can share a common database, since these virtual machines are in "total" isolation and do not communicate locally to each other. Like separate computers, they can only communicate via networks. The third limitation is that the virtual machine capability requires considerable duplication in peripherals. This is particularly evident in terms of I/O devices; since every virtual machine must have its peripherals which are difficult if not impossible to emulate efficiently. The last limitation causes a degradation of performance since each virtual machine is emulated, its performance is usually not as good as its real computer counterparts, and certainly not as good as its "upward" replacements.

7.4 DESIGN AND IMPLEMENTATION
OF SECURE OPERATING SYSTEMS

The operating system, which enforces protection of physical resources, program usage, and data access, must be secure itself. In other words, even if we know what algorithms and techniques are specified for logging, access control, monitoring, and isolation, how do we know that the software design will meet these specifications? Furthermore, if we accept the design, how can we be sure that the software produced implements the design intended?

7.4.1 Verification

Verification methods are used for checking the correctness of the software designs against algorithm (or program) specifications, and for checking the correctness of the software programs against their original designs. Unless the specifications are in error, the process of verification will make sure the software designed and program produced meet the intent of the specifications. The emphasis on intent is important. In software, specifications are seldom given as ways and procedures to produce the software products. Instead, specifications are mostly requirement and property statements. It is up to the designers to devise algorithms to meet the requirements and properties and the implementors to write programs to computerize the algorithms. The verification methods must be used to assure that the programs meet the intended requirements and properties.

One of the popular verification methods is the *inductive assertion technique.* Consider the case where we apply this technique to the verification of a program whose algorithm design is agreed to be correct. The basic steps are as follows:

1. We make the first assertion, called *input assertion,* at the program entry. Typically, the input assertion indicates the domain or joint constraints among the input variables.

2. We also have a final assertion, called *output assertion,* at the program exit. The output assertion expresses the result of the program's operation on the input variables and other variables in the program.

3. We make an assertion, called *loop assertion,* for each loop of the program. The loop assertions are required to construct proofs by induction of correctness of the loops.

As an example of how one proceeds to associate assertions with the program statements and to construct proofs of correctness, consider the flowchart as shown in Fig. 7–5. The boxes labeled INITIALIZATION, LOOP–BODY, and FINALIZATION are intended to be

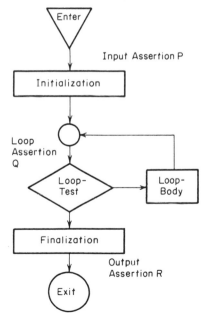

FIGURE 7-5. Flowchart with assertions.

loop-free program segments, and LOOP–TEST is a simple predicate whose truth is the condition for loop termination. P, Q, and R are the input assertion, loop assertion, and output assertion, respectively. To prove the correctness of the program as illustrated by the flowchart, it is sufficient to prove the following lemmas:

Lemma a   Assuming that P is true before the execution of IN-ITIALIZATION, then Q will be true after the execution of INITIALIZATION.

Lemma b   Assuming Q is true and LOOP–TEST is false before the execution of LOOP–BODY, then Q will be true after the execution of LOOP–BODY.

Lemma c   Assuming that Q is true, and LOOP–TEST is true before the execution of FINALIZATION, then R will be true after the execution of FINALIZATION.

Thus, for each possible path between two assertions, a lemma must be proved. This lemma must show that the program statements that are executed between the assertions do not make those assertions false. We say that the program statements between two assertions are proven *correct* if the program statements do not invalidate either assertion. We call this lemma that must be proven a *verification condition*. Thus, verification conditions must be proved to insure that program statements between assertions do not falsify those assertions.

In addition to the proof of the verification conditions, we must also prove that every loop of the program will eventually *terminate*. By a loop termination, we mean that at some time the loop test of the loop will be true. In referring to the flowchart in Fig. 7–5, the LOOP–TEST must be true in order for the loop to terminate.

The way to prove the termination of loops is often quite simple. By the statement of the loop test, we know under what criterion the loop will terminate. By expressing this criterion as an assertion, we need only prove, at some point during the execution of the loop body, the assertion will be true. We will call this lemma a *loop terminating condition*.

Thus, a program is *verified* if every condition (verification or loop termination condition) is proved. In other words, *program verification by inductive assertion* requires proofs for every condition of the program. The conditions are often easy to prove and the application of induction is straightforward. For a sample program depicted in Fig. 7–6 there are five conditions; one for the input assertion, one for the output assertion, one for the loop assertion where the loop test is false, one for the loop assertion where the loop test is true, and one for the loop termination condition.

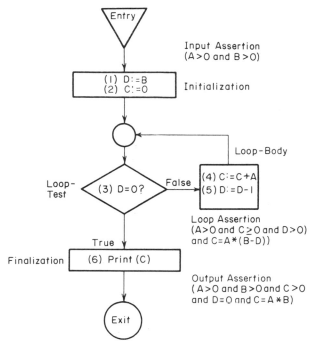

FIGURE 7-6. Flowchart of a multiplication program of two nonzero positive integers using repeated addition.

Although program verifications may be a necessity in producing secure software, there are limitations to the induction assertion techniques.

1. Comparing the loop assertion in Fig. 7–5 with the loop assertion in Fig. 7–6, these two loop assertions are attached at different places. We note that the program can be verified by using either placement without the other. However, for more complicated program logic, the placement of an assertion is critical. Clever placements of assertions may result in shorter proofs and in simpler inductions.

2. If a program uses data structures such as a single or multiple linked list of data elements, it is difficult to develop proofs and exercise inductions on the data structures directly. Instead, an equivalent data structure may have to be introduced to expedite the proofs and inductions. Thus, we have not verified the original data structures. Rather, we verify something we believe to be equivalent.

3. For any practical program, the resulting proof is longer than the program, making program verification a tedious and error-prone process. It is not clear whether this property is inherent in the inductive

assertion technique or is a general limitation of the verification techniques.

7.4.2 The Kernel Concept

Since the operating system is usually very large and complex, and since verification methods tend to produce long proofs, verification of the entire operating system may not be possible or even desirable. It is therefore hoped that perhaps one can isolate those few primitives which are essential to the secure operation of the operating system. By implementing these primitives into program modules and then verifying them rigorously, it is hoped that the essential security of the operating system can be assured even if the rest of the system has not been verified.

The difficulty in pursuing this concept is the definition of the concept itself. In other words, what constitutes the *kernel* of an operating system?

As we have seen from previous discussion, the computer system security depends upon the security of real, virtual, and secondary memories, and on the file subsystem. In addition, it depends on the security of those modules which perform logging, access control, and threat monitoring. Thus, to a large degree, the kernel of the operating system may have to include those modules which manage and control the real, virtual, and secondary memories, maintain and search the file subsystem, and perform access controls and threat monitoring. Since most of the system modules are interdependent on each other, the size of the kernel tends to be large. One study shows that the secure kernel of a general-purpose operating system consists of approximately 30,000 lines of program statements. This is not promising.

Efforts have been directed to re-examine the structure and design of the operating system with a view toward a reduction of the number of dependencies among system modules, and the development of more explicit module interfaces for characterizing the dependencies. It is hoped that with fewer dependencies and clearer interfaces, the size of a secure kernel can be reduced considerably. Such operating system design tends to aid the kernel verification effort. Furthermore, if the operating system has simple functionality and is small in size, the kernel verification effort is minimal. Nevertheless, the very reason for approaching the operating system design with the kernel concept is to tackle large and complex systems for essential security. If an operating system is indeed small, we do not need a kernel. Instead, we may verify the entire system.

7.4.3 Penetration Tests

Verification methods allow the operating system designer and implementor to claim that the system is a correct product. However, a correct product may be a "weak" product in that there are holes and spots whose security can be breached easily. This is not the fault of the verification methods. In fact, if the original specifications have holes and if the designer and implementor are too blind to discover them, these are the "correct" holes being designed and implemented into the operating systems. A *penetration test* is used to identify the holes and weak spots. One of the requirements in conducting the penetration test is that the design and program logic of the operating system is assumed to be known to the penetrator. In fact, in many penetration studies, the design and program documentation are provided to the testers (the professional penetrators). In addition, these are very bright testers. Extensive and concerted penetrations may allow the designer and implementor to fix up the holes and patch up the weak spots.

At their best, penetration tests may, on the basis of their intensity and comprehensiveness, allow the *security certification* of an operating system with some quantitative measures or scales. At their least, the tests may answer a series of yes, no, or maybe questions for a checklist of penetration possibilities. Whether an operating system is *certified* by a scale or by a checklist, the idea is to gain some degree of *security confidence* in the operating system. On the other hand, absolute security (i.e., complete confidence) in the system is not possible, since there may always be another penetration test which has been overlooked.

7.5 POSTSCRIPT

The discussion of operating system security has been divided into identification and surveillance, access control, isolation, and design and implementation. The basic access matrix model is now classic and is discussed in all the surveys described later. The capability approach [Fabry 74], [Dennin 76b], [Redell, 74a], [Redell 74b] is used in one form or another in the Hydra system [Cohen 75], [Jones 75b], [Wulf 74], [Wulf 75], in the Cambridge CAP Computer System [Cook 78], [Herber 78], [Needha 74a], [Needha 74b], [Needha 77a], [Needha 77b], at SRI [Neuman 74,] [Neuman 77], at Livermore [Donnel 75], and modelled in [Cosser 74]. The access list approach is typified by the work of [Saltze 74a] and [Saltze 75]. Refinement and restructuring of this approach for security purposes are continued in [Bratt 75], [Janson 74], [Janson 75],

and [Montgo 76]. Authority items have been used in the earlier work of
[Hsiao 75a]. Most systems intended to be secure use a form of logging
and monitoring. See, for example, [Burke 76], [Gaines 78], and [Hoff-
man 77a]. Amplification has been studied by [Jones 73], [Dennin 75],
[Dennin 76a], and [Hartso 76b]. A related but slightly different problem
is the *confinement* problem [Cohen 75], [Harris 75], [Harris 76], [Lipner
75]. If an access right is passed to one program, how do you prevent
that program from passing the right even further?

In order to secure different users' programs from each other, some
form of isolation is necessary [Dennin 74]. The multiple space approach has been used in OS/VS-2 [McPhee 74]. More commonly, the
virtual machine approach is employed [Belady 74], [Goldbe 74], [Hsu
76], [Popek 74c]; also see specific proposals made in [Chande 76],
[Donova 75], [Donova 76], and [Wagues 75]. There has also been a pro-
posal to use virtual machines to eliminate the problems of the periods
processing required by the Department of Defense [Weissm 75].

A number of efforts have been devoted to the application of
veritification methods for secure kernel design and implementation. By
far the largest effort is perhaps the one funded by the Air Force Electronics Systems Division. The original plan calls for a 4½ year study on
four major tasks: (a) restructure an existing Multics with a view toward
code reductions for a secure kernel; (b) design a new multics kernel
from scratch; (c) design a secure front-end communications computer
for Multics; and (d) prove the correctness of the aforementioned
tasks *a*, *b*, and *c* with verification methods. The time period scheduled
for the study spans 1976 to 1980 [Adlema 76a], [Adlema 76b], [Bonnea
76], with Honeywell, M.I.T., and SRI as principal investigating part-
ners. In addition, there is some "in-house" work. However, from the
literature published since, it seems that MIT pursued task *a* while
MITRE undertook tasks *b*, *c*, and *d*. The Air Force Electronics Systems
Division has done some evaluation work.

The work at M.I.T. on restructuring an existing multics is noted in
[Ciccar 76], [Janson 74], [Janson 75], [Luniew 77], [Montgo 76], [Schroe
75], and [Schroe 77]. The work at MITRE on the new multics kernel
design and specification is published in three volumes [Shill 77],
[Within 78], [Woodwa 78]. The work on a secure communications
front-end and minicomputer is documented in [Millen 76], [Harper 78],
and [Schill 75]. Proposals for proving correctness of the secure Multics
kernel can be found in [Kallma 78]. Evaluations of both operational
and system security on an existing Air Force Multics are documented in
[Burke 74a], [Davis 76], [Gasser 76b], [Karger 74], and [Reynol 76].

Other notable efforts on verification of secure operating systems or kernels are centered at SRI [Neuman 74], [Neuman 77], UCLA [Popek 74b], [Popek 76], [Popek 78a], and USC [Carlst 76]. Tutorials, surveys, and general discussion of verification methods can be found in [Hantle 76] and [Walter 75b].

The efforts in modelling a whole or parts of a secure operating system are many. They are mostly mathematical, graphic, and abstract models in terms of access control to resources and capabilities. They are found in [Andrew 75], [Bell 73], [Bell 74a], [Cohen 77], [Conn 74], [Conn 75], [Dennin 75], [Dennin 76a], [Dennin 77], [Ekanad 76], [Feiert 77], [Fenton 74], [Gorski 78], [Harris 75], [Harris 76], [Jones 76], [Lipton 77], [Popek 74a], [Popek 78b], [Robins 75], [Spier 74a], [Snyder 77], [Vanvle 74], [Walter 74], and [Walter 75a]. Simulation models are provided in [Burris 76b].

Work on retrofitting of IBM VM/370, OS/MVT,OS/VS2, and KVM/370 is documented in [Gladne 75], [Gold 77], [McPhee 74], and [Schaef 77].

The study of centralized and decentralized secure computer networks can be found in [Lientz 75], [Winkle 74], and [Gaines 75].

Penetration and evaluation studies are reported in [Attana 76], [Carlst 75], [Lackey 74], and [Linde 75]. General discussion on operating system security issues (such as integrity, military application, encapsulation, errors, certification reliability) are found in [Attana 74], [Beach 77], [Bell 74b], [Biba 77], [Bisbey 74], [Bisbey 75], [Dennin 77], [Ellis 74], [Honeyw 75], [IBM 74], [Lampso 77], [Linden 74], [Linden 76b], [Neuman 78], [Rotenb 74], [Saltze 74b], [Saltze 75], [Sevcik 74], [Shanka 77], [Stork 75], and [Yasaki 74]. The use of programming language constructs such as types and type extensions as a means for protection specification and enforcement by operating system are noted in [Ambler 77], [Ferrie 74], [Jones 78], and [Yuval 76].

For glossary and reference manuals on security, see [NBS 76a], [NBS 76b], and [White 75b].

REFERENCES

Adlema 76a

Adleman, N., et al., "Multics Security Integration Requirements." Honeywell Information Systems, Inc., March 1976, ESD–TR–76–354 (NTIS AD–A041514).

> Like [Adlema 76b], this is one of the "earliest" documents on Air
> Force Electronic Systems Division's plan to develop a secure Multics

kernel and a secure communications front-end for Multics. Unlike [Adlema 76b], this report weights the alternative approaches and plots the milestones of all the developmental efforts from 1976 to 1980.

Adlema 76b

Adleman, N., Gilson, J.R., Sestak, R.J., and Ziller, R.J., "Security Kernel Evaluation for Multics and Secure Multics Design, Development and Certification." Honeywell Information Systems, Inc., August 1976, ESD–TR–76–298, (NTIS AD–A038261).

This is one of the "earliest" documents concerning an ambitious plan put out by the Air Force Electronic Systems Division. The plan calls for the design, verification, and implementation of a secure Multics system using the kernel approach, a secure communications front-end for the Multics kernel, and a restructuring of an existing Multics operating system for security purposes.

Ambler 77

Ambler, A.L., and Hoch, C.G., "A Study of Protection in Programming Languages." *Proceedings of ACM Conference on Language Design for Reliable Software,* 1977, pp. 25–40.

A simple example, the prison mail system, is used to compare the security capabilities of the languages Pascal, Concurrent Pascal, Euclid, Clu, and Gypsy. Conclusions reached are (a) access to objects should be passed rather than an object itself, (b) selective hiding of declarations is desirable, and (c) selective access to operations as well as data is important.

Ames 74

Ames, S. R., "File Attributes and Their Relationship to Computer Security." Dept. of Computing and Information Science, Case Western Reserve University, June 1974 (NTIS AD–A002 159).

Andrew 74

Andrews, G. R., "COPS—A Mechanism for Computer Protection." Computer Science Dept., Cornell University, Ithaca, New York, CU–CSD–74–241, October 1974 (NTIS PB–236 760).

Andrew 75

Andrews, G. R., "Partitions and Principles for Secure Operating Systems." *Proceedings of ACM Annual Conference,* October 1975, Minneapolis, Minnesota, pp. 177–180.

Andrews proposes a model for the design of a secure operating system in this paper. This model is composed of two parts, the first of which is the model of the type of action users would like the operating system to perform. To perform these actions in a secure manner several different mechanisms are used. These form the second part of Andrew's model as the security kernel. Andrews then outlines the components and functions of each of these two portions of the model.

Once the model has been defined several principles which must be adhered to by the system are then described. These affect what Andrews feels are the four logical partitions in the operating system: the user interface, user called processes, background services, and the operation of the security kernel.

Attana 74

Attanasio, C. R., "Operating System Architecture and Integrity." *IBM Data Security Forum* (IBM 74), September 1974.

Attanasio discusses the results of attempts to penetrate the IBM OS/MVT and VM/370 systems. By comparing the results, he outlines the relative strengths and weaknesses of each system. It is hoped by the author that these provide insight into the causes of security flaws and solutions to designing secure systems.

Attana 76

Attanasio, C. R., Markstein, P. W., and Phillips, R. J., "Penetrating an Operating System: A Study of VM/370 Integrity." *IBM Systems Journal,* Vol. 15, No. 1, 1976, pp. 102–116.

This paper reports on the methodology used and the results of a project to penetrate a VM/370 system. The flaw hypothesis methodology used is reported in more detail in [Linde 75]. The results of the penetration attempts showed the I/0 facility of VM/370 was the most vulnerable area to attack. The security strengths of the VM/370 were found to lie in its design simplicity. Another report of this penetration effort is included in [Goldbe 74].

Beach 77

Beach, M. H., "Computer Security for ASSIST." Masters thesis, U.S. Army Command and General Staff College, Fort Leavenworth, Kansas, June 1977 (NTIS AD–2043 446).

The application of current computer security research to the ASSIST military intelligence handling system is considered.

Belady 74

Belady, L. A., and Weissman, C., "Experiments with Secure Resource Sharing for Virtual Machines." *Proceedings IRIA International Conference on Protection in Operating Systems,* Rocquencourt, France, August 1974, pp. 27–33.

Bell 73

Bell, D. E., and La Padula, J., "Secure Computer Systems: A Mathematical Model." Mitre Corp., Bedford, Massachusetts, MTR–2547, Vol. II, November 1973 (NTIS AD–771 543).

Presented in this paper is one of the earliest developed mathematical models of a secure computer system. This model along with its refinements [Bell 74a] have provided much of the basis for later work in secure systems and both are recommended reading for the individual interested in the theoretical aspects of secure computer systems.

This paper discusses several access types: read, write, append, execute and control. Furthermore, the property, referred to by the authors as the "*-property," is defined. This property states that "if a subject user of user process S has write or append access to some objects and read or write access to some objects, then the classifications of the objects to which S has write or append access must exceed or equal the classifications of the objects to which S has read or write access."

The report is organized such that the first section presents an introduction and the second an informal view of the model. The formal presentation of the model is given in Section III with the rules of operation for the model proven correct in Section IV. The final section concerns itself with design considerations.

Bell 74a

Bell, D. E., "Secure Computer Systems: A Refinement of the Mathematical Model." Mitre Corp., Bedford, Massachusetts, MTR–2547, Vol. III, April 1974. (NTIS AP 780 528).

In this report three refinements to a mathematical model of a secure computer system are discussed. The first deals with the control access attribute which allows users to pass or rescind access rights to other users. In the original model this was an explicit attribute whereas the refinement allows hierarchical, implicit control.

The second refinement covers a topic of "current classification." In the previous model a check was made of every object accessed by a subject when another access was attempted. The refinement eliminates this by classifying a user's access status.

The final refinement allows an authorized subject to be exempt from the security checking of the so called "*-property."

The report does contain three appendices: access rules, proofs of correctness, and a glossary of notation used which are useful when reading this report or [Bell 73].

Bell 74b

Bell, D. E., Fiske, R. S., Gasser, M., and Tasker, P. S., "Secure On-Line Processing Technology—Final Report." Mitre Corp., Bedford, Massachusetts, MTR–2638, August 1974 (NTIS AD–785 378).

Bell 76

Bell, D. E., and La Padula, L. J., "Secure Computer Systems: Unified Exposition and Multics Interpretation." Mitre Corp., Bedford, Massachusetts, MTR–2997, March 1976 (NTIS AD–A023 588).

Biba 77

Biba, K. J., "Integrity Considerations for Secure Computer Systems," The Mitre Corp., Bedford, Massachusetts, April 1977; ESD–TR–76–372 (NTIS AD–A039324).

> This report prepared for the Air Force Electronic Systems Division attempts to characterize the notion of computer system integrity, to classify sources and types of integrity threats and to motivate the notion of integrity policies and enforcement. Several policies are examined. Possible enforcement mechanisms of the policies are discussed. It is an interesting report because it covers many policies and mechanisms which were found in a contemporary operating system. By discussing these features around a central problem (i.e., the integrity problem) the reader may gain some relative comparison and overall perspective on the policies and mechanisms involved.

Bisbey 74

Bisbey, R. L., II, and Popek, G. J., "Encapsulation: An Approach to Operating System Security." *Proceedings of ACM Annual Conference,* Vol. 2, November 1974, San Diego, California, pp. 666–675.

Bisbey 75

Bisbey, R. L., II, Popek, G. J., and Carlstedt, J., "Protection Errors in Operating Systems: Inconsistency of a Single Data Value Over Time." Information Science Inst., University of California, Marina del Rey, California, December 1975, (NTIS AD–A020 481).

Bonnea 76

Bonneau, C. H., "Security Kernel Specification for a Secure Communication Processor." Honeywell Information Systems, Inc., September 1976, ESD–TR–76–359 (NTIS AD–A045 452).

> This report consists of 26 pages of descriptive information and 43 pages of rather detailed specification of the kernel for a secure communications processor based on a Honeywell Level 6/40 minicomputer. A review of the work by the Air Force Electronic Systems Division is included as Appendix C of the report. This work was terminated by the Air Force in 1976.

Bratt 75

Bratt, R. G., "Minimizing the Naming Facilities Requiring Protection in a Computing Facility." Massachusetts Institute of Technology, Project MAC, ESD–TR–76–161, September 1975 (NTIS AD–A031 909).

Browne 76

Browne, P. S., "Computer Security—A Survey." *AFIPS Conference Proceedings–1976 NCC,* Vol. 45, 1976, p. 53–63.

> The paper briefly describes the various aspects of computer security ranging from operational and physical security to the technical issues of identification, authorization, integrity, and audit trails. The paper includes a good bibliography of 134 articles each with a short annotation. Although not detailed, the paper does provide a well-organized coverage of the issues involved.

Burke 74a

Burke, E. L., "Concept of Operation for Handling I/O in a Secure Computer at the Air Force Data Services Center (AFDSC)." Mitre Corp., Bedford, Massachusetts, MTR–2733, April 1974 (NTIS AD–780 529).

Burke 74b

Burke, E. L., "Synthesis of a Software Security System." *Proceedings of ACM Annual Conference,* November 1974, Vol. 2, San Diego, California, pp. 648–658.

> Described in this paper are the techniques used in the design and verification of a security kernel for a PDP–11/45. These techniques, developed at the Mitre Corporation, are based on two ideas: a mathematical model of the kernel operation and proof of correctness methodology to verify the correctness of the implementation of the model. Burke discusses the four representations of the kernel: mathematical model, formal specification, algorithmic representation, and machine language used for verifying that one representation corresponds to the previous. An example of applying these techniques to the PDP–11/45 kernel is presented.

Burke 76

Burke, E. L., "Discovering Illicit Computer Usage." *Proceedings IEEE CompCon International Conference,* San Francisco, California, February 24–26, 1976, P. 178.

> Burke states that in order to detect illicit use of the computer it is first necessary to provide uncompromisable security mechanisms which may be used to build features such as audit trails. These mechanisms would allow observation of illegal activities. A reference monitor is then described and its application as a security mechanism discussed. Related work is reported in detail elsewhere (Walter 75a).

Burris 76b

Burris, H. R., "Simulation Method for Multi Level Data Security Analysis." *Proceedings on Simulation of Computer Systems,* National Bureau of Standards, Boulder, Colorado, August 1976, pp. 53–59.

Burris outlines a game-theoretic approach to computer security. He presents a methodology for simulating a security system in which the data sets are partitioned into several classes. The particular security class to which a data set is assigned is determined by its value to an intruder attempting to gain unauthorized access to it.

Carlst 75

Carlstedt, J., Bisbey, R., II, and Popek, G., "Pattern-Directed Protection Evaluation." Information Sciences Inst., University of Southern California, Marina del Rey, California, June 1975 (NTIS AD–A012 474).

Based on errors found in the OS/360, GCOS, Multics, TENEX, and Exec-8 operating systems, patterns of error types have been developed to help in the location and removal of similar errors in other systems. Computer tools have been developed to help search for these patterns.

Carlst 76

Carlstedt, J., "Protection Errors in Operating Systems: Validation of Critical Conditions." Information Sciences Inst., University of Southern California, Marina del Rey, California, May 1976 (NTIS AD–A026 442).

Carlstedt describes in this paper a class of operating system errors that he refers to as "validation errors." These are errors that occur when the operating system is insufficient in guaranteeing the correctness of a critical condition. The paper outlines several examples where these errors occur in current systems. The most well known of these is when a user program passes a parameter to the operating system and parameter is not checked for correctness. Carlstedt specifies categories and mechanisms for validation.

In order that validation be done in a reasonable manner, it is necessary to determine which points in the system are "most" critical. Carlstedt addresses the problem of specifying critical conditions and determining what is "fundamentally critical."

Chande 76

Chandersekaran, C.S., and Shankar, K.S., "On Virtual Machine Integrity." IBM Systems Journal, Vol. 15, No. 3, 1976, pp. 264–269.

The authors of this letter refute some of the conclusions of [Donova 75] and disagree with the way some of the terms used in that paper were defined. In particular, Chandrasekaran and Shankar disagree with [Donova 75] that a penetrator of a hierarchically structured system will first have to subvert the operating system and then the virtual machine to be successful. Their argument is based on the fact that subversion could be done through data channel programs. Also, the authors disagree with [Donova 75] in its use of terms security, reliability, integrity, and correctness. They provide other definitions and explain the distinctions.

Ciccar 76

Ciccarelli, E., "Multiplexed Communication for Secure Operating Systems." S.M. thesis, Massachusetts Institute of Technology, Cambridge, September 1977.

Cohen 75

Cohen, E., and Jefferson, D., "Protection in the Hydra Operating Systems." *Proceedings ACM Fifth Symposium on Operating Systems Principles,* November 1975, University of Texas, Houston, Texas, pp. 141–160.

> Cohen and Jefferson present the capability protection mechanism in the Hydra Kernel system described in [Wulf 74] and [Wulf 75]. The protection mechanisms in Hydra are based on the following five principles which are explained in detail by the authors:
>
> 1. Information can be divided into distinct objects for the purpose of protection.
> 2. Objects are distinguished by type.
> 3. Access to objects is controlled by capabilities.
> 4. Each program should execute with the smallest set of access rights necessary.
> 5. All knowledge about the representation and implementation of operations for each type of object should be hidden in modules called subsystems.
>
> The authors explain that capabilities are the actual protection mechanism used in Hydra. They explain that capabilities are represented as capability lists (C-lists) which are associated with an executing program and contain the name of objects and access rights of that program to the objects. The concept of capabilities has also been extended so that objects themselves may contain C-lists. This may then be used to define new objects in terms of already existing objects. Users are thus allowed to define their own subsystems which are not provided by Hydra. This is explained in the paper along with the methods used by Hydra to help solve several protection problems such as confinement and mutual suspicion.

Cohen 76

Cohen, E.S., "Problems, Mechanisms and Solutions." Ph.D. dissertation, Carnegie-Mellon University, Pittsburgh, Pennsylvania, August 1976 (NTIS AD–A034 855).

Cohen 77

Cohen, E., "Information Transmission in Computational Systems." *Proceedings of Sixth ACM Symposium on Operating Systems Principles, Operating Systems Review,* Vol. 11, No. 5, 1977, pp. 133–139.

> A formalism for describing information flow [Dennin 76a] is described. The formalism based on ideas from classical information theory

can be used to prove properties of information flow. The work is based on [Cohen 76].

Conn 74

Conn, R.W., and Yamamoto, R.H., "A Model Highlighting the Security of Operating Systems." *Proceedings of ACM Annual Conference*, 1974, Vol. 1, San Diego, California, pp. 174–179.

A model of operating systems in which a graph model is used is presented in this paper. In the formulation of these graph models the nodes are program modules or data structures and the access or shared resource paths are represented as the arcs. The authors discuss the development of the appropriate model and then show how an existing operating system (RTSS) may be analyzed using the model. It is felt by the authors that this technique will be useful in determining the security flaws within operating systems.

Conn 75

Conn, R.W., "Flow Models for Operating System Security." Lawrence Livermore Laboratory, University of California/Livermore, California, February 1975 (NTIS UCRL–76314).

Cook 78

Cook, D., "The Cost of Using the CAP Computer's Protection Facilities." *Operating System Review*, Vol. 12, No. 2, April 1978, pp. 26–30.

A process running on the CAP computer is running in a specific protection domain. In order to access a protected procedure a process switch to a new domain is required. Thus one view of the CAP system is that it has multiple states as opposed to the standard two-state machine (problem state, supervisor state). A rough measure of the cost of the CAP protection system is then to measure the number of domain switches resulting from the execution of a procedure call that would be equivalent to a call on a supervisor routine in a standard system. The particular programs studied were the Algol 68C compiler and the system generation program. See [Needha 77a], [Needha 77b], and [Needha 77c] for information on CAP.

Cosser 74

Cosserat, D.C., "A Data Model Based on the Capability Protection Mechanism." *Proceedings IRIA International Conference on Protection in Operating Systems*, Rocquencourt, France, August 1974, pp. 35–53.

Davis 76b

Davis, R.C., "A Security Compliance Study of the Air Force Data Service Center Multics System." The Mitre Corp., Bedford, Massachusetts, December 1976, ESD–TR–76–165 (NTIS AD–A034985).

The U.S. Department of Defense (DOD) Directive 5200.28 consists of specific requirements in the areas of personnel security; physical and communications security; hardware and software security; audit log and file security; safeguard, erasure and declassification procedures; and security test and evaluation programs. The Mitre report claims that the security features of an operational Air Force Data Service Center Multics system comply with the DOD directive.

Dennin 74

Denning, D.E., Denning, P.J., and Graham, G.S., "Selectively Confined Subsystems." *Proceedings IRIA International Conference on Protection in Operating Systems*, Rocquencourt, France, August 1974, pp. 56–61.

Dennin 75

Denning, D.E., "Secure Information Flow in Computer Systems." Ph.D. dissertation Purdue University, Lafayette, Indiana, May 1975.

Denning explores the mechanisms that may be used to enforce secure information flow from objects of one security class to objects of another. A mathematical model is proposed from which these mechanisms may be studied. This model is based on a lattice structure of the security classes which Denning details. From this lattice structure she examines the problems of guaranteeing secure information flow. A mechanism for doing so when security classes are statically bound to memory locations is studied. This is then extended to systems in which the security classes are dynamically boind to locations. [Denning 76a] is based on this work.

Dennin 76a

Denning, D.E., "A Lattice Model of Secure Information Flow." *Communications of the ACM*, Vol. 19, No. 5, May 1976, pp. 236–243.

This paper is based on the author's Ph.D. dissertation [Dennin 75] in which she formulates a model to control the flow or dissemination of information implied by a set of access rights. The model is based on a set of security classes and a flow relation on pairs of these classes. Each object is assigned a security class which may be static or dynamic and each process a class determined by the owner of the process or previous security classes. A lattice structure is formulated and examples are given as to how security is enforced.

The author surveys mechanisms used for static binding of security classes to objects [Walter 74], [Walter 75a] and breaks these down into compile time and run time checks preferring the former. She then briefly surveys methods for dynamic binding of security classes [Fenton 74] noting that a system based purely on dynamic binding is practical.

Dennin 76b

Denning, P. J., "Fault-Tolerant Operating Systems." *ACM Computing Surveys*, Vol. 8, No. 4, December 1976, pp. 355–558.

This readable tutorial examines the use of capability architecture (Fabry 74) to support what Denning feels are the four principles that confine errors and thereby increase system reliability. These are process isolation, resource control, decision verification, and error recovery. The application of these principles in the design of the operating system along with the necessary hardware support will allow the implementation of reliable systems in the author's eyes. Denning notes the lack of hardware to support the system he envisions, but feels that with the cost of hardware going down plus the completion of current projects, this problem will be reduced. Denning discusses the implementation of these principles with regard to several operating system functions including interrupts, resource control, scheduling and others.

Dennin 77

Denning, D.E., and Denning, P.J., "Certification of Programs for Secure Information Flow." *Communications of the ACM,* Vol. 20, No. 7, July 1977, pp. 504–513.

Based on the lattice model of secure information flow [Dennin 75], [Dennin 76a] the authors present a compile-time mechanism that will certify that a program contains no violations of the "flow policy." Although the authors do not feel that the need for run-time checks is completely eliminated, this scheme will reduce the amount necessary.

The paper briefly reviews the lattice model and then discusses the mechanism to be used for certification. This involves the programmer specifying the security class of all variables and files used in his program. The compiler would then perform security checks that would guarantee that information would not flow from a file or variable of a high security class to one of a lower class. The handling of procedure class and exceptional conditions are also described. The paper briefly addresses the applications and limitations of this mechanism.

Donnel 75

Donnelly, J.E., "DCAS—A Distributed Capability Access System." Lawrence Livermore Laboratory, August 1975 (NTIS UCID–16903).

Donova 75

Donovan, J.J., and Madnick, S.E., "Hierarchical Approach to Computer System Integrity." *IBM Systems Journal,* Vol. 14, No. 2, 1975, pp. 88–202.

The concept of protecting the users of a computer system by isolating one from another is examined in this paper. The use of a virtual machine monitor [Goldbe 74] in conjunction with several independent operating systems is shown to achieve security at a level not available in systems where users share the general purpose operating system. The authors feel that this high level of security is accomplished through redundant security mechanisms—those in the virtual machine monitor and those in the operating system. Included in the paper is an analytical examination of the reliability and security provided by virtual machines. An example is included using the VM/370 system to illustrate the use of a virtual machine to develop a shareable yet secure system.

A criticism of this paper is included in [Chande 76].

Donova 76

Donovan, J.J., and Madnick, S.E., "Virtual Machine Advantages in Security, Integrity and Decision Support Systems." *IBM Systems Journal,* Vol. 15, No. 3, 1976, pp. 270–278.

In this letter Donovan and Madnick respond to the criticisms of their earlier paper [Donova 75] contained in [Chande 76]. They clarify certain points and misconceptions which may have arisen from [Donova 75] and disagree with criticism that their use of terms protection and security interchangeably was incorrect and misleading. They include examples of actual implementations of virtual machine systems to examine benefits other than security afforded from the use of virtual machines.

Ekanad 76

Ekanadhem, K., "Context Approach to Protection." Ph.D. Dissertation, SUNY at Stony Brook, New York, December 1976.

A model of protection systems is developed around the concept of conditional capabilities in this paper. Contexts, representing the conditions on capabilities, are presented as an efficient manner in which to implement the capabilities. The protection mechanisms that evolve from this use of contexts and capabilities are discussed and a hierarchical operating system is presented.

Ellis 74

Ellis, C.A., and Nutt, G.J., "Preliminary Thoughts on Degrees of Security in Multiprocessor Systems." Dept. of Computer Science, University of Colorado, Boulder, CU–CS–03674, January 1974 (NTIS PB–235 292).

Feiert 77

Feiertag, R.J., Levitt, K.N., and Robinson, L., "Proving Multilevel Security of a System Design." *Proceedings of Sixth ACM Symposium on Operating Systems Principles, Operating Systems Review,* Vol. 11, No. 5, 1977, pp. 57–65.

Two formal definitions of multilevel security are presented. The first is a generalization and abstraction of the models in [Bell 74a] and [Walter 75]. The second is a restriction of the first, more useful for the specification of a system design.

Fenton 74

Fenton, J. S., "Memoryless Subsystems." *Computer Journal,* Vol. 17, 1974, pp. 143–147.

Suppose a user U would like to use a program P on confidential data C. Assuming P is pure code U would also specify a work area W for use by P for temporary storage. The memoryless subsystem problem is then to prevent any information from C being passed to an another user through the work area. This paper presents an abstract computer model which is then shown to solve the problem.

Ferrie 74

Ferrie, J., Kaiser, C., Lancioux, D., and Martin, B., "An Extensible Structure for Protected System's Design." *Proceedings IRIA International Conference on Protection in Operating Systems*, Rocquencourt, France, August 1974, pp. 83–105.

Flato 76b

Flato, L., "Navy Sinks 1108." *Computer Decisions*, Vol. 8, No. 7, July 1976, pp. 35–36.

In May of 1976 a confidential report from the Naval Research Laboratory was leaked to Congress. Flato explains that this report deals with the results of computer penetration exercises undertaken by scientists at the laboratory. The object of their penetration attempt was the Navy's Univac 1108 Exec VIII system. The scientists were able to subvert the system with relative ease by taking advantage of several aspects of the Exec VIII design philosophy according to the report, the specific suggestions made by the report to improve security are included in the article.

Gaines 75

Gaines, R.S., "Introduction by Session Chairman." *Proceedings of ACM SIGCOMM/SIGOPS Interprocess Communications Workshop*, Santa Monica, California, March 1975, pp. 57/58.

Gaines reports on the discussion portion of the session in which Popek presented his paper "On Data Secure Computer Networks" [Popek 75]. The discussion centered on this paper and the confinement problem which Gaines briefly explains.

Gaines 78

Gaines, R.S., and Shapiro, N.Z., "Some Security Principles and Their Application to Computer Security." *Operating Systems Review*, Vol. 12, No. 3, July 1978, pp. 19–28.

After examining the ideas of general security, the authors try to apply these ideas to the problems of computer security. The basic methods for increasing security of an object are to place a barrier between an intruder and the object, to provide a mechanism for detection of an intruder, to provide a guard who is able to apply counterforce and use reasoning and deductive powers, and to conceal the object or information need to obtain the object.

The authors then point out that the chief method for computer security has been the barrier, i.e., the access control mechanism. Almost no attention has been given to any of the other approaches.

Gasser 76b

Gasser, M.S., Ames, S.R., and Chmura, L.J., "Test Procedures for Multics Security Enhancements." Mitre Corp., Bedford, Massachusetts, MTR–3005, December 1976 (NTIS AD–A034 986).

Procedures to test enhancements made by the Air Force to a Honeywell 6180 Multics system are described in this report. The security of the Multics system is discussed followed by descriptions of the actual test procedures and the portions of Multics that were examined. A majority of this report is appendices that include the actual test commands, program documentation, and listings.

Gat 76

Gat, I., and Saal, H.J., "Memoryless Execution: A Programmer's Viewpoint." *Software—Practice and Experience,* Vol. 6, 1976, pp. 463–471

A possible solution to the memoryless subsystem problem [Fenton 74] is presented. The required hardware support is then discussed.

Gladne 75

Gladney, H.M., Worley, E.L., and Myers, J.J., "An Access Control Mechanism for Computing Resources." *IBM Systems Journal,* Vol. 14, No. 3, 1975, pp. 212–228.

In the early 1970s, the IBM San Jose Research Laboratory developed a system to better manage the increasing number of data sets on their IBM 360/195. This paper details the objectives and methods used in the development of the Installation Management Facility.

One of the major objectives was to increase the security and integrity of data sets beyond that normally provided by OS/MVT. This was done by implementing a directory, called an inventory data set, which contained entries for all users, organized into groups. These group and user entries are connected to data set entries for which access is allowed. The authors describe in some detail the inventory data set that includes the command for manipulating it. The authors also describe the experience the San Jose Laboratory has had with the system.

Gold 77

Gold, B.D., Linde, R.R., Schaefer, M., and Scheid, J.F., "VM/370 Security Retrofit Program." *Proceedings of ACM Annual Conference,* 1977, Seattle, Washington, pp. 411–417.

The System Development Corporation is developing a security retrofit for IBM's VM/370 which is intended to allow programs with different military classifications to operate concurrently on the same computer. The approach is to create a secure kernel KVM/370 based on [Bell 74a] and to then formally verify this kernel. Each security level will be supervised by a nonkernel control program. Thus there is no assurance of security within a security level, the kernel will be able to assure security between levels. This paper gives an overview of the project and includes a discussion of how the security flaws described in [Attana 76] can be overcome.

Goldbe 74

Goldberg, R.P., "Survey of Virtual Machine Research." *Computer,* Vol. 7, No. 6, June 1974, pp. 34–45.

Goldberg presents a readable, yet comprehensive, survey of virtual machines. The paper is divided into three major sections in which the author examines recent work on virtual machines in terms of principles, performance, and practice.

The first section of the paper explains the concepts of a virtual machine (VM) and virtual machine monitor (VMM). The idea is that a small amount of code, responsible simply for the sharing of hardware, runs on the bare machine as a VM. On top of this copies of the operating system or possibly different operating systems would run with only slight modification. Each user can thus have his "own" operating system and will not have to be concerned about the effect of other users on him. The most well known of these systems is IBM's VM/370.

The section on performance outlines the sources of overhead in using a virtual machine. Possible solutions to some of these problems that arise are also included.

The final section discusses some of the possible uses for such systems. These include smoothing the transition from an old operating system to a new release or the allowance of privileged software development at the same time as normal users have the system. Goldberg concludes that virtual machines have come of age and provide one method to solve the problem of nonsecure computer systems.

Górski 78

Górski, J., "A Modular Representation of the Access Control System." *Operating Systems Review,* Vol. 12, No. 3, July 1978, pp. 61–77.

A security model based on objects, subjects, access attributes, and protection states is presented. The model is specified using the formalism of module specification given by Parnas.

Hantle 76

Hantler, S.L., and King, J.C., "In Introduction to Proving the Correctness of Programs." *Computing Surveys,* Vol. 8, No. 4, December 1976, pp. 331–353.

Harper 78

Harper, S.R., "Computer Program Specification for Security Kernel for PDP–11/45." Mitre Corp., Bedford, Massachusetts, MTR–3178, Vol. I & II; ESD–TR–78–288, Vol. I & II (NTIS AD A054247 & AD A034 220).

Complete program specification of a security kernel for a PDP–11/45 is given. The implementation is based on the design of [Schill 75]. The procedure required for validation is discussed. The system is operational. Volume I gives the specifications and Volume II gives the programs.

Harris 75

Harrison, M.A., Ruzzo, W.L., and Ullman, J.D., "On Protection in Operating Systems." *ACM Proceedings Fifth Symposium on Operating Systems Principles,* November 1975, University of Texas, Houston, Texas, pp. 14–24.

This is an earlier version of (Harris 76).

Harris 76

Harrison, M.A., Ruzzo, W.L., and Ullman, J.D., "Protection in Operating Systems." *Communications of the ACM,* Vol. 19, No. 8, August 1976, pp. 461–471.

The authors present a formal model of computer protection systems in this paper. This model is used to prove several theorems. The model incorporates six primitive operations for creating and destroying objects and subjects along with entering and deleting access rights into an access matrix. Examples of these operations are given with several being drawn from the UNIX operating system for the DEC PDP–11.

Once these operations have been explained the authors discuss the problem of an owner of some object who gives away an access right to an object having that right then passed to some user the owner does not consider "authorized." This "safety " problem, as the authors refer to it, is analyzed from the viewpoint of Turing machines and is found to be undecidable. The implications of this are discussed.

Heinri 76

Heinrich, F.R., and Kaufman, D.J., "A Centralized Approach to Computer Network Security." *AFIPS Conference Proceedings,* NCC Vol. 45, 1976, pp. 85–90.

The design of a network security system is outlined in this paper. Heinrich and Kaufman first briefly review some basic network concepts and then describe four general security threats to computer networks. These are those to network communication, those from counterfeit network resources, forged user identification, and unauthorized access by legitimate users. The authors then present a network system design which uses a "network security center" to control connections between network resources. Also included in the design are cryptographic devices incorporating the NBS data encryption standard. This design is then analyzed with respect to its ability to safeguard against the four security threats described earlier.

Herber 78

Herbert, A.J., "A New Protection Architecture for the Cambridge Capability Computer." *Operating Systems Review,* Vol. 12, No. 1, January 1978, pp. 24–28.

The addition of a global naming scheme, typed-objects, type extension and revocation to the basic CAP architecture [Needha 77a], [Needha 77c] is discussed.

Hoffma 77a

Hoffman, L.J., *Modern Methods for Computer Security and Privacy.* Prentice-Hall, Inc., Englewood Cliffs, New Jersey, 1977. (See Chapter 1.)

Hollin 76

Hollingworth, D., and Bisbey, R.L., II, "Protection Errors in Operating Systems: Allocation/Deallocation Residuals." Information Sciences Inst., University of Southern California, Marina del Rey, California, June 1976.

The authors state that a common vulnerability in operating systems that can lead to security violations is that of residuals. They define residuals as "data or access capabilities left after the completion of a process and not intended for use outside the context of that process." It is explained that if data or process capabilities become accessible to another process a security violation may occur.

There are two types of residuals studied in this paper. The first are those resulting from incorrect allocation/deallocation of cells which are defined as logical or physical entities which may contain information.

The second are those resulting from errors in access capability allocation/deallocation. The authors examine several types of processes in computer systems and present a method for discovering where residuals may occur.

Honeyw 75

Honeywell Information Systems, "Proceedings Computer Security and Privacy Symposium." April 1975, Order Number DE20, Rev. 0.

Contained in these proceedings are 20 papers covering computer system operational and physical security along with the privacy aspects of computers. The two-day symposium was held to "furnish up-to-date information on state-of-the-art hardware and software security technology." The proceedings are divided into three major sections along the lines of the sessions. The first is that covering the joint session in which papers were presented to provide an overview of computer security and privacy. The second section contains papers presented at the technical session on computer system security. The papers in the third section deal with the topic of data center management.

Hsu 76

Hsu, N., "Protection Properties and Hardware Architecture for Recursive Virtual Machines." Ph.D. dissertation, University of Wisconsin-Madison, May 1976.

In his thesis Hsu investigates two problems with existing virtual machines systems which are those of resource allocation and protection. Hsu develops the idea of "execution environment hierarchy." That is, a bare machine provides an execution environment for a virtual machine monitor (Goldbe 74) which in turn provides an execution environment for operating systems running on it. Within this context Hsu develops rules for resource allocation and a protection mode. The necessary architecture for supporting these concepts is then presented.

Huber 76

Huber, A., "A Multiprocess Design of a Paging System," M.S. thesis, May 1968; Tech. Report 171, M.I.T.

IBM 74

IBM Corporation, *IBM Data Security Forum.* Denver, Colorado, September 1974, Document No. G520–2965–0.

This publication contains 36 papers that were presented at the 1974 IBM Data Security Forum. The sessions of the forum included those on Architecture, Data Access Control, Data Base Management and Policy, Data Base and Operations. Government, Operating Systems, and Program Integrity and Hardware. Some of the papers are listed separately in this bibliography (see [Attana 74]).

Janson 74

Janson, P.A., "Removing the Dynamic Linker from the Security Kernel of a Computing Utility." Massachusetts Institute of Technology, Cambridge, MAC–TR–132, 1974 (NTIS AD–781 305).

This M.S. thesis describes the removal of the dynamic linker from the revised security kernel for Multics. It is reported that this removal led to a 10% reduction in the size of kernel while the performance was not noticeably affected. See also [Janson 75].

Janson 75

Janson, P. A., "Dynamic Linking and Environment Initialization in a Multi-Domain Process." *Proceedings Fifth Symposium on Operating Systems Principles, Operating Systems Review,* Vol. 9, No. 5, November 1975, pp. 43–50.

Jeffer 74b

Jeffrey, S., and Branstad, D.K., "Security Considerations in Software Systems." *Proceedings 3rd Texas Conference on Computing Systems,* Austin, Texas, November 1974 (NTIS PB–257 009).

> This brief paper addresses the considerations which must be kept in mind when designing and implementing secure systems. The topics covered include control of design, control of implementation, security and quality control, security validation, security certification, and the role of standards.

Jones 75a

Jones, A. K., and Lipton, R. J., "The Enforcement of Security Policies for Computation." *Proceedings Fifth Symposium on Operating Systems Principles, Operating Systems Review,* Vol. 9, No. 5, November 1975, pp. 197–206.

> Formal definitions of a program, a protection mechanism, and a security policy are given. A particular mechanism which provides for keeping track of what input values have affected each program variable is introduced. This mechanism is shown to be theoretically acceptable as long as running time of a program is not observable. It is then compared to other possible mechanisms.

Jones 75b

Jones, A. K., and Wulf, W. A., "Towards the Design of Secure Systems." *Software—Practice and Experience,* Vol. 5, 1975, pp. 321–336.

> The protection mechanisms of the Hydra Kernel system [Cohen 75], [Wulf 74], [Wulf 75] are discussed. In particular, mechanisms to transfer capabilities and to amplify capabilities (allow a trusted called program to have more access rights than the calling program) are included. The second part of the paper shows several security policies that can be implemented using these mechanisms.

Jones 76

Jones, A. K., Lipton, R. J., and Snyder, L., "A Linear Time Algorithm for Deciding Subject-Object Security," *Proceedings 17th Annual Foundation of Computer Science Conference,* Houston, Texas, 1976, pp. 33–41.

This paper extends the Take–Grant model of [Lipton 77] which includes only subjects to systems of two classes—subjects and objects where only subjects are able to initiate changes of access rights.

Jones 78

Jones, A. K., and Liskov, B. H., "A Language Extension for Expressing Constraints on Data Access." *Communications of the ACM,* Vol. 21, No. 5, May 1978, pp. 358–367.

An extension to strongly typed programming languages such as Simula 67, Clu and Alphard is described. By associating a set of access rights with a data type in a manner comparable to a capability protection mechanism, it is possible to check for security violations at compile time.

Kallma 78

Kallman, D. K., and Miller, J. K., "Security Kernel Verification Techniques: Algorithmic Presentation." The Mitre Corp., Bedford, Massachusetts, April 1978, MTR–3289; ESD–TR–78–123 (NTIS AD–A054098).

This report prepared for the Air Force Electronic Systems Division suggests a technique, in the sense of Dijkstra's levels of abstraction, to produce programming language representations of the kernel at each level of the kernel specification.

Karger 74

Karger, P. A., and Schell, R. R., "Multics Security Evaluation: Vulnerability Analysis," Air Force Electronic Systems Division, ESD–TR–74–193, Vol. II, June 1974 (NTIS AD–A001 120).

This is a report on the results of penetration efforts made on the Air Force Data Services Center's HIS 645 Multics.

Lackey 74

Lackey, R. D., "Penetration of Computer Systems—An Overview." *The Honeywell Computer Journal,* Vol. 8, No. 2, 1974, pp. 81–85.

Lampso 77

Lampson, B. W., Needham, R. M, Randall, B., and Schroeder, M. D., "Protection, Security, Reliability *Operating Systems Review,* Vol. II, No. 1, January 1977, pp. 12–14.

The authors present lists of concepts and techniques related to protection, security, and reliability that (a) need to be done, (b) are difficult and results are not expected in the short run, and (c) are basically misconceived.

Larson 74

Larson, D. L., "Computer Data Security." Masters thesis, Naval Postgraduate School, Monterey, California, June 1974 (NTIS AD–7837 81).

Lauer 74

Lauer, H. C., "Protection and Hierarchical Addressing Structures." *Proceedings IRIA International Conference on Protection in Operating Systems*, Rocquencourt, France, August 1974, pp. 137–148.

Lientz 75

Lientz, B. P., and Weiss, I. R., "Effects of Security Measures on Network Performance," Graduate School of Management, UCLA, Los Angeles, November 1975 (NTIS AD–A018 762).

Lientz and Weiss address the costs of imposing security measures on a computer network environment. The experiments performed tested three types of networks: centralized, semicentralized, and distributed, all utilizing IBM 370 systems. The experiments were designed to measure the trade-offs between percentage of secure work load and degradation with respect to cost, workload, and response time for the three types of networks. The report includes several graphs comparing the results.

Linde 75

Linde, R.R., "Operating Systems Penetration." *AFIPS Conference Proceedings-1977 NCC*, Vol. 44, 1975, pp. 361–368.

In order to determine the security weaknesses or vulnerabilities in operating systems the System Development Corporation (SDC) has been studying and attempting to penetrate several computer systems. In the first part of the paper, Linde explains the methodology used in these attacks known as the Flaw Hypothesis Methodology. This consists of four steps according to Linde: gain knowledge of the operating system control structure, generate a flaw hypothesis, confirm the hypothesis, and make generalizations as a result of this flaw.

The second portion of the paper is concerned with the generic vulnerabilities of the system. Such things as I/O control and access control are considered usual places for system flaws to occur and are examined by Linde.

Appendices are included which outline the system flaws and the specific methods used in these attacks in some detail.

Linden 74

Linden, T. A., "Different Goals for Protection," *Proceedings IRIA International Conference on Protection in Operating Systems*, Rocquencourt, France, August 1974, pp. 149–153.

Linden 76a

Linden, T.A., "Security Analysis and Enhancements of Computer Operating Systems." The RISOS Project, Lawrence Livermore Laboratory, Livermore, California, April 1976, (available as NBSIR 76–1041) (NTIS PB–257 087).

Linden 76b

Linden, T.A., "Operating System Structures to Support Security and Reliable Software." *Computing Surveys*, Vol. 8, No. 4, December 1976, pp. 409–445.

> Linden asserts that inclusion of security considerations into the design of computer systems has become a challenging goal for their designers. He presents two concepts, that of small protection domains and extended-type objects as being able to support the security in operating systems. Additionally, the use of capability based addressing [Fabry 74] [Dennin 76b] for implementing these concepts in an efficient manner is presented.
>
> Linden explains a small protection domain as the environment a user or his procedures execute in such that access is limited to those objects necessary to complete the current task. The author notes this is based on the "principle of least privilege." An extended-type object is described as one in which the system has allowed the user to define new types in terms of existing ones and then create objects of this new type. Linden states that the use of extended type objects allows the protection features of the operating system to be extended.

Lipner 74b

Lipner, S.B., "A Panel Session—Security Kernels." *AFIPS Conference Proceedings-1974, NCC*, Vol. 43, 1974, pp. 973–980.

> This report from the panel on security kernels provides an excellent introduction to the kernel concept and several viewpoints of the kernel idea. Lipner gives a good introduction followed by brief expositions by several acknowledged experts in the area of operating system security. They include Wulf of Carnegie-Mellon University [Wulf 74], [Wulf 75], Schell of Air Force Electronic Systems Division, Popek from UCLA [Popek 74b], Neumann from the Stanford Research Institute, Weissman from the System Development Corporation, and Linden from the Department of Defense.

Lipner 75

Lipner, S. B., "A Comment on the Confinement Problem." *Proceedings Fifth Symposium on Operating Systems Principles, Operating Systems Review*, Vol. 9, No. 5, November 1975, pp. 192–196.

Solutions of the confinement problem (can a borrowed program steal unauthorized information?) based on security kernel research are discussed. In particular experience with a PDP–11/45 kernel [Schill 75] is reported.

Lipton 77

Lipton, R. J., and Snyder, L., "A Linear Time Algorithm for Deciding Subject Security." *Journal of the ACM*, Vol. 24, No. 3, July 1977, pp. 455–464.

A simple protection mechanism—the take and grant system—is analyzed. Suppose a system is made up of the programs (w, x, y, z) which may have read, write, or call access rights to each other. The protection mechansim then consists of (a) x may "take" an access right that y has if x can read y; (b) x may "grant" an access right that it has if it can write in y; (c) x may "create" a new program y to which it has all access rights; (d) x may "remove" any right that it has; and (e) x may "call" z with parameter y which is implemented conceptually by the creation of a new program w which may read z and which has the same access rights to y as does x. The paper then describes under what conditions access rights can be passed from one program to another. Unlike the general security problem [Harris 76] it is shown that this determination can be made in time proportional to the number of programs and program to program access rights.

Lujana 75

Lujanac, P., "Letter." *Operating System Review,* Vol. 9, No. 1, January 1975, p. 2.

In this letter, Lujana comments and provides a bibliography on the problem of database recovery, a topic which was not included in [Saltze 74b].

Luniew 77

Luniewski, A., "A Certifiable System Initialization Mechanism." S.M. Thesis, Massachusetts Institute of Technology, Cambridge, January 1977, MAC TR–180.

McPhee 74

McPhee, W.S., "Operating System Integrity in OS/VS2." *IBM Systems Journal,* Vol. 13, No. 3, 1974, pp. 230–252.

McPhee in his study of OS/VS2 integrity, examines the flaws in operating systems that allow user programs to compromise operating system integrity problems:

1. System data in the user area.

2. Nonunique identification of a system's resources.
3. System violation of storage protection.
4. User data passed as system data.
5. User supplied address of protected control blocks.
6. Concurrent use of serial resources and
7. Uncontrolled sensitive system resources.

McPhee discusses each of these problems in general and then describes the techniques used in OS/VS2 for solving these problems. The paper also includes comments on the responsibilities of the installation to support the security mechanisms in OS/VS2.

Millen 76

Millen, J.K., "Security Kernel Validation in Practice." *Communications of the ACM,* Vol. 19, No. 5, May 1976, pp. 243–250.

A security kernel for a DEC PDP–11/45 has been designed by the Mitre Corporation. Millen describes the abstract model of the kernel and techniques used in the first stage of the proof which is verifying the specifications of the kernel in terms of axioms developed for secure systems.

Montgo 76

Montgomery, W., "A Secure and Flexible Model of Process Initiation for a Computer Utility." S.M. thesis, Massachusetts Institute of Technology, Cambridge, June 1976, MAC TR–163.

NBS 76a

National Bureau of Standards, "Glossary for Computer Systems Security." February 1976 (NTIS NBS–FIPS PUB 39).

NBS 76b

National Bureau of Standards, "Security Analysis and Enhancements of Computer Operating Systems." National Bureau of Standards, Final Report, April 1976, NBSIR 76–1041.

Needha 74a

Needham, R. M., and Walker, R. D. H., "Protection and Process Management in the CAP Computer." *Proceedings IRIA International Conference on Protection in Operating Systems,* Rocquencourt, France, August 1974, pp. 155–160.

Needha 74b

Needham, R.M., and Wilkes, M.V., "Domains of Protection and the Management of Processes." *The Computer Journal,* Vol. 17, No. 2, May 1974, pp. 117–120.

Needha 77a

Needham, R.M., and Walker, R.D.H., "The Cambridge CAP Computer and Its Protection System." *Proceedings of the Sixth Symposium on Operating Systems Principles, Operating Systems Review,* Vol. 11, No. 5, 1977, pp. 1–10.

The architecture of a secure computer, CAP, implemented at the University of Cambridge using a combination of hard logic and microprogram is described. The architecture is based on capabilities to access any physical segment of memory. A process may access up to 16 segments. A capability unit contains the base, limit, and access status of each active segment which have been computed by microprogram. The operating system is divided into two levels, the master coordinator, which is responsible for scheduling and dispatching and the second level which contains other operating system functions.

Needha 77b

Needham, R.M., and Birrell, A.D., "The CAP Filing System." *Proceedings of the Sixth Symposium on Operating Systems Principles, Operating Systems Review,* Vol. 11, No. 5, 1977, pp. 11–16.

The CAP [Needha 77a] file system is described. Security is based on equating a file with the preservation of a capability. By handling directory capabilities like storage capabilities, hierarchical and shared directories are possible.

Needha 77c

Needham, R.M., "The CAP Project—An Interim Evaluation." *Proceedings of the Sixth Symposium on Operating Systems Principles, Operating Systems Review,* Vol. 11, No. 5, 1977, pp. 17–22.

After reviewing the CAP system [Needha 77a], [Needha 77b], the author concludes that the following questions still exist: (a) Are the protection features useful to users developing elaborate subsystems? (b) What are the costs and effectiveness of the protection features in regular computation? (c) Does the explicitness and precision of protection features ease system restructuring? (d) How should premature termination of a computation be handled?

Neuman 74

Neumann, P.G., Fabry, R.S., Levitt, K.N., Robinson, L., and Wensley, J.H., "On the Design of a Provably Secure Operating System." *Proceedings IRIA International Workshop on Protection in Operating Systems,* Rocquencourt, France, August 1974.

In this paper the authors describe the methodology used and the design of an operating system at the Stanford Research Institute. The

operating system was designed to be general purpose and provide at least
the sharing flexibility of Multics. In addition, the system was meant to be
provably secure. The authors describe how in order to meet these goals
they included a formal proof methodology within the design of the
system. The actual design of the system is outlined in the paper. It is explained that the system is hierarchically structured and the protection
mechanisms are capability-based. A discussion of system initialization,
fault recovery and monitoring is also included.

Neuman 77

Neumann, P.G., Boyer, R.S., Feiertag, R.J., Levitt, K.N., and Robinson,
L., "A Provably Secure Operating System: The System, Its Applica-
tions, and Proofs." Final Report, Project 4332, SRI International, Menlo
Park, California, February 1977.

A detailed description of the design of the Provably Secure Operating
System (PSOS) developed at SRI is presented. Included are (a) a formal
methodology for the design, implementation, and verification of such a
system; (b) the specification of the capability-based operating system
itself; (c) the design of several application subsystems including support
for multilevel security classifications, for confined subsystems, for a
secure relational database system, and for monitoring of security; and (d)
the statement and proof of properties of these designs.

The methodology has been divided into stages (a) the choice of the
visible interface which is decomposed into modules, objects and functions; (b) the hierarchical design of each module in terms of lower levels;
(c) the specification of each function at each node of the hierarchy; (d) the
definition of mappings among the data representations at connecting
nodes; and (e) the writing of implementation programs for the functions at
each node. On-line tools have been developed to support the first four of
these stages.

The operating system itself is designed to prevent unauthorized ac-
quisition or alteration of information, to prevent the unauthorized
leakage of information, and to prevent the unauthorized denial of service.
The multilevel security model is based on [Bell 74a]. The report includes
the formal specifications of the basic design, the secure object manager,
the confined subsystem manager, and the data managment subsystem. It
also includes illustrative implementations and implementation proofs of
the basic system.

Neuman 78

Neuman, P.G., "Computer System Security Evaluation." *AFIPS Conference Proceedings-1978 NCC*, Vol. 47, 1978, pp. 1088–1095.

Two approaches to improved computer security have been suggested:
(a) remedial-classify patterns of security violations and (b) preventive—use a formal methodology in the design and implementation of the

operating systems. This paper suggests a combination of remedial methods [Bisbey 75], [Carlst 75], [Carlst 76] with preventive methods [Neuman 74], [Neuman 77]. It then evaluates the design of PSOS (a Provably Secure Operating System) [Neuman 77] and two existing operating systems, Multics and UNIX using this approach.

Popek 74a

Popek, G.J., "Protection Structures." *Computer*, Vol. 7, No. 6, June 1974, pp. 22–23.

Popek presents a survey of the problems and solutions involving controlled access and sharing in computer systems. In this paper, he discusses several control disciplines such as isolation, mutually suspicious subsystems, and the problems of confinement. From this he introduces the concept of a model of protection and examines several of these. The implementation of such models is then presented with comments on kernels, virtual machines and the uses of cryptography.

Popek 74b

Popek, G.J., and Kline, C.S., "Verifiable Secure Operating System Software." *AFIPS Conference Proceedings-1974 NCC*, Vol. 43, 1974, pp. 145–151.

The development of a security kernel of an operating system at UCLA which is to be proved correct is reported in this paper. In the initial sections of the paper Popek and Kline discuss the general idea of security kernels and then present the concept of virtual machines on which the UCLA kernal design is based.

The latter portions of the paper discuss the UCLA–VM system and the progress of verifying the correctness of the code. Furthermore, the authors discuss the costs of such a security kernel with respect to construction, user convenience, and performance. The authors conclude that it is practical to have verified software security in multiuser computer systems.

Popek 74c

Popek, G.J., and Goldberg, R.P., "Formal Requirements for Virtualizable Third Generation Architectures." *Communications of the ACM*, Vol. 17, No. 7, July 1974, pp. 412–421.

This paper develops a model of third-generation computer architecture. Using this model, Popek and Goldberg outline the formal requirements necessary to support a virtual machine type of system. The authors distinguish between a virtual machine and a hybrid virtual machine. They state that the structure of a hybrid virtual machine is similar to a virtual machine only more instructions are interpreted by the virtual machine monitor. They show that while few third-generation computers will support virtual machines, many will support hybrid virtual machines.

Popek 75

Popek, G. J., and Kline, C. S., "A Verifiable Protection System." *Proceedings of the 1975 International Conference on Reliable Software, SIGPLAN Notices* Vol. 10, No. 5, June 1975, pp. 294–304.

This paper discusses some of the problems encountered in the design of the UCLA Virtual Machine System based on a security kernel. In particular which of the following functions may be removed from the kernel? Virtual memory facilities, CPU scheduling, input/output, I/O scheduling, user authentication, facilities for modifying access rights, facilities for controlled sharing, file access control, or interrupt and trap routines.

Popek 76

Popek, G.J., and Farber, D., "On Computer Security Verification." *Proceedings IEEE CompCon International Conference,* San Francisco, California, February 1976, pp. 140–142.

Theoretical methods for verifying software have been applied to the security kernel of the UCLA virtual machine system [Popek 74b]. Popek and Farber discuss the methods used and their success in this paper.

The first stage of the verification process is composed of three parts as explained by the authors. The first is the development of a high level abstract machine. Next the abstract machine is interpreted in such a manner to reflect the UCLA kernel, and finally I/O assertions for the kernel primitives are developed. The second involves developing precise semantic definitions for the PASCAL language while the third stage involves verifying the actual code. The authors provide several comments about the verification process.

Popek 78a

Popek, G.J., and Kline, C.S., "Issues in Kernel Design." *AFIPS Conference Proceedings-1978 NCC,* Vol. 47, 1978, pp. 1079–1086.

A nice summary of the results of research on security kernels is presented. Discussed are the effects of design constraints such as the security policy, system functions, hardware effects, and performance constraints; the principles of kernel design including "least privilege" and "least common mechanism"; the decomposition of secure code; the internal kernel architecture including hardware selection; and the problem of confinement.

Popek 78b

Popek, G.J., and Farber, D.A., "A Model for Verification of Data Security in Operating Systems." *Communications of the ACM,* Vol. 21, No. 9, September 1978, pp. 737–749.

This paper describes the abstract machine used in the UCLA security kernel [Popek 74b], [Popek 76]. This abstract machine is essentially a finite state machine described by states and instructions which transform states. The system has been implemented on a DEC PDP 11/45 using an extension of Pascal.

Redell 74a

Redell, D. D., and Fabry, R. S., "Selective Revocation of Capabilities." *Proceedings IRIA International Conference on Protection in Operating Systems*, Rocquencourt, France, August 1974, pp. 197–209.

Redell 74b

Redell, D.D., "Naming and Protection in Extendible Operating Systems." Massachusetts Institute of Technology, Cambridge, Project MAC, MACTR–148, November 1974 (NTIS AD–A001 721).

Reynol 76

Reynolds, G. E., "Multics Security Evaluation: Exemplary Performance Under Demanding Workload." Air Force Electronic Systems Division, November 1976; ESD–TR–74–193, Vol. IV (NTIS AD–A038 231).

Benchmark tests of four computer systems with security features are conducted. These systems are IBM 370–155, HIS 635 with GCOS, HIS 6180 with Multics and GCOS, and HIS 6180 with Multics only. The test programs are written in Fortran and tests are mathematical computations and matrix manipulation. The main purpose of the test runs is to see whether the performances of the systems involved are hindered by the presence of built-in security features. The finding is negative. Multics running on HIS 6180 has best performance still.

This report is Volume 4 of a four-part series. For Volume 2, see [Karger 74]. For Volume 3, see [Downey 74]. Volume 1, however, does not seem to exist.

Robins 75

Robinson, L., "On Attaining Reliable Software for a Secure Operating System." *Proceedings of the 1975 International Conference on Reliable Software, SIGPLAN Notices*, Vol. 10, No. 6, June 1975, pp. 267–284.

First the general methodology developed at SRI for the design, implementation, and proof of large software systems is described. Then the requirements for a secure operating system are discussed. Finally, the methodology is applied to the design of the secure operating system.

The methodology consists of defining a hierarchy of abstract machines using Parnas modules. Each abstract machine is then implemented by abstract programs executing on lower level machines. A proof technique is then provided to verify the implementations. The proposed operating system structure includes 13 levels including hardware capabilities and interrupts at the lowest level to user commands at the highest. Some of the intermediate levels are scheduled processes, segments, directories, linkage tables, and user processes. Three of the levels of the operating system are then illustrated in simplified form.

Rotenb 74

Rotenburg, L. J., "Making Computers Keep Secrets." Ph.D. dissertation Massachusetts Institute of Technology, Cambridge, February 1974, NSF–OCA–GJ34671–TR–115 (NTIS PB–229 352).

Rotenberg, in his Ph.D. dissertation, presents the design of a secure computer system that includes specification of hardware and software protection mechanisms. An interesting hardware device, the Privacy Restriction Processor, is described as holding the restriction set of segments accessed by a process.

The dissertation also provides an analysis of the impact computers and information technology have had on society. He uses this to develop a set of requirements on computers. Among these are that (a) computers should be secured (b) no one individual should have a large amount of power over a computer performing social functions, (c) computers should be auditable, and (d) databases should be easily bound to a "caretaker program" or reference monitor.

Saltze 74a

Saltzer, J. H., "Protection and the Control of Information in Multics." *Communications of the ACM,* Vol. 17, No. 7, July 1974, pp. 388–402.

Saltzer explains that a major and essential portion of a computer system are the mechanisms which control the transfer of information among users. These mechanisms of the Multics system are presented in this paper. Saltzer states that this controlled sharing of information was an original goal of the Multics system design. Saltzer explains the following five principles which guided the design of the actual mechanisms used in Multics:

1. Base the protection mechanisms on permission rather then exclusion.
2. Check every access to every object for current authority.
3. Do not keep the design secret.
4. Principle of least privilege.
5. Natural user interface.

The rest of the paper is devoted to describing Multics' use of mechanisms such as access control list, memory protection, and authentication of users. The final section discusses the weaknesses and vulnerabilities of the Multics protection mechanisms.

Saltze 74b

Saltzer, J. H., "Ongoing Research and Development on Information Protection." *Operating System Review,* Vol. 8, No. 3, July 1974, pp. 8–24.

In this enlightening paper, Saltzer explains nine areas of computer security research that were underway at the time of publication. These categories were system penetration exercises, user interface studies, proofs of correctness, mathematical models of protection kernels, protection mechanisms, security in data communications networks, database facilities, authentication mechanisms, and Department of Defense operational problems. The rest of the paper describes the activities of some of the major organizations performing research into one or more of these areas.

A comment on another category of research, database recovery, is contained in [Lujana 75].

Saltze 75

Saltzer, J. H., and Schroeder, M. D., "The Protection of Information in Computer Systems." *Proceedings of the IEEE,* Vol. 63, No. 9, September 1975, pp. 1278–1308.

This paper, written as a tutorial, discusses the protection of data in computer systems from unauthorized access. The paper is organized into three major sections. The first describes functions, design principles, and examples of elementary protection and authentication mechanisms. The second explores the principles of modern protection architecture and the relation between capability systems and access control lists systems in detail. The section ends with a brief analysis of protected subsystems and objects.

The final section reviews the state of the art and current research projects. Although rather lengthy, the paper provides one of the most comprehensive overviews of computer protection methods. A glossary of terms related to computer security is included.

Schaef 77

Schaefer, M., Gold, B. D., Linde, R. R., and Scheid, J. F., "Program Confinement in KVM/370." *Proceedings of ACM Annual Conference,* 1977, Seattle, Washington, pp. 404–410.

The KVM/370 system is intended to provided multilevel military security [Gold 77]. This paper discusses how to prevent covert transmission of data from a higher security level to a lower level; for example, by knowing the times required for certain input/output operations.

Schell 76

Schell, R. R., and Karger, P. A., "Security in Automatic Data Processing (ADP) Network Systems." Air Force Electronic Systems Division,

Hanscomb AFB, Massachusetts, ESD–TR–77–19, December 1976 (NTIS AD–A037 210).

Schill 75

Schiller, W. L., "The Design and Specification of a Security Kernel for the PDP–11/45." Mitre Corp., Bedford, Massachusetts, MTR–2934, May 1975 (NTIS AD–A011 712).

> The design of a prototype security kernel for the PDP-11/45 is described. The purpose of the prototype is to demonstrate how to go from a mathematical model of a secure system [Bell 74a] to an implementation both generally as well as specifically on the PDP 11/45. The design consists of four levels. Level 0, the hardware, provides three execution domains (kernel, supervisor, and user) and three access rights (write, read, or execute; read or execute; or no access). It also provides a segmented main memory. Level 1, sequential processes, creates the process abstraction. Level 2 creates the segmented virtual memory. Level 3, security, adds the association of subjects and objects and completes the implementation of the security model.
>
> The implementation is intended for validation, but has not been validated. As a prototype it is very small, only 900 lines of code.

Schill 77

Schiller, W. L., "The Design and Abstract Specification of a Multics Security Kernel." The Mitre Corp., Bedford, Massachusetts, November 1977, MTR–3294, Vol. I; ESD–TR–77–259, Vol. I (NTIS AD A04876).

> This report prepared for the Air Force Electronic Systems Division presents an overview of the design, verification and specification of a secure Multics operating system utilizing the kernel approach. It is followed by Volumes 2 and 3 with high-level design and formal specification of main and secondary functions of the Multics kernel. See [Within 78] and [Woodwa 78] for Volumes 2 and 3, respectively.

Schroe 75

Schroeder, M. D., "Engineering a Security Kernel for Multics." *Proceedings Fifth Symposium on Operating Systems Principles,* November 1975, University of Texas, Houston, Texas, pp. 25–32.

> Described in this paper are the partial results of a research project whose goal is to design a security kernel for the Multics system. Schroeder first describes past efforts, goals of the projects, and why Multics is suited for this type of effort. The major portion of the paper is then spent outlining three categories of activities underway as part of this project. Schroeder explains that the first is to remove unnecessary pieces of code from the kernel, the second is to restructure of the parts of kernel that are

necessary, and the final category of activities is to modularize the parts of the kernel so that it may be verified more easily.

Schroe 77

Schroeder, M. D., Clark, D. D., and Saltzer, J. H., "The Multics Kernel Design Project." *Proceedings of the Sixth ACM Symposium on Operating Systems Principles, Operating Systems Review,* Vol. 11, No. 5, 1977, pp. 43–56.

Summarized are the results of a project to apply security kernel technology, information flow control, and verification of correctness to a large operating system, Multics. Since the central supervisor consists of 54,000 lines of code (mostly PL/I) and the security mechanisms are somewhat ad hoc, the project was designed to simplify the supervisor and to provide a set of mechanisms that could be described by a simple, understandable model. It was then intended to reimplement and verify a new supervisor.

The first step of the project was to add to Multics the security controls required by the Mitre model [Bell 74] which was then installed at various test sites. Experiments were then conducted on ways to reduce the complexity of the system, for example by developing a file system and processor multiplexing organization based on the ideas of abstract data types. Trial implementations were carried out on four projects: (*a*) removal of the dynamic linker [Janson 74], (*b*) removal of some of the name management mechanism [Bratt 75], (*c*) modification of the answering service [Montgo 76], and (*d*) the redesign of the memory management algorithm [Huber 76]. Other projects not then completed included (*e*) modification of the connection to multiplexed networks [Ciccar 76] and (*f*) the redesign of the system initialization mechanism [Luniew 77]. It is estimated that these modifications would reduce the kernel from 54,000 to 28,000 lines, an improvement, but still leaving a large kernel. In addition a considerable reduction in complexity was reported. In terms of performance it is reported that these modifications have no significant impact. The project was terminated before formal specifications of a new kernel could be completed.

The authors then report on several conclusions. (*a*) The kernel concept and the use of abstract data types can significantly simplify the central supervisor. (*b*) The kernel of a general-purpose operating system will be large. (*c*) Minor hardware adjustments and minor variations in user interface semantics can make major differences in the implementation complexity. (*d*) All desired functions must be considered in the initial design.

Sevcik 74

Sevcik, K. C., and Tsichritzis, D. C., "Authorization and Access Control Within Overall System Design." *Proceedings IRIA International Con-*

ference on Protection in Operating Systems, Rocquencourt, France, August 1974, pp. 221–224.

Shanka 77

Shankar, K. S., "The Total Computer Security Problem: An Overview." *Computer,* Vol. 10, No. 6, June 1977, pp. 50–73. (See Chapter 3.)

Snyder 77

Snyder, L., "On the Synthesis and Analysis of Protection Systems." *Proceedings of Sixth ACM Symposium on Operating Systems Principles, Operating Systems Review,* Vol. 11, No. 5, 1977, pp. 141–150.

> This paper demonstrates the richness of the Take–Grant security model of [Jones 76] and [Lipton 77]. Three different protection designs which allow sharing are presented.

Spier 74a

Spier, M. J., "A System Theoretic Look at the Complexity of Access Control Mechanisms." *Proceedings IRIA International Conference on Protection in Operating Systems,* Rocquencourt, France, August 1974, pp. 225–241.

Spier 74b

Spier, M. J., Hastings, T. N., and Cutler, D. N., "A Storage Mapping Technique for the Implementation of Protective Domains." *Software Practice and Experience,* Vol. 4, 1974 pp. 215–230..

> The Department of Software Engineering at the Digital Equipment Corporation undertook an exploratory implementation of a secure operating system in 1972 using a DEC PDP–11/45. The system was based on a kernel/domain architecture. In particular, it was used to study the storage mapping technique and the intermodule call/return mechanism. The goal was to demonstrate that current systems could be made to keep one errant module from interferring with other modules. The author concludes that such an approach is definitely feasible as soon as supportive hardware is available.

Stork 75

Stork, D. F., "Downgrading in a Secure Multilevel Computer System: The Formulary Concept." Mitre Corp., Bedford, Massachusetts, MTR–2924, May 1975 (NTIS AD–A011 696).

> This report describes a secure multilevel database system which could be used on a PDP–11/45 with the security kernel developed by Mitre [Schill 75], [Harper 78]. One particular problem of a database system is to provide a secure method to allow downgrading, i.e., transformation of information in one object from one security level to a lower

level. Two downgrading methods are possible—change the level of the existing information or copy the information into another lower level object. The latter approach was chosen because it would require fewer changes to the kernel.

Vanvle 74

Van Vleck, T. H., "Access Control to Computer System Resources." *Proceedings CompCon 74 Eighth IEEE Computer Society International Conference,* February 1974, pp. 65–68.

Needs for implementation and design constraints on access control mechanisms for multiple access computer systems are described in this paper. Specific mechanisms described include identification, access matrices, and auditing along with comments on minimizing the cost involved. Van Vleck includes examples from Multics.

Wagues 75

Waguespack, L. J., Jr., "Virtual Machine Multiprogramming and Security." Ph.D. dissertation, University of Southwestern Louisiana, Lafayette, June 1975.

Waguespack's research investigates four topics within the context of operating system resource management and process control. In his thesis he does the following:

1. Examines the conditions required to support multiprogramming.
2. Defines computer security.
3. Presents the design of a secure multiprogrammable machine.
4. Explores the characteristics and relationships between multiprogramming processes and multiprogramming interpreter.

The concept of a kernel or nucleus to support virtual machines is developed. Waguespack extends this in such a manner as to present the detailed design of a self-virtualized machine.

Walter 74

Walter, K. G., Ogden, W. F., Rounds, W. C., Bradshaw, F. T., Ames, S. R., and Shumway, D. G., "Primitive Models for Computer Security." Dept. Computing and Information Sciences, Case Western Reserve University, Cleveland, January 1974.

Early in 1973 Case Western Reserve University began work on development of a mathematical model of a secure computer system. This report contains a description of the basic model along with its application to a directory file system. This work along with the results of subsequent research is contained in [Walter 75a].

Walter 75a

Walter, K. G., Odgen, W. F., Gilligan, J. M., Schaeffer, D. D., Schaen, S. I., and Shumway, D. G., "Initial Structured Specifications for an Uncompromisable Computer Security System." Report 1172, Case Western Reserve University, Cleveland, July 1975.

In the spring of 1973 researchers at Case Western Reserve University began working in conjunction with the Electronic Systems Division of the Air Force to develop a mathematical model of a secure computer system. This model was to be used in the design of a security kernel for the Air Force's Multics computer system. This report contains the final results of the study and is made up of seven sections: an introduction, basic structure of the model, its application to a directory file and mailbox system, formalization of dynamic security, security events, the security perimeter, and conclusions.

In section two the basic model is developed around a set of objects and subjects which the authors call repositories and agents, respectively. A set of four axioms is then outlined. The first two simply state that there is a set of security classes in which there exists a linear ordering. The second formulates the idea that agents can only observe repositories whose security class is less than theirs. In addition, agents may only modify repositories whose security class is greater than or equal to that of the agents. These axioms are then used to prove that information cannot be transferred from a repository of a high security class to a repository of a lower class. From this primitive model several successive ones are developed to specify the file directory structure, interprocess communication, and other system functions.

Walter 75b

Walter, K. G., "Structured Specification of a Security Kernel." *Proceedings of the 1975 International Conference on Reliable Software, SIGPLAN Notices,* Vol. 10, No. 6, June 1975, pp. 285–293.

This paper summarizes the results reported in [Walter 74] and [Walter 75a].

Weissm 75

Weissman, C., "Secure Computer Operation with Virtual Machine Partitioning." *AFIPS Conference Proceedings-1975 NCC,* Vol. 44, 1975, pp. 929–934.

Weissman describes an operational procedure used for security known as periods processing which involves allowing only one security class of jobs to run during a particular period of the day. He notes that this is the method approved by the Department of Defense for processing information of different security classes on the same computer. He then compares virtual machines with periods processing and asserts that virtual machine systems provide the needed security for military operations and yet still provide sharing of computer resources not found in a periods processing environment.

A discussion of a project undertaken by IBM and the System Development Corporation to analyze the security of VM/370 is presented. Methods to security-harden VM/370 to make it secure are then presented. This paper makes a good case for the use of virtual machines for security reasons.

White 75a

White, J. C., "Design of a Secure File Management System." Mitre Corp., Bedford, Massachusetts MTR–2931, April 1975 (NTIS AD–A010 590).

White 75b

White, R., "Computer Security Technology Reference Manual." TRW Systems Groups, Inc., RADC–TR–75–283, November 1975 (NTIS AD–A019 439).

Winkle 74

Winkler, S., and Danner, L., "Data Security in the Computer Communication Environment." *Computer,* Vol. 7, No. 2, February 1974, pp. 23–31.

The authors of this paper note the growing use of computer systems in which components are spread over a wide area. For these components to interact there became a need to merge computer and communication technology. While this has provided faster and more accessible systems, problems of data security have also evolved. This paper addresses these problems.

The authors define the computer communication environment as consisting of "computers, computer communication elements, a communications link, and programs for processing data and controlling the transmission of that data." The authors then discuss several computer system configurations that include multiterminal systems, intelligent terminal systems, and computer networks. The problems of data security within each of these systems are described and the advantages and disadvantages of various solutions are outlined. The paper also includes comments on the need for operational and physical security. Problems of identification and authentication are briefly addressed.

Within 78

Withington, P. T., "Design and Abstract Specification of a Multics Security Kernel." The Mitre Corp., Bedford, Massachusetts, March 1978, MTR–3294, Vol. II; ESD–TR–77–259, Vol. II (NTIS AD–A053148).

This report prepared for the Air Force Electronic Systems Division is the second volume dealing with the design and specification of a secure Multics utilizing the kernel approach. It deals with four major functions of the kernel, the interpreter, the storage system, process management, and I/O system. Compatibility of the kernel design with the existing Honeywell Multics is discussed. Furthermore, the syntax and semantics of the specification language for specifying the design and for subsequent verification are discussed. See [Woodwa 78] for Volume 3. See [Schill 77] for Volume 1.

Woodwa 78

Woodward, J. P. L., "Design and Abstract Specification of a Multics Security Kernel." The Mitre Corp., Bedford, Massachusetts, March 1978, MTR–3294, Vol. III; ESD–TR–77–259, Vol. III (NTIS AD–053149).

This report prepared for the Air Force Electronic Systems Division is the third volume dealing with design and specification of a secure Multics utilizing the kernel approach. There are three kernel functions, the initialization of the kernel to a secure state, the interface between the kernel and a user responsible for system security, and the reconfiguration of hardware via a secure system module. See [Within 78] for Volume 2 and [Schill 77] for Volume 1.

Wulf 74

Wulf, W., Cohen, E., Corwin, W., Jones, A. K., Levin, R., Pierson, C., and Pollack, F., "HYDRA: The Kernel of a Multiprocessor Operating System." Communications of the ACM, Vol. 17, No. 6, June 1974, pp. 337–345.

Hydra, which is the kernel of an operating system, has been implemented on the C.mmp (Carnegie Mellon Multi-Mini-Processor) which consists of up to 16 DEC PDP–11's. This paper discusses the design philosophy of Hydra, an overview of the Hydra environment, the protection mechanism, and concludes with an example of how the system and subsystems can be used. The protection mechanisms, generally based on the concept of capabilities, are detailed in [Cohen 75].

Wulf 75

Wulf, W., Levin, R., and Pierson, C., "Overview of the Hydra Operating System Development." Proceedings ACM Fifth Symposium on Operating Systems Principles, November 1975, U. of Texas, Houston, Texas, pp. 122–131.

At Carnegie Mellon University a kernel of an operating system has been developed. This kernel, Hydra, is designed to run on a set of up to 16 DEC PDP–11 minicomputers. This paper discusses the hardware aspects of this system and the philosophy behind the design of the Hydra kernel. Included in this portion of the paper is a section on the protection mechanisms within Hydra which are generally based on capabilities.

These mechanisms within Hydra are further detailed in [Wulf 74] and [Cohen 75].

Yasaki 74

Yasaki, E. K., "News in Perspective/A New Science Emerges: Plugging Holes in Operating Systems." *Datamation*, Vol. 20, No. 2, February 1974, pp. 90–92.

Yasaki's article comments on research being done at various places to find vulnerabilities in current operating systems and to design more secure systems. He reports on work at Lawrence Livermore Laboratories, System Development Corp., Mitre Corp., and others.

Yuval 76

Yuval, G., "An Operating Non-System." *Operating System Review*, Vol. 10, No. 3, July 1976, pp. 9–10.

Yuval, in this paper, advocates that programmers not be allowed to program in assembly language but only in higher level languages. By enforcing this restriction, secure operating systems will be easier to obtain. A method of enforcement is described.

Chapter 8

DATABASE SECURITY

For the purpose of drawing a sharp distinction between traditional *data processing* and modern *database management* let us view a data item as an *attribute-value pair*, the attribute indicating the type and characteristic of the value. This distinction has a profound impact on the complexity and difficulty of data security.

Traditional data processing treats data as a collection of values. To process the stored values, programs are written which not only must know the attributes of the values, but also must manipulate the values in accordance with their types. Different processing requirements call for various programs to be written. Furthermore, these programs may assign new attributes to the stored values and manipulate the values in different ways. New assignments of attributes and new manipulation of the values indicate that the data may yield new and useful information. To safeguard the sensitive information, the stored values must be protected, since without the values, neither the assignments nor the manipulation can take place. Furthermore, the programs and the programmers who wrote the programs must also be protected because they know the characteristics and types of the values. For data security, traditional data processing becomes essentially a *closed-shop operation* which precludes on-line access and interactive use of data. To authorize a user certain access to the data, the data processing shop must develop and run the programs for the user, and return the results to him. If the results are incomplete, it is not clear to the user whether he was not authorized for the "missing" information or whether the programs developed for him were inadequate. On the other hand, he is not capable of developing his own programs since he has little knowledge of the types, characteristics, or storage formats of the values. Even if he had developed his programs, he would not be allowed to run the programs in the closed shop.

Modern database management differs from traditional data processing in many respects. The database not only consists of all the stored values of the database, but also provides a *standard set of attributes* for the values. In other words, the database is kept in the computer system as a collection of attribute-value pairs. There are several reasons for doing so. The standard attributes allow the system administrator and users to have a *uniform view* of the types and characteristics of the database. This uniformity is important for *data integrity* during update and concurrent accesses because modern database management systems are meant to support on-line access, multiuser interaction, and dynamic update environments. *Data security consistency* requires the database management system to resolve overlapping or even contradictory protection requirements about the database. Without a uniform view, the owner of a database (whether he is a system administrator or a user) cannot begin to specify the protection requirements of the database. He is thus prevented from authorizing other users to access his database in a controlled and protected way. Without the requirements, the database system cannot assign protection attributes to the data and enforce the protection. Protection enforcement requires the database management system to identify the data in terms of its type and characteristic so that, in addition to exact values, data of certain type and characteristic can be secured in accordance with the specifications. The resolution of protection specifications on common data requires the database management system to distinguish data of one type from another and one characteristic from another, and to discriminate among various levels of data aggregates. Without such distinction, the database management system does not know whether a common piece of data is indeed the one which incurred the overlapping or conflicting requirements.

Since data represents information and information has intended meaning, such meaning should be represented in and managed by the database systems. In addition to the standard set of attributes, a modern database management system also provides a basic set of *semantic relations* of the data. There are several advantages to having built-in relations in the database system. The most obvious one is that the system (therefore the user) knows not only what the data are (in terms of their types and characteristics), but also knows how the data are used. If two pieces of data belong to the same relation, they are likely to be used in such a related way (see Fig. 8–1).

By keeping track of the relations, the database management system can facilitate the use of data effectively and efficiently since the storage and retrieval of the related data can now be optimized in terms of their relations.

Station-ID	(Number,	Name,	Status,	Place,	Person-in-Charge)
	127	ABCDE	ACTIVE	Moscow, IN	Jones
	223	ABXYZ	INACTIVE	Rome, NY	Smith
	224	PCPQR	UNKNOWN	Paris, IA	Lee
	346	ICAST	ACTIVE	Peking, PA	White
	509	MDFHI	INACTIVE	Newark, NJ	Hart

If Smith is fired as the person-in-charge of station number 223, then the removal of his entry in the relation will result in entries of the relation as follows:

Station-ID	(Number,	Name,	Status,	Place,	Person-in-Charge)
	127	ABCDE	ACTIVE	Moscow, IN	Jones
	224	PCPQR	UNKNOWN	Paris, IA	Lee
	346	ICAST	ACTIVE	Peking, PA	White
	509	MDFHI	INACTIVE	Newark, NJ	Hart

In the newly updated relation, we note the fact that the station in Rome, NY has been deleted along with its station chief.

FIGURE 8-1.   A data relation.

8.1 ACCESS DECISIONS

There are more subtle needs for keeping track of the data which can be seen by studying the example given in Fig. 8–1. If we intend to fire the person in charge of a station by deleting him from the (relation) Station ID, we inadvertently remove the station from the map (i.e., Rome). In other words, we are liable to lose data if we do not know the intended use (therefore, the relations) of the data. This problem, known as *update abnormality*, can be overcome if the relations of the station data are kept in an appropriate way as depicted in Fig. 8–2. Another subtle need for understanding relations is that the effectiveness of data security, to a large extent, is dependent upon the capability of the database management system to handle relations. Since relations are sensitive to the context in which the related data appear, protection of data requires the system to have a good understanding of context-sensitive issues. Let us elaborate on some of these issues in the following sections.

Station-ID   (Station Number,   Name,   Status,   Place)

Station Number	Name	Status	Place
127	ABCDE	ACTIVE	Moscow, IN
223	ABXYZ	INACTIVE	Rome, NY
224	PCPQR	UNKNOWN	Paris, IA
346	ICAST	ACTIVE	Peking, PA
509	MDFHI	INACTIVE	Newark, NJ

Station-head   (Station Number,   Person-in-Charge)

Station Number	Person-in-Charge
127	Jones
223	Smith
224	Lee
346	White
509	Hart

To delete SMITH, the entry is removed from station-head only, station-ID remains the same. Thus, we have a newly updated relation station-head as follows:

Station-head   (Station Number,   Person-in-Charge)

Station Number	Person-in-Charge
127	Jones
224	Lee
346	White
509	Hart

FIGURE 8-2. Overcoming the update abnormality.

8.1.1 Factors Influencing the Access Decisions

For database accesses, decisions may have to be based on a number of factors. There is *event-sensitive* information which for example, prevents access to be made by any user of the system in a particular group of users except between 7 A.M. and 7 P.M. and unless special terminal 72 is used. There is *value-sensitive* information where the access decision is based on the current value of the data. For example, a given user may not read the salary field (having the salary attribute) or any personnel record (any instance of the personnel relation) for which the salary value is greater than $20,000.00. There is *state-sensitive* information in which the dynamic state of the data base management system may play a major role. For instance, the user may open a particular file only at a time when the database in which the file resides is in an unlocked state. There is *pattern-sensitive* information which influences the access decision on the basis of the prescribed usage of the data. Consider the case where a user is authorized to call a sort program to sort a certain file and is allowed to read neither the program logic nor the file. In this case, the user is assigned the protection attribute execute-only. Further, the program is endowed only with the protection attribute to read data for the purpose of sorting. Although it reads data on behalf of the user, the program nevertheless cannot return the data to the user. Such a controlled way of utilization of data requires a high degree of sophistication in data security. There is also *history-sensitive* information. Individual accesses to the database of related items may allow the inference of supposedly protected information. Although the problem of using inference as a means to breach data security is not fully understood, the necessity of access history keeping by the database system for the purpose of arriving at certain particular inferences is known. For example, if we have a person–rank file and a rank–salary file in the database, any user can find any other person's salary by finding the rank of the person in the first file and locating the salary figure in the second file on the basis of the rank found in the first file. Such simple inference should not be allowed if the information on a person's salary is deemed to be confidential. A crude way to prevent such inference is to deny the user any access to the files. A more subtle way to disallow such inference and still allow controlled access to the database is to allow the user to access either one but not both files. To control subsequent access to the database, the database management system must keep track of past access history. History-sensitive information is therefore vital to data security.

8.1.2 A Case of Access-History-Sensitive Information

Consider the simple statistical database as depicted in the following table.

Nonconfidential			Confidential
Name	Sex	Profession	Overdraft
A	M	Lawyer	Yes
B	M	Journalist	No
C	M	President	No
D	M	Doctor	Yes
E	M	Lawyer	Yes
F	F	Lawyer	No
G	F	Senator	Yes
H	M	Lawyer	Yes
I	F	Doctor	No
J	M	Senator	No
K	F	Journalist	No
L	M	Budget director	Yes

Because information on overdrafts is considered confidential, the database management system may refuse to answer any query about a single individual's overdraft. However, the system may answer queries which involve over half the population of the database (in this example, seven or more individuals), since exact information on individuals may be disguished in the summaries on a large number of people. The following queries are therefore accepted by the system:

1. Give me the number of male professionals who are not budget directors.
   Answer: There are seven.
2. Give me the number of male professionals who either are not budget directors or have not had an overdraft.
   Answer: There are seven again.

By comparing the answers to the two queries, it is easy to infer that there are no male budget directors who had no overdrafts. In other words, Mr. L must have had an overdraft.

The security of a statistical database is therefore particularly sensitive to such things as the number of queries that the user puts forward to the database management system, the number of attributes that overlap among successive queries, and the number of attributes permitted in each query. To secure the statistical database from revealing exact information on individuals, the database management system must keep track of the aforementioned history-sensitive information so that the confidential information will not be compromised by inference.

8.1.3 Protection of Value-Sensitive Information

Several current experimental database management systems allow the protection of value-sensitive information.

A. View Mechanisms

Since attribute information about the characteristics and type of the data values are usually concentrated in the software templates known as *schemas,* the use of subschema can provide access control of values. By removing the attribute information of protected values from the schema, the remaining information in the schema constitutes a *subschema.* Furthermore, we may assign different subschemas for different users. Thus, these users have different *views* of the database since they do not see those values that are protected from them.

B. Query Modification

A second method of protection is by means of *query modification.* The following security specifications disallow a user the access to the HEW information of age under 50.

1. deny (NAME, SALARY, AGE) where DEPT = HEW.
2. deny (NAME, DEPT, SALARY) where AGE < 50.

Then protection is attained by having the system modify any query
about an employee to enforce these restrictions. Thus the request for
Smith's SALARY (retrieve SALARY where NAME = SMITH) would be
modified to include the restrictions about department and age. Effectively, the system would be required to process the query in a more
restrictive form (retrieve SALARY where NAME = SMITH and neither
DEPT = HEW nor AGE < 50).

It should be noted that both views and query modification have the
disadvantage that the system must retrieve information which is then
not passed on to the user. This problem is discussed more fully in Section 8.2.1.

8.1.4 Access Control in the Presence of Context Protection Requirements

The aforementioned sensitive information may be classified in two
categories: *context-dependent* and *context-independent*. The event,
value, and state-sensitive information is context independent in the
sense that the database management system merely examines the content of the event registers, the value fields, or the state of flip-flops in
order to make the on-the-spot access decisions. The system does not
need to have long "memory" to keep track of previous access decisions
in order to grant or deny a present request. The context-independent
access control mechanisms of the database management system are
therefore easier to design and implement. Furthermore, software implementation of (either the view or query modification) mechanism can
perform adequately without significant increase in response time, and
(security) cost.

The pattern and history-sensitive information is dependent on the
context in which the previous requests were made and granted, and the
present request is issued. Furthermore, the database management
system must know the relations of the data in order to exercise control
to related data in the context. Let us illustrate the importance of
context-dependent information for access decision making with an
example.

Assume there are five data items D_1 to D_5 which have the following
protection requirements:

1. If either item one is read or item two is executed, then item
    three cannot be read. Otherwise, item three can be read.
2. If item four is printed, then item five is not to be printed. If item

five is printed, then item four is not to be printed. In other words, only one of the items can be printed.

This database is depicted in Fig. 8–3a where a data item and protection attribute pair is represented by a node and relation between nodes is represented by an arrow. Thus, for example, requirement 1 is represented by the arrows from (D_3, R) to (D_1, R) and (D_2, E).

Sample Data Base: $\{D_1, D_2, D_3, D_4, D_5\}$,

   1. If either item one is read or item two is executed, then item three cannot be read. Otherwise, item three can be read.

   2. If item four is printed, then item five is not to be printed. If item five is printed, then item four is not to be printed. In other words, only one of the items can be printed.

Prior to any database–user interaction, the database is depicted as follows:

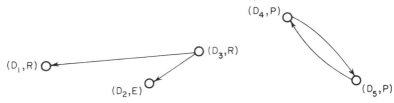

User

FIGURE 8-3.   (a) A sample database with context protection requirements.

Job one: (A) Execute D_2
          (B) Print D_5
          (C) Read D_1
Job two: (A) Print D_4
          (B) Read D_3

FIGURE 8-3.   (b) At the completion of Job one and before processing of Job two.

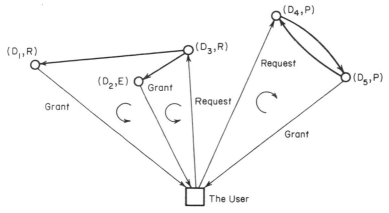

FIGURE 8-3.   (c) Requests generated by Job two.

Assume that the following two (much simplified) data management jobs are submitted:

Job one: (A) Execute D_2.
   (B) Print D_5.
   (C) Read D_1.
Job two: (A) Print D_4.
   (B) Read D_3.

It is obvious that the requests made by the first job may be granted without violating the protection relations. By the time Job two is being processed by the database management system, two new requests are made for data items D_3 and D_4, respectively. These two requests obviously cannot be granted, since granting of the requests will cause a breach of data security which was dictated by the protection requirements at the creation time of the sample data base. (See again Fig. 8–3a.)

It is also possible to represent a request for a data item by introducing an arrow from the user node to the data item and similarly to represent the granting of a request by reversing the arrow. Such a graph at the end of Job one is shown in Fig. 8–3b, while Fig. 8–3c represents the database after Job two requests data items D_3 and D_4.

What is not obvious is that this sample has a profound implication to the database system. How can the database system be designed and implemented so that the enforcement of such type of data security becomes automatic. This is still an open question. However, we do have some theoretical understanding of the problems involved which may lead to some effective solutions to context-dependent protection.

A. Violations of Context-Dependent Protection

The study of automatic recognition of violation in the context-dependent protection requirement has had some progress. Let us return to Fig. 8–3c. We observe that there is the potential of a *violation* of context-dependent protection requirement if the arrows among the user node and data item nodes form a *cycle*. More specifically, the request arrow leading from the user node to the data item D_4, the relation arrow from D_4 to D_5, and the grant arrow from D_5 to the user node form a cycle. Thus, graph-theoretically, the presence of a cycle indicates that a potential violation exists. Since there are three such cycles in the sample database, three potential violations exist. The capability of a database system to identify cycles allows the system to detect potential violations of these types.

B. Orderly Access Without Violation

As long as we represent the context dependent protection requirements among items of a database in terms of built-in directed graphs, this definition of violation enables the database access control mechanism to enforce the context dependent protection requirements and to detect violations. Violations exist when a user either maliciously or unintentionally attempts to access the protected data. Nevertheless, a regular user is permitted to use some data with appropriate protection attributes. Since the interrelationships among the various protection requirements may be very complex, a legitimate question that might be asked is, what is the maximum amount of data which may be accessed without any violation. Furthermore, it may be desirable to know the best access sequence in order to achieve this maximum.

To see how to answer the preceding questions consider the sample database with context-dependent protection requirements as depicted in Fig. 8–4a. The directed graph consists of 10 data item-protection attribute pairs (nodes) and 15 built-in protection requirements (arrows). Rewriting the graph (Fig. 8–4b) into different levels (arrows only go from top to bottom), it can be seen that the whole database can be accessed if the correct sequence of requests shown in Fig. 8–4c is made, i.e., e_3 and e_{10} first and e_7 last.

There is an algorithm which can be used to make the transformation shown in Fig. 8–4a to the one in Fig. 8–4b. With this sequence of requests, the user not only is granted the requested data but also has satisfied the context-dependent protection requirements for the data.

C. Some Data May Lead to Violations

Consider the protection requirement of a proprietary package in a database system environment. The proprietary package is meant to be

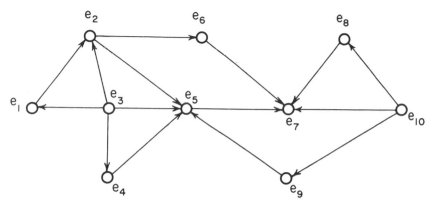

FIGURE 8-4. (a) The directed graph representation of a sample database with protection requirements.

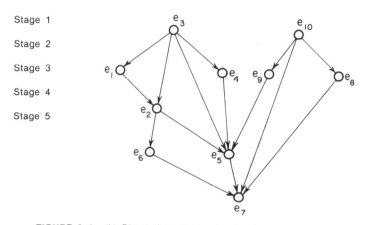

Stage 1
Stage 2
Stage 3
Stage 4
Stage 5

FIGURE 8-4. (b) Directed graph showing levels.

First request: $\{e_3, e_{10}\}$;
Second request: $\{e_1, e_4, e_8, e_9\}$;
Third request: $\{e_2\}$;
then: $\{e_5, e_6\}$, and
finally: $\{e_7\}$.

FIGURE 8-4. (c) The sequence of requests for the sample database in (a) without vio-lation.

used and shared by many users. However, due to its proprietary nature, access to the package must be controlled. There are two types of control. First, the protection of the package itself must be specified. In this case, no read, write, or print access rights should be given to regular users except the owner. The only access right that regular users can have is execute-only. Second, the use of the package must be monitored for accounting and other purposes. By invoking the owner-made monitor each time a proprietary package is used, the usage of the package can indeed be controlled and protected. It is therefore desirable for a database system to provide a mechanism for the automatic invocation of related programs. The first type of access control is available in conventional database systems where individual data items (programs or information) are associated with different protection attributes with respect to different users of the system. It is a form of context-independent protection. The second type of access control where invocation of another program before the present program can be executed is really a special case of a more general form of context protection requirement where access to one data item (program or information) cannot take place unless access to another data item has taken place. Thus, if these latter data items are well secured, then the other access will not lead to violation due to the system's ability to anticipate potential violations. With these studies, we are able to provide theoretical answers to the following questions.

Given a database with a set of context dependent protection relations, is it possible to find a maximal subset of the database such that permitted access to one item of the subset will not lead to any violation of a denied access to another item in the database? Given a database with a set of context protection relations, is it possible to find a sequence of accesses such that the protection requirement is enforced with no violation?

In summary, we have attempted to motivate the usefulness and the settings of the semantic relations in database applications and protection. We then show the properties of the context protection relations and algorithms that the access control mechanism of a database management system can employ to enforce the intended security in spite of such semantic relations and inferences in the database. Knowledge of the database semantics and the enforcement algorithms constitute the "intelligence" of the access control mechanism. We have pointed out that this type of access control mechanism can indeed treat shareable resources as a collection of semantically dependent entities. Security is achieved by denying access not just to the protected entities but also to the inferred entities which are semantically related to the protected ones. Modern database management systems have not yet incorporated such intelligent access control mechanisms.

8.2 ACCESS PATHS

After an access decision is made by the database management system, the granting of an access request will result in an actual access to the requested data. Ideally, the database management system should access those and only those data involved with the request. Such a desirable requirement is intended for performance and security reasons. For performance, the database management system is measured in terms of *precision*, i.e., the amount of data accessed versus the amount of data requested. Obviously, *absolute precision* means that every piece of data accessed is a piece of data requested. Every database management system designer and implementor aims to achieve absolute precision for that system, since high precision implies high performance. For security, the database management system is measured in terms of its capability to eliminate the *pass-through* problem. The pass-through problem occurs when the database management system, in order to get to certain data, must access some other data which have different protection requirements. The situation is critical if these latter protection requirements are more stringent than the requirements for the requested data. An example of the problem is to search for confidential documents by passing through a pile of classified documents with information being designated as top secret, secret, and confidential. In this case, highly classified documents with top-secret and secret designations are being looked at for the purpose of finding the more lowly classified, confidential documents. A goal of every designer and implementor is to build secure database systems which will incur no pass-through problem.

8.2.1 The Pass-Through Problem

The elimination of the pass-through problem makes it necessary for the system to access only those data whose protection requirements are the same as the requested one. Let us first relate the problem to databases, and consider the sample database with 10 records which are characterized by four attributes as depicted in Fig. 8–5a. We now structure the database in terms of the attributes, since attributes are the descriptors that the user employs to specify his request. For example, he may request all those records which deal with salary and rank. By linking the records in terms of the attributes, and by providing a directory to keep track of the unique attributes, we can gain a functional impression of how the database system makes access to the records. Naturally, the system receives the user request, identifies the attributes in the requests, consults the directories for the attributes, and accesses records by way of the linkages established for the attributes. In this way, the records accessed are indeed records with the requested attributes. This is depicted in Fig. 8–5b. Numbered circles are records mentioned in Fig. 8–5a. An arrow with a marked attribute between two

1. A_1, A_2, A_3, A_4 are attributes which characterize the records. These may be security attributes on troop movement, intelligence, aliens, and domestic.

2. There are 10 records identified by record numbers ranging from 1 through 10.

3. Other information in the individual records is not known.

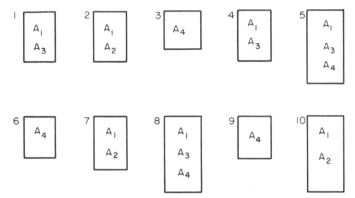

FIGURE 8-5.   (a) A sample database to illustrate the pass-through problem.

records represents the fact that these two records are characterized by the same attribute. The directory is a special record.

Now consider the security. If the owner desires to deny a user those records that have the following property:[1]

$$A_2 \wedge ((A_1 \wedge \bar{A}_4) \vee (\bar{A}_3 \wedge A_4)),$$

he essentially provides the user a partial view of his database as depicted in Fig. 8–5c. We note that the records 2, 7, and 10 do indeed possess the above property. Thus, these three records do not appear in the user's view.

Whenever the user makes a request, say, all records having either the attribute A_1 or the attribute A_2 or both, the data management system will access every record having A_1 or A_2 or both A_1 and A_2 as attributes. In this case, the system effectively has accessed five records, i.e., records 1, 2, 4, 7, and 10. However, for each record accessed, the system also checks the record against the above security property. Because records, 2, 7, and 10 do satisfy the property, they are denied to the user. Instead, the user is granted access to records 1 and 4.

Although the unauthorized records were made inaccessible to the user by the system, the mode of accessing is insecure. (a) The system retrieves records with different protection requirements. (b) The system

---

[1] A_1 be the attribute "troop movement," A_2 be "intelligence," A_3 be "aliens," and A_4 be "domestic." Then the property says essentially "all those intelligence records which either deal with nondomestic troop movement or are concerned with domestic nonalien matters."

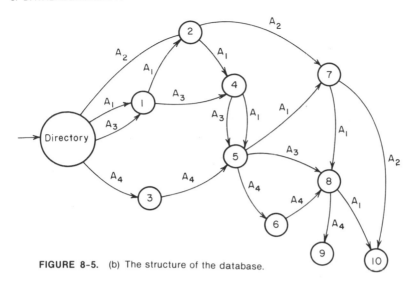

FIGURE 8-5. (b) The structure of the database.

Now consider the security specification $(U1, Q, \text{Deny})$ where $Q = A_2 \wedge ((A_1 \wedge \bar{A}_4) \vee (\bar{A}_3 \wedge A_4))$.

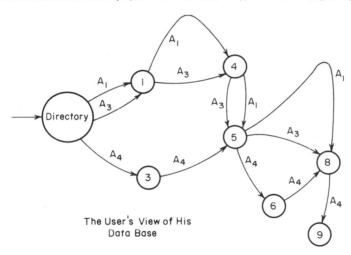

The User's View of His
Data Base

FIGURE 8-5. (c) An illusion of secure view.

brings these three records (along with two other records) to the main
memory for the purpose of checking against the security property. (c)
Upon discovering that these records are not authorized for the user, the
system rejects the records by destroying them in the main memory.
Problem (a) causes records with different protection requirements to be

handled in the same batch, thus, the pass-through problem. Problem (b) invites the possibility of security breach due to data spillage and system malfunction in the main memory. Problem (c) incurs imprecision, i.e., retrieving more than necessary.

It is interesting to note that if the database is organized in such a way that data of the same protection requirements are partitioned into groups and that the database management system knows the security property of each group, then for a given request the system can determine the groups whose security properties do not deny the request. In this way, the system will go to the secondary storage and access the records of those groups directly.

8.2.2 The Need for Compartmentalization

The partitioning of records into groups, so that records of a group have the same protection requirements and records of different groups have different requirements, requires a method for the compartmentalization of the database.

A. The Security Atom Concept

The *security atom concept* is a viable means of compartmentalization. A security atom of records is characterized by the *canonical expression* of the attributes of the records. By assigning different protection attributes to different security atoms, we can protect the records of an atom uniformly. Furthermore, by keeping track of the whereabouts of the security atoms, the system can access records of one atom without passing through records of another atom. Let us illustrate the last point with the same sample database depicted in Fig. 8–5a. This time we reorganize the database in accordance with the security atom concept. Without a detailed discussion, we note that for this database, the ten records can be characterized by only four canonical expressions. Thus, there are four corresponding security atoms. Records of an atom are linked together exclusively in the atom. The directory points to the security atoms individually and contains additional information as depicted in Fig. 8–6. Now, assume the user makes the same request as indicated earlier, i.e., all records having either the attribute A_1 or the attribute A_2 or both. Also assume the owner uses the same security specification

$$A_2 \wedge ((A_1 \wedge \bar{A}_4) \vee (\bar{A}_3 \wedge A_4))$$

to deny the user from access to records satisfying the specification. (See again Fig. 8–5a.) Then, in the newly compartmentalized database, the

Information about the four security atoms depicted in the following table is included in the new directory.

Security atom	Canonical expressions	Protection attributes	Addresses of records in the atom
1	$A_1 \wedge \bar{A}_2 \wedge A_3 \wedge \bar{A}_4$	Read-only	1, 4
2	$A_1 \wedge A_2 \wedge A_3 \wedge \bar{A}_4$	Read/Insert	2, 7, 10
3	$\bar{A}_1 \wedge \bar{A}_2 \wedge A_3 \wedge A_4$	Read/Insert/Delete	3, 6, 9
4	$\bar{A}_1 \wedge \bar{A}_2 \wedge A_3 \wedge A_4$	Execute-only	5, 8

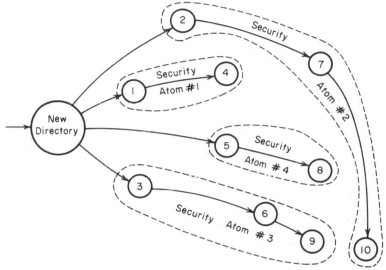

FIGURE 8-6. New organization of the database.

database management system will first determine the number of security atoms involved with the request $(A_1 \vee A_2)$. Such determination requires access only to the directory. In this example, we note that the security atoms # 1 and # 2 will have records satisfying the request. The system will then determine the number of the security atoms involved with owner security specification for the user. In this case, we note that the only expression which has a corresponding entry in the directory is $(A_1 \wedge A_2 \wedge A_3 \wedge A_4)$. Thus, the owner effectively denies the user from accessing any record in atom # 2. This, again can be determined from information in the directory.

By removing atom # 2 from the set of atoms which will have records satisfying the user request, the system finally arrives at the atom # 1. It is this atom whose records are authorized for the user request. We note in Fig. 8–6 that the system knows exactly the whereabouts of the atom # 1. Consequently, records 1 and 4 are accessed and given to the user in response to the read request.

B. Improved Access Precision

It is important to observe that pre-processing of the user request and owner's specification for the determination of the authorized security atoms enables the system to access the authorized atoms without passing through other atoms. This procedure not only eliminates the pass-through problem, but also improves access precision. However, for the sake of data security, preprocessing of user requests and owner security specification is a price we must pay. The approach of modifying the user request by other specifications (security or otherwise) in order to narrow down the access range is knows as the query modification technique which was introduced in the previous section. Except in this case, the user query is not only modified for security reasons, but the modification also improves the access precision.

8.2.3 Multilevel Security

The traditional need of *multilevel security* in the DOD environment requires that information of different levels of security should be kept and accessed in different compartments. Furthermore, these compartments should be allowed different degrees of physical security in proportion to the level of data security. For example, top secret information should be harder to access physically than confidential. This notion of multilevel security can be easily accommodated using the security atom concept. Since records of a security atom are always protected the same way, they together are always classified in one and only one level. In other words, classification levels themselves are protection attributes which may further aggregate the atoms into subfile entities for protection. The desirable thing about this use of security atoms is that these subfile entities are again mutually exclusive, access to records of one classification level will not pass through records of another level. This is because the combination of security atoms into a subfile entity merely forms a *security molecule*. No two security molecules will have a record in common since no single security atom will participate in more than one molecule. Physical security can now be achieved by placing records of different classification levels on different devices. This is possible because the security atom concept enables the logical separation of records on the basis of security requirements to be transformed into physical compartmentalization of records by hardware devices. In Fig. 8–7, we have two security atoms and one security molecule of different classification levels. Because access paths of these atoms are independent of each other, these atoms can be stored on separate devices for physical security as well.

Size of the subfile	Expressions	Security classification
Security molecule	$(A_1 \wedge \bar{A}_2 \wedge A_3)$	Top secret
Security atom	$(A_1 \wedge A_2 \wedge \bar{A}_3 \wedge \bar{A}_4)$	Secret
Security atom	$(\bar{A}_1 \wedge \bar{A}_2 \wedge \bar{A}_3 \wedge A_4)$	Confidential

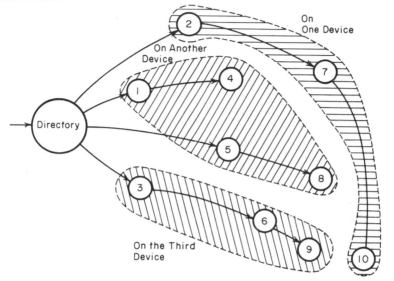

FIGURE 8-7. Multilevel security without the pass-through problem.

8.3 ACCESS AUTHORIZATION AND RESOLUTION

We introduce the *concept of ownership* to facilitate the transfer of protection attributes to different users. A user can grant and deny other users access to a data aggregate if he is the *owner* of the data aggregate. To become an owner of a data aggregate, the user must satisfy and comply with a set of rules and regulations which may vary from one installation to another. When a user becomes an owner of a data aggregate, the system assigns an *OWN* attribute for the aggregate in the *authority item* created for the user. The authority items are system data. (see Section 7.2 for the notion of the authority item.) In one model, the creator of an aggregate will automatically become the owner of the aggregate. As an owner of the aggregate, the user can grant and deny any other users access to that aggregate. In other words, a user with *OWN* attribute on an aggregate can assign any protection attribute to other users for the aggregate. In particular, he may cause another user to be a co-owner of the aggregate by assigning *OWN* attribute to the user. The exercise of data management operations by a user is dictated by the user's assigned attributes in his authority items.

8.3.1 The Authorization Hierarchies

It is important to note that the concept of ownership varies greatly among different database management environments. For example, the above notion of ownership establishes for the database management system *an authorization hierarchy* as depicted in Fig. 8–8, where the system administrator owns all the databases, can perform all data management operations, may authorize other users to use the databases, and is *subjected to further managerial rules and regulations.* (See Chapter 3 on Operational Security.) The owners, on the other hand, own private databases, can perform all data management operations on their own databases, and may authorize other users to access their databases. Finally, the nonowner users do not own the databases, can perform *some* data management operations, and may *not* authorize others to use the databases.

In addition to the above *three-level, co-ownership authorization hierarchy,* there are other authorization hierarchies: the *multilevel subownership authorization hierarchy* and the *two-level transfer-*

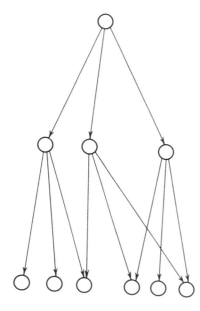

System administrator
1. Owns all databases
2. Can perform all data management operations
3. May authorize other users to use the databases
4. *Is subjected to further rules and regulations*

Database Owners
1. Own private databases
2. Can perform *all* data management operations
   on their databases
3. May authorize other users to use their databases

Nonowner users
1. Do not own the databases
2. Can perform *some* data management operations
3. May not authorize others to use the databases

FIGURE 8-8.   A three-level co-ownership authorization hierarchy.

ownership authorization hierarchy. The multilevel subownership authorization hierarchy establishes the following discipline:

1. Each database has an owner. The owner of a database may assign a portion of the database to a user and designate him as a subowner. The subowner can further divide his portion of the database into finer aggregates and designate others as (sub) owners of the partitions.

2. Subownership can only be removed by the owner who originally authorized the subownership.

3. Ownership and subownership can be established, replaced, and removed. However, co-ownership is not allowed.

4. Owners (or subowners) can perform *all* the database management operations on their private (portions of) databases.

This hierarchy has the distinction that at every level of data aggregates (e.g., records, subfiles, files, and databases), there is some single user who is directly responsible for the control of the data aggregates.

The two-level transfer-ownership authorization hierarchy enables the creator of a database to become immediately the owner of the database. The owner is the only one who may authorize others as users of his database with various protection attributes to data aggregates. Furthermore, he can transfer the ownership of his database to another user. Once transferred, he no longer can access the database. In fact, he is not even a user of the database. The advantage of this hierarchy lies in its simplicity. There are no subowners, making the concentration of authorization apparent. There are no co-owners, thereby precluding the awkward situation where two co-owners attempt to cancel or interfere with each other in terms of authorization.

8.3.2 Mechanisms and Policies

A. The Access Control Procedure

Regardless of the type of access the user may desire, and the authorization hierarchy he is in, the user is subjected to the following *access control procedure.* The procedure is the heart of access control mechanisms of the database management system:

1. Identify the user's request.

2. Check to see whether the user has access to the data aggregates involved. (Let us call the largest aggregates, files; next largest, subfiles; next, records; then, fields).

3. If the user has access to a file, then check to see whether the file is currently open for his use.

4. If the file is open, then check to see if the user has the proper file-level protection attribute with respect to the call (e.g., read-only for retrieval, write for input, etc.).

5. If the user has the correct attribute for using the file, set up certain necessary information for the system programs involved.

6. Call the proper system programs to perform the requested service.

7. Keep track of the status of the service. Since a data management service may not be completed without repeated calls, it is necessary to save some information for the continuation of the service at a later time.

8. Update and save the information that was originally set up for the system programs.

9. Continue the service on next open file, if Step 3 involves more than one open file.

10. Make sure that a record to be output is one belonging to the open portion of a file, not temporarily blocked from use by others, and not permanently protected from access.

11. Satisfy the procedural checking at record level.

12. Make certain that fields protected from access are removed from the output record.

13. Satisfy the procedural checking at field level.

Let us discuss some of the steps in the procedure.

Steps 1 and 4 require the system to identify the types of protection attributes which are necessary for carrying out the particular database management request. As was indicated in previous sections, the data management operations that a user can exercise are determined by the type of protection attributes assigned to him. To this end, the system consults the user's authority item. Since protection attributes regarding a file are always associated with the name of the file as a part of the entry in the authority item, the system can determine whether the user has proper attributes for making that request.

For Step 2, the system again consults the authority item. We note that only the names of the files accessible to the user are listed in the authority item. In other words, inaccessible files are completely invisible to the user.

Step 3 in the procedure provides for a file owner the first opportunity to employ authentication programs to screen all users of the file. Typically, a file authentication program consists of a set of owner-written routines which are loaded into the system by the file owner through the use of a special command at the file creation time.

The program may demand various inputs from the user. It then indicates whether there is a positive or negative authentication. Since programs written for authentication can use database management facilities, they can store and retrieve information regarding the number of file opening attempts and combination of user passwords. The program entry points for file-level checking are placed in the authority item. Thus, thoughtful use of authentication programs at file level can provide very good protection of the file as a whole.

Steps 5 through 9 are self-explanatory. We shall not elaborate here. In Step 10, the procedure carries the access control from the file level as in Step 3 to the subfile level. By using predicates of attributes and values as a means to partition a file into subfiles (say, the security atoms), the system can control access to the subfiles. However, in this case the partitions are virtual and no subfiles are actually being generated. The reasons for not physically making duplicate subfiles are to safeguard the integrity of the data base on the one hand and to facilitate update on the other hand. Virtual subfiles can be created readily by introducing new predicates. In fact, there can be a multiplicity of subfiles for various access control purposes as illustrated in Fig. 8–9.

On a needed basis, many subfiles may be defined for the same files. The multiplicity of subfiles for various access control re-

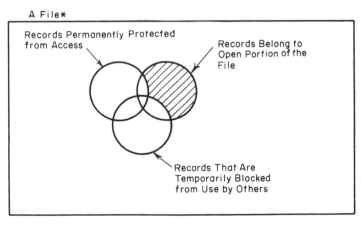

*The subfiles of records in a file specified by three types of expression.

FIGURE 8-9. Overlapping protection requirements.

quirements may grow large. However, the mechanism needed by the system to verify whether a record belongs to a subfile is straightforward. Basically, the checking of a record with respect to a predicate can be characterized by the following table:

Predicate intended for ...	Does the record satisfy the predicate?	Checking of the record
Permanent protection from use	Yes No	Not Passed Passed
Temporarily open for use	Yes No	Passed Not Passed
Temporarily blocked by others from use	Yes No	Not Passed Passed
.	.	.
.	.	.
.	.	.

In Step 11, the system allows programs incorporated by the owner to check records which become accessible to a user, whereas in Step 3, access control is at the file level, and in Step 10, access control is at the subfile level. By allowing the owner to develop his own record-checking program, records which are already accessible to other users can be subject to further checking and auditing.

In Step 12, the system performs a posteriori checking of protected field names. We note that the checking can only take place after the record has been retrieved from secondary storage into the system's working area. In contrast to a posteriori checking, a priori checking of field names and values at request time involves the removal of all the protected attributes and values from the predicates of the user's database management requests before the first step of the procedure is to be invoked. (See the section on Query Modification.) In this way, no access will be initiated by any invalid predicates. Step 13 is the last step in the procedure. It is in this step that access control is finally brought to the user at the field level. Because many access control requirements are dependent upon some combination of field names and/or values, matching of names and computing of values must take place dynamically. By incorporating these at the field level, the owner can have direct control of other user's access to an individual datum.

The implementation of the access control procedure in a database management system may vary widely depending on whether the implementation takes place in the software or in the hardware. The discussion on software versus hardware implementation is given in the Section 8.4. We do not repeat the discussion here. The implementation also depends on how much or how little is to be implemented. For example, few conventional systems provide either software means or hardware means for automatic invocation of file-level, record-level, or field-level authentication and checking programs. Subfile control for restricting access to the part of a file (which supports real-time conditions such as temporary blocking, permanent denial, and current opening) is not found in commercial systems.

B. Resolution and Disclosure Policies

Due to their semantic relations, some data may participate in several uses having different security requirements for the same data. Consider the case (depicted in Fig. 8–10) where two sets of data satisfy two different requests Q_1 and Q_2, respectively, and have two different sets of protection attributes, A_1 and A_2, respectively. For the common data (the shaded area of Fig. 8–10), the question is (a) whether to allow access based solely on the protection attributes in A_1 if they satisfy Q_1? (b) whether to allow access on the basis of the common attributes between A_1 and A_2? or (c) whether to allow no access since overlapping data may disclose to Q_2 information intended for Q_1 and vice versa?

To answer such questions requires the access control mechanisms of a database management system to have some *resolution* capability. This capability must be based on a *resolution policy*. Several such policies are possible. One aspect of the policy is whether or not one access attribute *implies* another, e.g., write implies read, secret clearance implies confidential clearance. In the case where two different requirements of protection attributes are applicable to the requested data, the *least-disclosure* policy states that access to the data is permitted based on the most stringent requirements (i.e., the "greatest

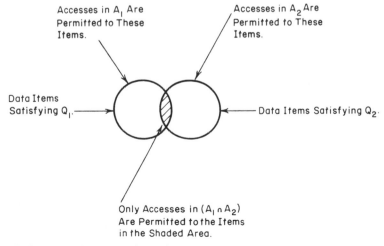

FIGURE 8-10. Access resolution for shared data.

common divisor" of the protection attributes). The *need-to-know* policy would allow access to be made on the basis of any protection attribute which is in the union of the protection attributes of the requirements. The *maximal-sharing* policy permits data access to be made if the user request is associated with the proper protection attribute which either matches or implies the protection attributes of the requirements (i.e., the "least common multiple" of the protection requirements.)

Consider the example in Fig. 8–10:

"Write some information into those satisfying Q_2."

If the user request is as above, then the least-disclosure policy will limit the writing into the unshaded data set of D_2. The need-to-know and maximal-sharing policies will allow the entire data set D_2 including the shaded portion to be written. The difference between the need-to-know policy and the maximal-sharing policy is that the former requires an exact matching of protection attributes (e.g., a requested read must match with an authorized read), whereas the latter is not limited to matching. Instead, a hierarchy of protection attributes are known to the policy. This hierarchy establishes a *partial ordering* so that a request with an attribute may be honored if the attribute is implied by an authorized attribute. For example, the attribute of reading secret information always implies the attribute of reading the confidential one.

8.4 IMPLEMENTATION AND PLACEMENT OF SECURITY FEATURES

The theoretical understanding and conceptual breakthrough in data security discussed in the previous sections for the most part can be realized in the computer system. Since a database management facility consists of three large elements, i.e., the databases, the software system, and the hardware components, we must develop an integrated approach to the incorporation of the concepts, algorithms, and procedures into these elements. Such an integrated approach is still not in sight. Thus, the design and implementation of a secure database management facility remains an art. However, there are promising indications.

8.4.1 New Secure Database Design Methodology

The design methodology of a secure database in particular and databases in general can be found in *data abstraction*. It is a process which allows multistage synthesis and analysis of the data abstractions so that at each stage of the abstraction the essential details of the abstraction become apparent, allowing the designer to perform analysis and synthesis of abstraction for the next stage. The most important contribution of this process is that there are only a *small* number of essential details at the given stage. These small numbers enable the designer to concentrate on the design instead of on the book-keeping of database details. Since real-world databases are large and complex, this design process allows orderly analysis and synthesis of the databases in a manageable way.

The uses of the security atom concept and security model concept in design and organization of databases are also promising.

8.4.2 The Use of Predicates for Control

Predicates have been used in data languages for specifying data aggregates so that subsequent access or update can be performed on the specified data. It is a means to address a data aggregate by the properties of the data aggregate. Such an addressing scheme enables the user to access or update the data by *content*, making progress towards content-addressable search and update of databases. However, recently researchers and designers have begun to realize that the predicates should also be utilized for the purpose of access control and security compartmentalization of databases. The fundamental gain in utilizing predicates for access control is that any data that are accessible or updatable can be controlled. Thus, controlled sharing of on-line, multiuser, and interactive databases may become a reality. The ultimate gain in utilizing the predicates for security compartmentalization is that any retrievable and manipulatable data can be compartmentalized for security purposes. In this way, not only will data in a compartment have the same protection requirement, but the compartments may be individually secured with additional physical means. Thus, for the first time, a clear and close relationship between data security and physical security of the database is allowed.

One of the major limitations of utilizing predicates for accessing, updating, controlling, and partitioning is that the software requirements are high. It is therefore not surprising that contemporary database management systems (DBMS) are large and complex (see Fig. 8–11.) The size and complexity causes the DBMS to be unreliable and inefficient. Such systems are likely to be insecure. To reduce its size and complexity, a contemporary DBMS sacrifices security by either relying on the operating system to provide all the security or by eliminating many data security features. The reliance on the operating system for security creates a situation of double jeopardy since the

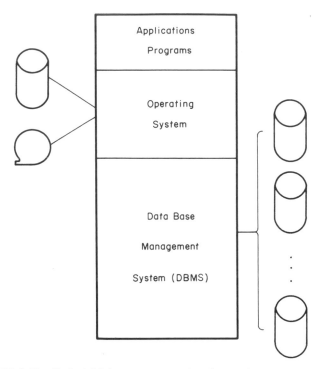

FIGURE 8-11. Typical database management environment.

operating system itself is a large piece of software. Consequently, a highly secure DBMS is not available.

8.4.3 Technology and Hardware Research Play an Important Role

Advances in technology have provided the database system designers and implementors with new options. These advances are beginning to show cost/performance advantages for the specialized hardware database machine over the large software DBMS running on a conventional computer.

In addition to the advances made in processor technology, such as microprocessors and microprogrammable mini's and micro's, there have been several advances in memory technology. In Fig. 8–12, we depict a broad spectrum of online memory technology. Further, the hardware research enables the designer and implementor to realize two things: (a) place logic on the memories, whether they are magnetic disk memories or electronic shift-register-like memories and (b) configure the new technology and modify the existing technology for specialized database management tasks such as security-related processing.

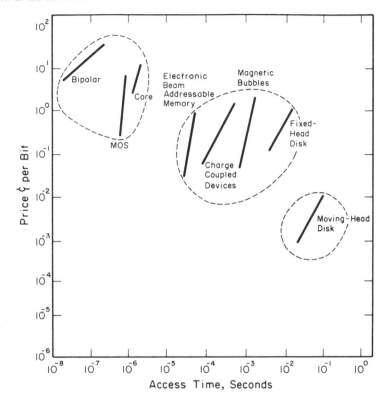

FIGURE 8-12. Technology price-performance projection over the next decade.

The hardware replacement of software components of the DBMS has several benefits:

1. The components are more reliable.
2. The components have improved performance.
3. Security mechanisms may be incorporated in the hardware without noticeable performance degradation (in other words, the hardware can absorb the software "overhead" which made the original introduction of the security procedures into software impractical).
4. The entire system is more reliable, higher in performance, and secured. This is because the replacement of the software by the new hardware allows the original system to have more available main memory, fewer peripherals, and more CPU cycles (see Fig. 8–13).

In Fig. 8–14, we depict a "hardwired" database management system, a *database machine*. The machine is typified by (a) the use of processor–memory pairs for both large database store and directory memory, (b) the use of functionally specialized boxes for query interpretation and optimization for security filtering and for other purposes,

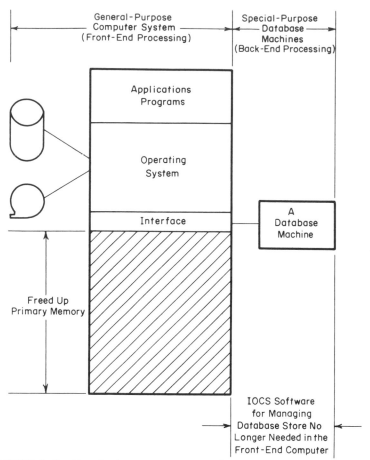

General-Purpose
Computer System
(Front-End Processing)

Special-Purpose
Database
Machines
(Back-End Processing)

Applications
Programs

Operating
System

Interface

A
Database
Machine

Freed Up
Primary Memory

IOCS Software
for Managing
Database Store No
Longer Needed in the
Front-End Computer

FIGURE 8-13.   New database management environment.

and (c) the use of built-in parallelism among the processor–memory pairs.

Item (b) allows a priori and a posteriori security checking to be built in the hardware. A priori checking such as query modification and security atom processing can greatly improve the system throughout and completely eliminate the pass-through problem. A posteriori checking is necessary for field-level security. With functionally specialized hardware, we can efficiently process the field values and allow the protection to be based on some function of these values.

Item (c) permits concurrent high-volume processing. It is important to note that with each hardware component absorbing the software overhead incurred in the original system, the hardware should have

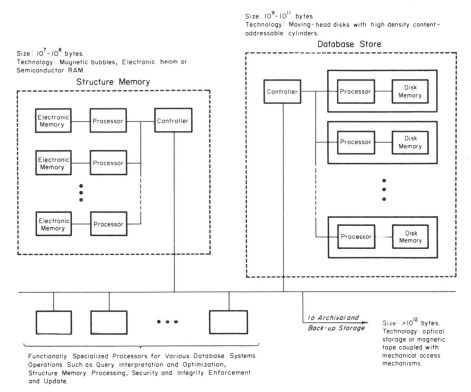

Size: $10^9 - 10^{11}$ bytes.
Technology: Moving-head disks with high density content-addressable cylinders.

Database Store

Size: $10^7 - 10^8$ bytes.
Technology: Magnetic bubbles, Electronic beam or Semiconductor RAM.

Structure Memory

Io Archival and Back-up Storage

Size: $>10^{12}$ bytes.
Technology: optical storage or magnetic tape coupled with mechanical access mechanisms.

Functionally Specialized Processors for Various Database Systems Operations Such as Query Interpretation and Optimization, Structure Memory Processing, Security and Integrity Enforcement and Update.

FIGURE 8-14. Future database machine. Structure memory—size: $10^7 - 10^8$ bytes; technology: magnetic bubbles, electronic beam, or semiconductor RAM. Database store—size: $10^9 - 10^{11}$ bytes; technology: moving-head disks with high density content-addressable cylinders.

enough raw performance to allow addition of new security features. The built-in parallelism through concurrent processing of many process–memory pairs with large memory blocks allow the database machine to employ new security provisions, to achieve high performance, and to support very large on-line store.

8.5 POSTSCRIPT

The study of the role of database semantics in security may have been originated in [Baum 75a] and [Hsiao 76a]. It indicates the limitation of protection through concealment due to semantic inferences. Furthermore, the study shows that the information-theoretic approach to access control is not practical. Access history keeping, a necessary part for preventing inferences is considered by [Hartso 75] and [Hartso 76b]. Theoretical study of statistical inferences can be found in [Chin

78], [DeMill 78], [Dennin 78], [Dobkin 76], [Haq 75], [Kam 77], and [Yu 77].

The use of the graph-theoretic approach to study context protection relations is influenced by the use of directed graphs in the study of operating system deadlocks. The concept of atom is not new. However, the extension of the atom concept to compartmentalization for security reasons is due to [McCaul 75b]. Authorization hierarchies are studied in terms of partial ordering of access privileges as lattices which are touched upon in [McCaul 75a] for database systems and expounded on in [Dennin 75] for information flows. The notion of the separation of mechanisms and policies is emphasized by [Jones 73]. The notion of amplification is also originally due to [Jones 73].

Other access decision factors such as the event-dependent factor are also considered by [Hartso 76a]. The use of preprocessing such as compilation to exercise value-dependent access control is due largely to an earlier work of [Conway 76]. Follow-up work can be found in [Kenned 74], [Summer 74], and [Woodwa 74]. Although the use of subschema or derived templates [Hsiao 75a] of structural information for the purpose of access control of values has been practiced for some time, such practice is now known as view mechanisms whose popularity may mainly be due to [Chambe 75]. Query modification allows the database management system to preprocess the user's request for access control reasons [Hsiao 75a]. This technique has also been used for some time. However, the term and its use perhaps owe their wide acceptance to [Stoneb 74] and [Stoneb 75].

Software mechanisms for data security are many. The use of data encryption for simple file structures can be found in [Bayer 76]. The inclusion in a host programming language of access control constructs has been suggested by [Conway 76], [Hartso 76a], [Hartso 76b], [Jones 75c], [Jones 76], [Stoneb 76b], and [Summer 74], and of privacy definition constructs has been proposed by [Fong 77] and [Goldbe, 75]. For data security, that control of program execution as well as program logic must be facilitated is suggested in [Minsky 74a], [Minsky 74b], [Minsky 74c], and [Minsky 76]. Authorization mechanisms can be found in [Griffi 76], [Stoneb 76a], and [Stoneb 76b]. Systems models are proposed in [Fernan 75], [Grohn 76], [Manola 75], [McCaul 75a], and [Schaef 75]. Software security cost is studied in [Hartso 76c] and [Hennin 76]; software engineering of secure systems can be found in [Hsiao 76d] and [Turn 74a]. The use of the verification technique to prove the correctness of secure programs can be found in [Horger 75].

Operational means for data security include audit-trail [Bjork 75] and [Burns 76]. The relationship between database management and the notion of databank in terms of security are expounded on in [Turn 73], [Turn 74b], [Turn 74c], and [Turn 75b]. References can be found on related topics such as physical integrity [Lorie 76] and [Lorie 77], reference monitor [Kirkby 77c], military applications [Mack 76] and [Manola 77], and civilian applications [Moore 77].

Research into specialized hardware for database management is picking up momentum. The technology base on which the database machine may be founded is described in [Kannan 77a]. A number of research proposals and experimental undertakings are reviewed and motivated in [Baum 76b], [Hsiao, 77c] and [Hsiao 77d], and are speculated on in [Hsiao 77e]. A specific database machine with built-in security provisions is outlined in [Baum 75b] and [Baum 76a], specified in [Baum 76c], [Hsiao 76b], and published in [Banerj 78e], [Banerj 79], [Kannan 77b], [Hsiao 77b], and [Kannan 78]. The storage requirements and the performance gains of the database machine in competing with conventional hierarchical, CODASYL, and relational systems are estimated in [Hsiao 77a], [Banerj 78d], and [Banerj 78b], and [Banerj 78c], respectively. The advocacy of the use of database machines in a computer network environment can be found in [Banerj 78a].

Other references related to data security that can be found in other chapters are listed herein. On operational and physical security, we have [Bushki 75], [NBS 75b], [Nielse 76a], and [Nielse 76b]. On data encryption, we have [Culpep 77], [Gudes 76], [Gudes 76b], [Stahl 74], and [Turn 73]. On operating systems security, [Ames 74], [Andrew 74], [Bell 73], [Bell 74a], [Bell 76], [Bisbey 75], [Burris 76b], [Dennin 76a], [Ekanad 76], [Gladne 75], [Hoffma 73], [Hoffma 77a], [IBM 74], [Jeffer 74b], [Katzan 73], [Lampso 77], [Larson 74], [NBS 76a], [Saltze 74b], [Stork 75], [White 75a], and [White 75b].

On privacy issues, [Bushki 75a], [Bushki 76a], [Bushki 76b], [Davis 76a], [Goldst 76], [Higgin 76], [Hoffma 77b], [Rennin 74a], [Rennin 74b], [Thomps 76], [Trigg 75], [Turn 75a], and [Ware 73].

REFERENCES

AFIPS 75

"Tutorial on Data Base Protection and Security." In conjunction with the 2nd USA–Japan Computer Conference, American Federation of Information Processing Societies and Information Processing Society of Japan, August 1975, Tokyo, Japan.

> The tutorial contains five papers covering various aspects of database security. Two of these are referenced separately—see [Fiesta 75] and [Hsiao 76a]—as they were published elsewhere.

Ames 77

Ames, S. R., Jr., "User Interface Multilevel Security Issues in a Transaction-Oriented Data Base Management System." *Data Base Engineering*, Vol. 1, No. 3, September 1977, pp. 7–14.

> This paper presents a general description of the system described more fully in [Ames 78].

ANSI 75

"ANSI–X3–SPARC's Interim Report: Study Group on Data Base Management Systems." *ACM SIGFDT*, Vol. 7, No. 2, February 1975.

> This document contains the report from the Standards Planning and Requirements Committee (SPARC) of the American National Standards Computers and Information Processing Committee (ANSI/X3) on database management systems. This report includes sections covering the topics of security, integrity, and recovery.

Banerj 78a

Banerjee, J., Hsiao, D. K., and Ng, F. K. "Data Network—A Computer Network of General-Purpose Front-End Computers and Special-Purpose Back-End Database Machines." *Proceedings of International Symposium on Computer Network Protocols*, Liege, Belgium, February, 13–15, 1978.

Banerj 78b

Banerjee, J., and Hsiao, David K., "The Use of a Database Machine for Supporting Relational Databases." *Proceedings of the 5th Annual Workshop on Computer Architecture for Non-numeric Processing.* Syracuse, New York, August 1978.

> Similar to [Banerj 78a] and [Banerj 78d] the storage requirement and performance gains in using a database machine, known as DBC, versus conventional software systems are studied. System R [Chambe 75] is used for comparative study. This paper should be followed by its continuation in [Banerj 78c].

Banerj 78c

Banerjee, J., and Hsiao, David K., "Performance Study of a Database Machine in Supporting Relational Databases." *Proceedings of the 4th International Conference on Very Large Data Bases*, Berlin, Germany, September 1978.

Banerj 78d

Banerjee, J., and Hsiao, David K., "A Methodology for Supporting Existing CODASYL Databases With New Database Machines." *Proceedings of 1978 National ACM* Conference, December, 1978, Washington, D.C.

> This paper demonstrates the capability of a database computer [Banerj 78e], [Banerj 79] to support a network database model such as that outlined by the CODASYL Database Task Group. Although this report is not directly concerned with the security features of such a model, the way in which the database computer can support these features is described.

Banerj 78e

Banerjee, J., Baum, R., and Hsiao, David K., "Concepts and Capabilities of a Database Computer." *ACM Transactions on Database Systems* (TODS), **3,** 4, December 1978.

> This paper provides the functional design of a special-purpose database computer (DBC). An overview of the architecture of the database computer is presented in this first report. The authors assert that the design described within overcomes many of the problems with conventional database systems implemented on general-purpose computers. Additionally, it is one of the first designs of a data-secure computer on which large on-line databases ($10^9 - 10^{10}$ bytes) may be implemented.
>
> The first portion of the paper describes many of the problems of database software and those facing the designers of a database computer. With this as background, concepts for the solving of the problems are presented.
>
> Next, the functional characteristics of the DBC are described and show the DBC as a back-end machine to a conventional general-purpose computer.
>
> The third section discusses the actual operation of the DBC. This is done in terms of a series of abstract models representing the components and data structures used. The access operations, security specifications, and management of data structures of the DBC are examined. The algorithms used are also presented.
>
> The final portion of the paper presents a reasonably high-level examination of the hardware used in the DBC. The DBC is made up of several processors which are combined to form two data flow loops. One, known as the *structure loop,* may be viewed as containing directory and security information about the actual database which is contained in the *data loop.* This report provides an overview of these two loops while the details are contained in the second and third reports [Hsiao 76b], [Hsiao 76c]. It should be noted that one important feature of the DBC design is that it uses presently available or currently emerging technology rather than depending on some major technological breakthrough in the distant future.

An elaborate appendix is included in the paper to illustrate the working of security and clustering mechanisms of the DBC.

Reports showing the capability of the DBC to support the known hierarchical, network, and relational data models are contained in [Hsiao 77a], [Banerj 78a], and [Banerj 78b], respectively.

Banerj 79

Banerjee, J., Hsiao, David K., and Kannan, K., "DBC—A Database Computer For Very Large Databases." *IEEE Transactions on Computers*, C–28, **6,** 1979.

A rather detailed hardware architectural description of the DBC is provided in this paper.

Baum 75a

Baum, R.I., and Hsiao, D.K., "A Semantic Model for Protection Mechanisms in the Database System." *Proceedings of the Eighth Hawaii Conference on System Science*, Hawaii, January 1975, pp. 175–179.

A database model derived from the concept of semantic connections is used to present what the authors refer to as concealment protection enforcement mechanisms. Baum and Hsiao explain that a concealment protection mechanism is one that selectively prevents user access to certain data items. They note that the restrictiveness of a mechanism may be thought of as "the number of nonexplicitly protected items that must also be protected to insure that a specific security policy is enforced." This paper examines several concealment protection policies focusing on their implementation and restrictiveness. It also points out the limitation of concealment protection mechanisms.

Baum 75b

Baum, R.I., "The Architectural Design of a Secure Database Management System." Ph.D. dissertation, The Ohio State University, Columbus, OSU–CISRC–TR–75–8, 1975.

Baum, in his dissertation, presents the design outline of the hardware architecture of a secure database management machine. He explains that the machine, a physically separate unit, may be interfaced with any computer system. The machine is made up of four major components: the directory memory, the intersector, the on-line mass storage, and the database management process command processor. Baum discusses the motivation for the design of each of these in detail. The most important feature is the design of a new type of memory which Baum refers to as segmented associative memories which are made up of blocks of content-addressable memories. Baum employs three different segment associative memories in his design.

This work is part of the initial research into a database computer,

known as DBC, being done at the Ohio State University. Other work subsequent to this is reported in [Baum 76c], [Hsiao 76b], and [Hsiao 76c].

Baum 76a

Baum, R.I., and Hsiao, D.K., "A Data Secure Computer Architecture."
Proceedings of Spring COMPCON 76, San Francisco, California,
February 1976.

Baum 76b

Baum, R.I., and Hsiao, D.K., "Data Base Computers—A Step Towards
Data Utilities." *IEEE Transactions on Computers*, C–25, 12, December
1976.

Baum 76c

Baum, R.I., Hsiao, D.K., and Kannan, K., "The Architecture of a
Database Computer Part I: Concepts and Capabilities." Technical
Report, the Ohio State University, Columbus, September 1976 (NTIS
AD–A034154).

> Material in this report was subsequently updated and published in
> [Banerj 78e].

Bayer 76

Bayer, R., and Metzger, J.K., "On the Encipherment of Search Trees and
Random Access Files," *ACM Transactions on Database Systems*, Vol.
1, No. 1, March 1976, pp. 37–52.

> Cryptography, while having long been used for communications pur-
> poses, may also be valuable in securing information in a large database.
> To this end, the authors propose a general encipherment technique for
> files maintained in a paged structure on secondary storage. The actual
> scheme proposed is to cleverly encipher each page individually. Two
> slightly different methods for obtaining the key to a particular page are
> proposed. This is discussed directly with respect to files organized as
> B-trees. An introduction to B-trees, their organization, and maintenance
> as well as other references is provided. Methods for breaking this en-
> cipherment and countermeasures to these threats are covered.
>
> Encipherment of B-trees as it affects access and update methods as
> well as paging mechanisms is discussed. The authors note that while
> specifically designed for B-trees the encipherment techniques they pro-
> pose may also be applied to other index trees and binary search trees.

Bjork 75

Bjork, L.A., Jr., "Generalized Audit Trail Requirements and Concepts
for Data Base Applicatons." *IBM Systems Journal*, Vol. 14, No. 3, 1975,
pp. 229–245.

Burns 76

Burns, K.J., "Keys to DBMS Security." *Computer Decisions*, Vol. 8, No. 1, January 1976, pp. 56–62.

> In a very general manner this paper briefly reviews the types of security features included in most database management systems. These include field level access control, audit trails, and user authentication procedures.

Chambe 75

Chamberlain, D.D., Gray, J.N., and Traiger, I.L., "Views, Authorization and Locking in a Relational Database System." *AFIPS Conference Proceedings-1975 NCC*, Vol. 44, 1975, pp. 425–430.

> The three concepts of views, authorization and locking are able to be supported by one mechanism. Within the context of SEQUEL language of the System R relational database system, the particular mechanism for doing this is described in this paper. The authors present examples of how SEQUEL is used, and in particular the way in which user views are defined. They then show how authorization and locking may be supported by including access qualifiers in the view definition.

Chin 78

Chin, F.Y., "Security in Statistical Databases for Queries with Small Counts." *ACM Transactions on Database Systems*, Vol. 3, No. 1, March 1978, pp. 92–103.

> The problem of security of a statistical database which allows queries for sums or averages, but only about classes containing at least two records is discussed. It is shown that if a key of one record is known then the keys of all records can be determined. It is also shown that if the value of a record with known key is determined, then the values of all the records can be determined. Estimates of the number of queries needed is given.

Conway 76

Conway, R., and Strip, D., "Selective Partial Access to a Database." *Proceedings of ACM Annual Conference*, October 20–22, 1976, Houston, Texas, pp. 85–89.

> The authors explain that in most database systems a user is allowed either total access to a field or none at all. This paper examines methods for allowing partial access to fields so that users can perform statistical operations on certain fields but are not allowed to obtain the exact value of a particular field.
>
> In particular, the authors explore three methods for accomplishing this. These are distortion, disassociation, and value class membership. Conway and Strip explain that distortion implies altering the value of a

field before giving it to a user. Disassociation is a technique in which the actual values are given to the user only after being disassociated with the record in which they occur. The final scheme of value class partition is simply the partitioning of the possible values of a field into mutually exclusive classes. The class into which a particular value fell would then be returned rather than the value itself. The authors discuss the utility and the amount of protection afforded by each method.

DeMill 78

DeMillo, R.A., Dobkin, D., and Lipton, R.J., "Even Data Bases That Lie Can Be Compromised." *IEEE Transactions on Software Engineering,* Vol. SE–4, No. 1, pp. 73–74.

A selection query is of the form "What is P for the following list of k records?" where P selects a value from one of the k records. P might be maximum, median, or a random value. It is shown that a sequence of such queries can always be used to determine the value of a particular record.

Dennin 78

Denning, D., "Are Statistical Data Bases Secure?" *AFIPS Conference Proceedings-1978 NCC,* Vol. 47, 1978, pp. 525–530.

This paper provides a good survey of the known methods for compromising statistical databases and of safeguards that can be used to prevent compromise.

Dobkin 76

Dobkin, D., Jones, A.K., and Lipton, R.J., "Secure Data Bases: Protection Against User Inference." Technical Report, TR 65, Department of Computer Science, Yale University, New Haven, Connecticut, April 1976.

The authors address the problem of database users inferring the content of a specific record from earlier responses to queries. A model with which to study this problem is presented in the paper. The authors then study and make a determination of the smallest amount of information necessary to permit statistical inference of information contained in the same record.

Fernan 75

Fernandez, E.B., Summers, R.C., and Lang, T., "Definition and Evaluation of Access Rules in Data Management Systems." *Proceedings of International Conference on Very Large Data Bases,* Framingham, Massachusetts, 1975.

A data model for authorization is presented in this paper in which units of data may be grouped into classes which in turn may be grouped

into classes of classes and so on. The authors explain that these classes
need not be disjoint allowing for partially ordered sets for authorization
purposes. Methods for evaluating access requests are discussed and applications of this model are considered.

Fong 77

Fong, E., "A Data Base Management Approach to Privacy Act Compliance." National Bureau of Standards, Special Publication 500–10,
June 1977.

This report outlines an approach for complying with the Privacy Act
of 1974 [Privac 74] through the use of database management systems
(DBMs) in automating many of the requirements of the Act.
Fong states that the requirements of the act regarding:

1. collection of information,
2. maintenance and use of information,
3. data subject access to an amendment of information,
4. nonroutine use and disclosures of information, and
5. public notice regulations

are able to be automated. She presents the necessary files and procedures
to be supported by the DBMs for doing so.
The final section of the paper addresses the questions regarding the
appropriateness of using DBMs to comply with the Privacy Act. The
positive and negative aspects of doing so are discussed. Additionally,
Fong describes problems not solved by the procedures presented in the
paper.

Goldbe 75

Goldberg, R.P., "How to Implement Systems Which Comply with the
Privacy Act of 1974." *Proceedings of Fall Compcon 1975*, IEEE Computer Society.

Griffi 76

Griffiths, P., and Wade, B., "An Authorization Mechanism for a Relational Database System." *ACM Transactions on Database Systems*,
Vol. 1, No. 3, September 1976, pp. 242–255.

The authors assert that in multiuser database systems there must be a
means to allow users to share data while at the same time providing the
means to protect user's data from unauthorized access. In addition, the
ability to grant and revoke access rights to the database must be dynamic
in nature. Within the context of the System R relational database system
developed at IBM's San Jose Research Laboratory, the authors address
these issues.
In this paper, the authors describe the facilities for owners of relations (i.e., tables) to grant access privileges to other users and to revoke
those privileges. In particular, the authors discuss the problem that occurs

when user A grants privileges to some relation to user B who then grants privileges to user C. If A now revokes the privileges B has, what happens to C's privileges.

Grohn 76

Grohn, M.J., "A Model of a Protected Data Management System." I.P. Sharp, Ltd., Ottowa, Canada, June 1976 (NTIS–AD–A035 256).

The Bell–LaPadula model (Bell 76) is extended to apply to a relational database management system. The extensions include integrity considerations, i.e., data modification and enhanced directory operations. A formal description of the model is included.

Haq 75

Haq, M. I., "Insuring Individual's Privacy from Statistical Data Base Users." *AFIPS Conference Proceedings-1975 NCC*, Vol. 44, 1975, pp. 941–946.

The author investigates the problem of users of a statistical database combining some specific knowledge of an individual along with responses to statistical queries to find out more about that individual. In particular, the author establishes what conditions are necessary so that a user who asks only statistical queries cannot obtain more information about an individual than is already in his possession.

Hartso 75

Hartson, H. R., "Languages for Specifying Protection Requirements in Database Systems: A Semantic Model." Ph.D. dissertation, The Ohio State University, Columbus, August 1975, OSU–CISRC–TR–75–6.

Hartson's dissertation develops an access control model that provides the semantics for protection languages. Two processes—the authorization process and enforcement process are explored.

The concept of keeping a history of user accesses on which to partially base the decisions on future accesses is included in the model. Additionally, a feature for allowing the invocation of auxiliary procedures is provided.

The final portions of the dissertation are concerned with the nature and constructs of protection languages. The actual features of these languages are developed in some detail.

Much of the work of this dissertation is reported in two papers [Hartso 76a], [Hartso 76b], and reproduced in the book by Hoffman [Hoffma 77a].

Hartso 76a

Hartson, H. R., and Hsiao, D. K., "A Semantic Model for Database Protection Languages." *Systems for Large Data Bases*, North-Holland Publishing Co., Amsterdam, 1976, pp. 27–42.

This paper, based on [Hartso 75], develops a model of an access control protection system. This model recognizes two distinct processes within a protection system. The first is the authorization process through which protection requirements are given to the system and stored. The second process is that of enforcement which using the protection requirements makes the access decisions. The authors note that most other models are strictly concerned with the enforcement process with no concern paid to the authorization process. This model remedies this deficiency with one result being the emergence of protection languages.

The paper descrbes the five-dimensional security space used by the model. It is explained that an access request made by a user is then a four-tuple—(u, e, R, s). That is a user (u) attempts to access certain resources (R) in a manner (e) while the system is in some state (s). Authorization is specified by a fivetuple (a, U, E, R, S), where an authorizer (a) specifies a group of users (U) who may perform certain operations (E) on resources (R) while the system is in one of the states (S).

It is then shown that this model can be used to define conditions with which access can depend on user information, data content, access history, and system states. The algorithm used for the enforcement process is outlined and an example is provided. The results of this paper are expanded upon in [Hartso 76b].

Hartso 76b

Hartson, H. R., and Hsiao, D. K., "Full Protection Specifications in the Semantic Model for Data Base Protection Languages." *Proceedings of ACM Annual Conference,* October 1976, Houston, Texas, pp. 90–95.

Beginning with a review of the model of semantics for protection languages presented in an earlier paper [Hartso 76a], this paper describes advanced protection features of the model. In particular, history keeping of user accesses and allowance for additional procedures to be executed are discussed. The paper also examines the process of extended authorization or amplification [Jones 73]. This is the situation in which control is passed from one program to another having greater access rights and safe access must be guaranteed. Examples are included to explain each of these features of the model and the enforcement process.

Hartso 76c

Hartson, H. R., Hennings, J. M., and Hsiao, David K., "A Study of Access Control Costs in Data Base Systems." *Proceedings Fifth Texas Conference on Computing,* Austin, Texas, October 1976. (See also [Hennin 76].)

Hennin 76

Hennings, J. M., "Toward an Understanding of Cost-Effective Access Control in Data Base Systems." Masters thesis, The Ohio State University, Columbus, 1976.

With the inclusion of security features in a computer system naturally comes increasing costs. In his thesis, Hennings investigates these costs with respect to overhead in storage and processing requirements. A model is developed based upon Hartson's work [Hartso 75] with which effective access control and resultant costs are examined.

From the model and concepts outlined in the first part of the thesis, an actual implementation of a secure system is studied. An analysis of the cost-effectiveness of this system is provided and actual measurements of performance overhead are reported. A summary of the work is published in [Hartso 76c].

Hinke 75

Hinke, T. H., and Schaefer, M., "Secure Data Management System." System Development Corp., November 1975, RADC–TR–266 (NITS, AD–A019 201).

Design considerations of a relational data management system for the Multics kernel are given. The design pays particular attention to those security-related problems involved either in the common database management functions or in the dedicated database management subsystems. No references are made to some of the existing relational system designs such as McAims (which interfaces with Multics), System R and Ingres (both of which have security provisions). See [Chambe 75], [Griffi 76], and [Stoneb 74].

Horger 75

Horger, W. A., "Data Base Module Verification—A Certification Method for Data Secure Systems." Masters thesis, OSU–CISRC–TR–75-3, Ohio State University, Columbus, June 1975.

Horger investigates the use of an inductive assertion technique to verify the correctness of programs which manipulate multiply linked lists. These lists, known as the generalized file structure, are able to support most typical file organizations such as indexed sequential, inverted, and multilist. Examples of uses of the inductive assertion technique are given throughout the report.

Hsiao 74

Hsiao, D. K., Kerr, D. S., and Stahl, F. A., "Research on Data Secure Systems." *AFIPS Conference Proceedings-1974 NCC,* Vol, 43, 1974, pp. 994–996.

This brief paper outlines the major research projects underway at The Ohio State University in data secure system at the time of publication. These include

1. development of a model of data security,
2. context protection and consistent control,

264 COMPUTER SECURITY

3. design and implementation tools for data secure systems,
4. design and Implementation of secure database management software.
5. data secure computer architecture.

Hsiao 75a

Hsiao, D. K., *Systems Programming—Concepts of Operating and Database Systems.* (see Chapter 6), Addison-Wesley Publishing Co., 1975.

Hsiao 75b

Hsiao, D. K., "Recent Advances in Information Secure Systems Research." *Proceedings of 4th Texas Conference on Computing Systems,* University of Texas, Austin, November 1975, pp. 2A–2.1:2A–2.9. (See [Hsiao 74].)

Hsiao 76a

Hsiao, D. K., and Baum, R. I., "Information Secure Systems." *Advances in Computers,* Vol, 14, Academic Press, Inc., New York, 1976, pp. 231–272.

A progress report of the work outlined in [Hsiao 74].

Hsiao 76b

Hsiao, D. K., and Kannan, K., "The Architecture of a Database Computer Part II: The Design of Structure Memory and Its Related Processors." Technical report, The Ohio State University, Columbus, October 1976 (NTIS AD–A035178).

This report details the portion of the database computer (DBC) known as the structure loop and its processors that were overviewed earlier in [Baum 76c].

The structure loop is essentially a sophisticated directory of the actual database. The information (structure and security information) stored in the structure memory would probably be 10^7–10^9 bytes. The concept of a partitioned content addressable memory (PCAM) is presented and three technologies: magnetic bubbles, charge-coupled devices, and electron beam addressable memories are examined for possible use.

This report is somewhat detailed and it is recommended that [Baum 76] be read for an introduction into the concepts involved.

Hsiao 76c

Hsiao, D. K., and Kannan, K., "The Architecture of a Database Computer Part III: The Design of the Mass Memory and Its Related Components." Technical report, The Ohio State University, Columbus, December 1976 (NTIS AD–A036217).

This report represents the final in a series of three outlining the architectural design of the database computer (DBC). In the first [Baum 76c], an overview of the entire DBC was given showing the DBC as logically made up of two information loops. The first is the structure loop detailed in [Hsiao 76b]. The second, detailed in this report, is the data loop. The major component of this loop is the on-line mass memory which actually contains the database. The mass memory is made up of modified movable-head disks which allow for content addressability and parallel-in-tracks read out by cylinder.

The other components of the data loop are known as the DBC controller and the security filter processor. The latter is responsible for one of two types of access control available to the user of the DBC.

Hsiao 76d

Hsiao, D. K., "A Software Engineering Experience in the Management, Design and Implementation of a Data Secure System." *Proceedings of The Second International* Conference on Software Engineering, San Francisco, California, October 1976, pp. 532–538.

In this paper, the design and implementation of an experimental system for solving access control problems in [Manola 77] is described.

Hsiao 77a

Hsiao, D. K., Kerr, D. S., and Ng, F. K., "DBC Software Requirements for Supporting Hierarchical DataBases." Technical report, The Ohio State University, Columbus, April 1977 (OSU–CISRC–TR–77–1).

The capability of the database computer [Baum 76c], [Hsiao 76b], [Hsiao 76c] to support a hierarchical database model, specifically IBM's Information Management System (IMS), is shown in this report.

Hsiao 77b

Hsiao, D. K., Kannan, K., and Kerr, D. S., "Structure Memory Designs for a Data Base Computer." *Proceedings of ACM Conference 1977,* Seattle, Washington, October 1977.

This paper summarizes a part of the work presented in [Hsiao 76b].

Hsiao 77c

Hsiao, D. K., "Data Base Computer—Why and How." *Data Base Engineering,* IEEE Computer Society, Vol. 1, No. 2, June, 1977, pp. 4–7.

This paper in the form of questions and answers argues strongly that the time to build database machines is here.

Hsiao 77d

Hsiao, D. K., and Madnick, S. E., "Data Base Machine Architecture in the Context of Information Technology Evolution." *Proceedings of the 3rd VLDB Conference,* Japan, October 1977.

The authors attempt to show the evolution leading to the arrival of database machines is natural and inevitable.

Hsiao 77e

Hsiao, D. K., "Future Database Machines." *Future Systems,* Infotech State of the Art Report, November 1977 (U.S. distributors: Auerbach Publishers, Ltd.).

In addition to arguing for the arrival of the database machines, the author attempts to predict the future in database machine development.

Jones 73

Jones, A. K., "Protection in Programmed Systems." Ph.D. dissertation, Carnegie-Mellon University, Pittsburgh, Pennsylvania, June 1973.

The notion of amplification is articulated. An arguement for the separation of policy and mechanism for protection is also included.

Jones 75c

Jones, A. K., and Lipton, R. J., "The Enforcement of Security Policies for Computation." Technical report, "Computer Science Dept., Carnegie-Mellon University, Pittsburgh, Pennsylvania, May 1975 (NTIS AD–A013 114).

Jones 76

Jones, A. K., and Liskov, B. H., "An Access Control Facility for Programming Languages." Technical Report, Dept. Computer and Information Science, Carnegie-Mellon University, Pittsburgh, Pennsylvania, May 1976.

The authors propose facilities that are to be included in programming languages to support controlled sharing of information. The mechanism introduced is such that compile time checks may be made as to whether a program will make authorized accesses. The authors present their scheme in the context of "object oriented" languages such as Simula 67. See [Conway 76].

Kam 77

Kam, J. B., and Ullman, J. D., "A Model of Statistical Databases and Their Security." *ACM Transactions on Database Systems,* Vol. 2, No. 1, March 1977, pp. 1–10.

The authors examine the problem of information about an individual being inferred from a database from which only statistical queries may be made. In this paper, Kam and Ullman attempt to establish how specific the queries may be before individual information is obtained by way of a simple and abstract model. They show that when the database contains arbitrary integers, nothing can really be inferred. When the numbers in the database lie in some fixed range though, it is shown that the value of individual records can often be determined.

Kannan 77a

Kannan, K., and Hsiao, D. K., "The Role of Emerging Technologies in Building Large On-line Database Systems." *Proceedings of the 1977 IEEE Workshop on Picture Data Description and Management,* Chicago, April 1977.

Specific technologies mentioned include change coupled devices, magnetic bubbles, and electronic beam addressable memory.

Kannan 77b

Kannan, K., Hsiao, D. K., and Kerr, D. S., "A Microprogrammed Keyword Transformation Unit for a Database Computer." *Proceedings of the 10th Annual Workshop on Microprogramming,* New York, October 1977.

This paper summarizes the design and results in the report [Hsiao 76b].

Kannan 78

Kannan, K., "The Design of an On-line Mass Memory for Very Large Data Bases." *Proceedings of the 1970 Symposium on Computer Architecture,* Palo Alto, California, March 1978.

This paper summarizes the design and results in the report [Hsiao 76c].

Kenned 74

Kennedy, J., "Cost of Execution-Time Data-Development File Access." Technical report, Electronics Research Laboratory, University of California, Berkeley, ERL–453, June 1974.

In this report, Kennedy discusses experiments performed at Berkeley to determine the cost of modifying I/O routines to provide execution time security checking. These experiments, motivated by an earlier work of Conway, Maxwell, and Morgan (see also [Conway 76]), used the Fortran system on a CDC 7600. The system I/O routines were changed so that when a READ or WRITE statement was executed, the access privileges to the file were checked with three possible results. These were (a) access not allowed, (b) access is data independent and allowed, and (c) access is data dependent and further checks are made.

Several different experiments were run with results showing a low cost (1–2%) for implementing run-time data independent checks. When data dependent control was tested, CPU costs rose upwards of 30%. [Woodwa 74] discusses similar experiments.

Kirkby 77a

Kirkby, G., and Grohn, M., "On Specifying the Functional Design for a Protected DMS Tool." I. P. Sharp Limited, Ottawa, Canada, March 1977, ESD–TR–77–140 (NTIS AD A045 537).

A two-level functional design for a database management system intended to satisfy the security model of [Grohn 76] is given. The higher level specifies relational and other operators that would be useful for the implementation of an end user interface for a particular database. These operators are then defined in terms of a set of lower level primitives. Formal specifications for these primitives are then given.

Kirkby 77b

Kirkby, G., and Grohn, M., "Validation of the Protected DMS Specifications." I. P. Sharp Limited, Ottawa, Canada, April 1977, ESD–TR–77–141 (NTIS AD–A045 538).

The formal validation that the specifications of [Kirkby 77a] satisfy the database security model of [Grohn 76] is discussed. Many of proofs are included.

Kirkby 77c

Kirkby, G., and Grohn, M., "The Reference Monitor Technique for Security in Data Base Management Systems." *Data Base Engineering,* IEEE Computer Society, Vol. 1, No. 2, June 1977, pp. 8–16.

The authors describe a mathematical model of secure database systems. The model is essentially an extension of the Bell–LaPadula model [Bell 73] to encompass relational data bases. From this model a database management security kernel was developed. This kernel was used to implement reference monitors, that is, the hardware–software interface between system users and the database itself. The model is such that all access to the database must go through the reference monitor.

Lorie 76

Lorie, R. A., "Physical Integrity in a Large Database." IBM Research, R J 1767(25575), April 26, 1976.

In this paper, Lorie outlines a two-level method for backup and recovery of a database in case of system failure.

In presenting these techniques, Lorie views the database as a collection of segments each made up of a set of pages. The first level of backup and recovery is applied when the contents of main storage are lost. The method is to maintain a "dual mapping" between pages in main storage and their location on disk-one for the current state and another for a backup state. The second level is to prevent loss when the contents of the disk are destroyed. This involves keeping track of and copying onto tape the pages that were modified since the last backup.

Lorie 77

Lorie, R. A., "Physical Integrity in a Large Segmented Database." *ACM Transactions on Database Systems,* Vol. 2, No. 1, March 1977, pp. 91–104. See [Lorie 76].

Mack 76

Mack, J. L., and Wagner, B. N., "Secure Multilevel Data Base Systems: Demonstration Scenarios." Mitre Corp., Bedford, Massachusetts, Technical report, MTR–3160, Vol. 2, Rev. 1, October 1976 (NTIS AD–A032 956).

> The Mitre Corporation has been involved in a project to implement a secure file management system on a DEC PDP–11/45 using a security kernel. In this report Mack and Wagner outline three demonstrations designed to enhance the effectiveness of the system.
> The first demonstration was a text editing one to show "a user's ability to access different levels of protected files through a text editor and utility exerciser." The second demonstration was an air surveillance test in which the system was used to track aircraft. This test was to show how the system could be used for "precisely controlled, selective downgrading of compartmented data." The third demonstration was of a tactical air defense situation in Europe with similar purposes as the second scenario. The authors describe each of these tests and discuss the value and limitations of each.

Manola 75

Manola, F. A., and Wilson, S. H., "Data Security Implications of an Extended Subschema Concept." *Proceedings of 2nd USA–Japan Conference,* Tokyo, Japan, 1975, pp. 481–487. Also appears as a technical report, Naval Research Laboratory, Report 7905, July 15, 1975, (NTIS AD–A013 248).

> In this paper the authors explain that a database user interacts with a logical view of the database, which may be only a portion of the database, and in general is quite different from its physical representation. This user view is known as a subschema with respect to the CODASYL database model. The authors examine the data security features of the CODASYL model and their limitations. Extensions to the model are then proposed that will further enhance security. This paper is also included as a part of a tutorial in (AFIPS 75).

Manola 77

Manola, F. A., and Hsiao, D. K., "An Experiment in Data Base Access Control." *Proceedings of 1977 IEEE Conference on Software and Application* (COMPSAC), Chicago, November 1977.

A military environment implies a classification of users and information. The authors show that two conditions—the lack of enforcing administrative control in an automated way, and the tendency to over classify information can cause redundancy in the hardware, software, and data used in an automated information system. This paper describes an existing Navy database application and an experimental database system used to solve the problems encountered.

The experimental system, known as the Highly Secure Database Management System (HSDMS), was developed at The Ohio State University. Several, fairly typical, military database environments were implemented on the system in what was felt to be a successful demonstration that was given early in 1976. The authors state that the primary goal of the experiment was to show the applicability of advanced access control features of the experimental system to a real-world problem. The benefits that were found include

1. elimination of redundant hardware, software, and data;
2. automated enforcement of administrative controls;
3. freer access to systems by wider classes of users with different access control requirements;
4. elimination of unnecessary security clearance costs due to over classification.

McCaul 75a

McCauley, E. J., III, "A Model for Data Secure Systems." Ph.D. dissertation, The Ohio State University, Columbus, March 1975, OSU–CISRC–75–2.

McCauley addresses the problems of access control and protection in database management systems. A three-level model of a database system is developed. At the highest level is the "conceptual" model in which protection concepts and terms are defined. The second level, known as the "structural" model, is used to describe the general database structure with security as a major consideration. The "engineering" model is the final level in which McCauley relates the theoretical results of the first two levels to typical database management systems.

McCauley feels his major contributions included (a) the protection rules rather than the mechanisms are emphasized in the conceptual model; (b) this model is an improvement over previous work; and (c) the idea that the database management system be "driven" by the protection requirements is an advancement. He further studies the protection rules as lattices and articulates the security atom concept. The latter appears in [McCaul 75b].

McCaul 75b

McCauley, E. J., III, "Highly Secure File Organization." *Proceedings of 2nd USA–Japan Conference*, Tokyo, Japan, 1975, pp. 497–501.

Minsky 74a

Minsky, N., "Comments on Privacy of Data Bases," Technical Report, Department of Computer Science, Rutgers University, April 1974.

Minsky 74b

Minsky, N., "On the Resolution Power of Privacy Protection in Data Base Systems." Technical report, Department of Computer Science, Rutgers University, New Brunswick, New Jersey, SOSAP–TR–9, June 1974.

Minsky 74c

Minsky, N., "Protection of Data Bases, and the Process of User Data Base Interaction." Department of Computer Science, Rutgers University, New Brunswick, New Jersey, September 1974.

Minsky 76

Minsky, N., "Intentional Resolution of Privacy Protection in DataBase Systems." *Communications of the ACM*, Vol. 19, No. 3, March 1976, pp. 148–159.

Minsky defines intentional resolution of privacy protection as "the ability to restrict the use of information retrieved from a database." He examines this concept and shows that it cannot be achieved within what he calls "the traditional approach to privacy protection." That is, where access control is accomplished by monitoring information transmitted to and from a user's program. In order to provide intentional resolution of privacy protection Minsky explains it is necessary to control the internal behavior of the users program. The author then describes a model for user–database interface which includes the introduction of protection mechanisms in programming languages. Once this model is developed, Minsky discusses several protection problems and proposed solutions.

Moore 77

Moore, G. B., Kuhns, J. L., Trefftzs, J. L., and Montgomery, C. A., "Accessing Individual Records From Personal Data Files Using Non-Unique Identifiers." Operating Systems, Inc., Woodland Hills, California, February 1977 (NTIS PB–263 176).

The use of the Social Security Number (SSN) as a unique identifier has been restricted by the Privacy Act of 1974 [Privac 74]. This report describes a technique which would enable individual records to be retrieved via identifiers that do not include the SSN. The authors discuss state-of-the-art retrieval techniques, weighting of personal data items and "a methodology for establishing error/omission rate for combinations of nonunique identifiers that are candidates for use as retrieval keys." Half of the report consists of appendices which contain the precision tables (confidence factors) for the various combinations of keys.

Rzepka 77

Rzepka, W. E., "Considerations in the Design of a Secure Data Base Management System." USAF Rome Air Development Center, Rome, New York, March 1977, RADC–TR–77–9 (NTIS AD–A039 169).

> The security related requirements for a military database management system suggested are (a) enforcement of the military levels of classification and need-to-know principles; (b) prevention of denial of service; (c) prevention of unnecessary disclosure of information; (d) minimization of the over-classification of data; (e) utilization of operating system security controls: (f) enforcement of the *-property of [Bell 73]. This report describes problems that arise in the data organization, the indexing, the data structures, the coordination of data sharing, and the handling of multilevel input data which are based on the requirements for security.

Schaef 75

Schaefer, M., "Secure Data Management System Preliminary Mathematical Model." System Development Corp., Santa Monica, California, February 1975 (NTIS AD–A007 784).

Stoneb 74

Stonebraker, M., and Wong, E., "Access Control in a Relational Data Base Management System by Query Modification." Proceedings of ACM Annual Conference, November 1974, Vol. 1, pp. 180–192.

> This paper is one of the earliest in which the access control mechanisms of the INGRES relational database system are described. These mechanisms are based on the concept of query modification. The authors explain that this means that a user query is changed to a form that is guaranteed to have no access violations. This is done in a high-level language so that further processing of the request need not be concerned with protection violations. The authors describe the query language used in INGRES (QUEL) and then discuss the actual access control algorithm. Several examples are given to illustrate how the method works.

Stoneb 75

Stonebraker, M., "Implementation of Integrity Constraints and Views by Query Modification." Proceedings of 1975 SIGMOD Workshop on Management of Data, San Jose, California, May 1975.

> Stonebraker discusses the problem of a database being "corrupted" by an improper update from either an authorized or unauthorized user. In

this paper he describes the query modification mechanisms being used in the INGRES relational database system to prevent this corruption [Stoneb 74]. Also, the author explains how the query modification techniques can be used to support user "views."

Stoneb 76a

Stonebraker, M., Wong, E., and Held, G., "The Design and Implementation of INGRES." *ACM Transactions on DataBase Systems,* Vol. 1, No. 3, September 1976, pp. 189–222.

Stoneb 76b

Stonebraker, M., and Rubenstein, P., "The Ingres Protection System." *Proceedings ACM Annual Conference,* October 1976, Houston, Texas, pp. 80–84.

This paper, generally based on [Stoneb 74], discusses the protection mechanisms of the INGRES relational database system. Included in this paper is a discussion of the protection language used by the database administrator. In addition, the protection of physical files is examined along with several design decisions affecting protection.

Summer 74

Summers, R. C., Coleman, C. D., and Fernandez, E. B., "A Programming Language Approach to Secure Data Base Access." Technical Report, IBM Los Angeles Scientific Center, TR G320–2662, May 1974.

The use of compilers to enhance database security is described in this paper. The features and additions needed in the PL/1 language to provide the actual compiler with enough information to make the security checks are outlined. Examples of how these features may be used are also included. Although the paper was written with PL/1 in mind, the authors feel the concepts could be extended to other languages with similar data structuring capabilities.

Tsichr 74

Tsichritzis, D. C., "A Note on Protection in Data Base Systems." *Proceedings IRIA International Conference on Protection in Operating Systems,* Rocquencourt, France, August 1974, pp. 243–248.

Turn 73

Turn, R., "Privacy and Security in Databank Systems." *AFIPS Conference Proceedings-1973,* Vol. 43, June 1973.

Turn 74a

Turn, R., "Toward Data Security Engineering." Rand Corp., Santa Monica, California, Paper P-5142, January 1974.

Turn, in this paper, discusses the various aspects of what he refers to as data security engineering. This includes designing a complete set of security techniques, measuring the effectiveness of these techniques, and establishing guidelines for their implementation. Turn describes the environment in computer installations within which security must be provided. He then discusses methods for protection along with ways of measuring their effectiveness.

Turn 74b

Turn, R., Remarks on the Instrumentation of Databank Systems for Data Security." Rand Corp., Santa Monica, California, Paper P–5151, January 1974.

Turn feels that while access control mechanisms are necessary for the protection of databases, they are not sufficient. The problem is that they are passive, that is designed to thwart an attempted intrusion, but nothing more. Turn proposes an active security subsystem which will take some action upon discovering an intrusion. This action may take the form of locking the terminal or notifying security personnel. Turn describes the information requirements of this subsystem along with the two other functions of auditing and threat monitoring.

Turn 74c

Turn, R., "Privacy Protection in Databanks: Principles and Costs." Rand Corporation, Santa Monica, California, Paper P–5296, September 1974 (NTIS AD–A023 406).

Turn 75b

Turn, R., "Cost Implications of Privacy Protection in Databank Systems." Rand Corporation, Santa Monica, California, Paper P5321, April 1975 (NTIS AD–A022 186).

Vonbue 74

Von Buelow, R. F., Gates, R., and Shasberger, W. W., "Data Management System Test Methods for Security and Restart/Recovery." System Development Corp., Santa Monica, California, RADC–TR–74–171, July 1974 (NTIS AD–783 280).

Woodwa 74

Woodward, F. G., and Hoffman, L. J., "Worst-Case Costs for Dynamic Data Element Security Decisions." *Proceedings of ACM Annual Conference,* July 1974, Vol. 2, pp. 539–544.

Woodward and Hoffman discuss an experimental system developed at the University of California at Berkeley—data dependent and independent file access decisions are made at run time. This system intercepts the first file I/O request from a Fortran program and makes one of three decisions: (a) access is allowed and no further checks need be made, (b) access is not allowed and the job should be aborted, and (c) all accesses are data dependent and checks will need to be made on all additional request. Once this is done, the job is either terminated or the I/O request is passed to the appropriate system routine. The cost of such a system is discussed in terms of initial I/O request, subsequent I/O requests, and memory.

Much of this work was prompted by conclusions reached in 1972 work of [Conway 76].

Yu 77

Yu, C. T., and Chin, F. Y., "A Study on the Protection of Statistical Data Bases," *ACM SIGMOD International Conference on Management of Data,* Toronto, Canada, August 1977, pp. 169–181.

This paper presents in detail one method for providing security in statistical databases. The problem is to allow statistical access to the databases while preventing users from infering actual values of data items. The actual method is that of value-class membership also discussed in [Conway 76]. The concept is, divide into equal regions the possible values of a data item. When a query is made, the region in which the data item falls is returned rather than the actual value. Two methods for implementing such a system are described in this paper.

AUTHOR INDEX

(Page numbers of the pages in which the reference is cited are not italicized. The page in which the reference appears has its page number italicized.)

Author	Reference Entry	Page Number
G		
Gaines, R. S.	Gaines 75	181, *193*
——	Gaines 78	180, *193*
Gait, J.	Gait 77	143, *153*
——	Gait 78	144, *153*
——	Branst 77	*146*
Gardner, M.	Gardne 77	144, *153*
Gasser, M. S.	Bell 74b	*184*
——	Gasser 76a	99, *101*
——	Gasser 76b	180, *194*
Gat, I.	Saal 78	*132*
——	Gat 76	*194*
Gates, R.	Vonbue 74	*274*
Gerberick, D. A.	Ombuds 76	*34*
Gilligan, J. M.	Walter 75	*215*
Gilson, J. R.	Gilson 76	78, *81*
——	Adlema 76b	*182*
Gladney, H. M.	Gladne 75	181, *194*, *253*
——	Gladne 78	*81*
Glaseman, S.	Glasem 77	77, 78, *80*
Gold, B. D.	Gold 77	181, *194*
——	Schaef 77	*211*
Goldberg, E. M.	Dial 75	*8*
Goldberg, R. P.	Goldbe 74	180, *195*
——	Goldbe 75	252, *260*
——	Popek 74c	*207*
Goldstein, R. C.	Goldst 75	25, *29*
——	Goldst 76	25, *29*, *253*
Goldwater, B. M., Jr.	Goldwa 77	25, *30*
Górski, J.	Górski 78	181, *195*
Graham, G. S.	Dennin 74	*190*
Gray, J. N.	Chambe 75	*258*
Griffiths, P.	Griffi 76	252, *260*
Grohn, M. J.	Grohn 76	252, *261*
——	Kirkby 77a	*268*
——	Kirkby 77b	*268*
——	Kirkby 77c	*268*
Gudes, E.	Gudes 76	143, *153*, *253*
H		
Hantler, S. L.	Hantle 76	181, *195*
Haq, M. I.	Haq 75	252, *261*
Harper, S. R.	Harper 78	180, *196*
Harrison, M. A.	Harris 75	180, 181, *196*
——	Harris 76	180, 181, *196*
Hartson, H. R.	Hartso 75	251, *261*

Author	Reference Entry	Page Number
——	NBS 75a	34
——	NBS 75b	99, 104, 253
——	NBS 75c	24, 34
——	NBS 76a	129, 144, 204, 253
——	NBS 76b	181, 204
——	NBS 77	129, 143, 158
National Commission on Electronic Fund Transfers	Nation 77a	25, 33
——	Nation 77b	25, 33
Needham, R. M.	Lampso 77	200
——	Needha 74a	179, 204
——	Needha 74b	179, 204
——	Needha 77a	179, 205
——	Needha 77b	179, 205
——	Needha 77c	205
Neumann, P. G.	Neuman 74	179, 181, 205
——	Neuman 77	179, 181, 206
——	Neuman 78	181, 206
Ng, F. K.	Banerj 78a	254
——	Hsiao 77a	265
Nielsen, N. R.	Nielse 75	77, 86
——	Nielse 76a	77, 87, 144
——	Nielse 76b	77, 87, 144, 253
Nolan, R. L.	Goldst 76	29
Notz, W. A.	Feista 75	152
Nutt, G. J.	Ellis 74	192
Nycum, S. H.	Nycum 76	78, 88
——	Parker 74a	76, 88

O

Oestreicher, D. R.	Ames 78	145
Ogden, W. F.	Walter 74	215
——	Walter 75a	215
Ombudsman Committee on Privacy	Ombuds 76	24, 34
Orceyre, M. J.	Orceyre 78	77, 88

P

Parker, D. B.	Parker 74a	76, 88
——	Parker 74b	77, 88
——	Parker 76a	76, 77, 89
——	Parker 76b	77, 89
——	Parker 76c	8, 11, 76, 77, 89
——	Parker 78	77, 89

SUBJECT INDEX

Hsiao, David K.

Computer security

DATE DUE

NOV 2 0 1981		DEC 0 4 1987
MAY 3 1982 RL		APR 1 5 1988
		DEC 1 0 1989
OCT 2 5 1982		
APR 1 1 1983		APR 1 4 1991
NOV 2 8 1983		
APR 2 3 1984		MAR 2 5 1992
NOV 1 3 1984		NOV 1 1 1993
DEC 1 1 1984		DEC 1 5 1993

658.4

H QA 76.9 .A25 H74
Hsiao, David K.,
Computer security   658.4
H873C 121037111